the cinema of ROBERT LEPAGE

DIRECTORS' CUTS

the cinema of

ROBERT LEPAGE

the poetics of memory

aleksandar dundjerovic

 **WALLFLOWER PRESS** LONDON & NEW YORK

First published in Great Britain in 2003 by
Wallflower Press
5 Pond Street, London NW3 2PN
www.wallflowerpress.co.uk

Copyright Aleksandar Dundjerovic 2003

A catalogue for this book is available from the British Library

ISBN 1-903364-33-7 (paperback)
ISBN 1-903364-34-5 (hardback)

Book design by Rob Bowden Design

Printed in Great Britain by Antony Rowe, Chippenham, Wiltshire

CONTENTS

ACKNOWLEDGEMENTS

Grateful acknowledgement is made to Robert Lepage for providing interviews, access to his work and material. I should like to thank the following individuals and institutions for their tremendous support, assistance and permission to use their material and facilities: Lynda Beaulieu and RTI, Ex Machina archives, Aurele Parisien and McGill-Queen's University Press, Cinématheque Québecoise, Professor Bill Chambers and Liverpool Hope University College, Marcel Dubois and Service des archives de la ville de Québec, the special collection and archives of Université de Sherbrooke Library, and Professor Jonathan Rithenhous and Bishop's University.

I would like to thank my editor Yoram Allon for his endless understanding, patience and tireless attention to detail; his tremendous support throughout the development of this work has been greatly appreciated. The ideas presented in this book started while I was doing my PhD thesis and in discussions with my mentor Professor David Bradby who introduced me to the work of Robert Lepage. I would also like to thank the following individuals for their invaluable assistance in the development of this book: Jorgen Wendeln, Krzysztof Blusz, Tanya Krzywinska, Christie Carson, Mary Richards, Hannah Patterson and Mike Nikolic. I am particularly grateful to Ita O'Keefe for the reading of material and all her invaluable suggestions, and Emma Smith my research assistant.

Finally I would like to thank to my wife Ilva Navarro-Batman for her inspiration and understanding, my father Aleksandar Dundjerovic Sr. for his encouragement, and my daughter Theodora Dundjerovic for her love, and to whom I dedicate this book.

LIST OF ILLUSTRATIONS

INTRODUCTION

Long before Robert Lepage came to the world of cinema, he had been internationally recognised as a director, writer, actor and designer of imaginative and innovative theatre work. He went on to achieve both national and international critical acclaim with his film-making, having taken up the medium in the mid-1990s. This is the first book-length study of Lepage's film work, and it offers comprehensive analysis of his four films to date: *Le Confessionnal* (1995), *Le Polygraphe* (1996), *Nô* (1998) and *Possible Worlds* (2000).

Lepage's films are inextricably linked to his theatre work, not only by the way they transform narratives from theatre to cinema but also by introducing theatrical vocabulary into cinematic language. In this, he follows in the tradition of many celebrated film directors who have drawn upon their own interdisciplinary experience – particularly that of theatre – such as Sergei Eisenstein, Orson Welles, Jean Cocteau, Andzrej Wajda and Mike Leigh.

Lepage thinks about theatre in a cinematic way: based on a Québecois tradition of collectively creating 'text' for theatre and dance performance, his theatre practice is thus fundamental to his creation of film narratives. Thematically and stylistically, his films reflect the concerns and preoccupations that permeated much of the 1990s: shifts in social, individual and political boundaries and borders; conflicts between the personal and the collective, and the national and global; the phenomenon of creative expression through a hybrid of arts, culture and new technology (particularly the use of internet and digital systems). The aim of this book is to respond to these interests by engaging with Lepage's film-making through the perspective of his personal world, his creative process borrowed from performance art, and the film's social and cultural context. Robert Lepage is a film auteur, and his work will be examined from the viewpoint of *new auteurism*, which recognises the interrelationship of the personal style of a film auteur with important underlying social, political, cultural, economic and technological factors.

Cultural context: existing in between worlds

Robert Lepage's film narratives, as with those of other Québecois directors, reflect the social and political conditions dominant in Québecois 'national' cinema. The prevailing question of what constitutes national cinema is of course a complex one, particularly within the context of the North American film industry, where actors, directors and funding are usually culled from a variety of 'nations'.

The tension between global and national narratives is a significant driving force in Lepage's theatre and film work. National cinema, like any other national art, is an embodiment of national allegorical specificity. In the main, the themes and narratives of Québecois films have ideological aims: to re-order the past, construct a national identity and reflect a fictionalised collective self. Such political factors are intrinsically linked with notions of national selfhood and important influences on the development of the institutional structures (exercised through funding agencies) of a Québecois national cinema.

Approaching film-making with the experience of international theatre, Lepage's aim is not to make films only for the Québecois and French-speaking world, nor simply to expand on the political debates around national identity. He is interested in telling stories to an international audience about the relationships between personal and collective identity, the social centre and its periphery, past and present, reality and memory, truth and myth.

Key questions in Québecois cinema, which Lepage's work responds to, are thus how personal memory represents collective identity and imagined collective memory forms individual identity. He entered the terrain of Québecois cinema after a new generation of film-makers – Denys Arcand, Jacques Leduc, Léa Pool, Raúl Ruiz, among others – had shifted the emphasis of their work. Previously combining documentary with fictionalised notions of the 'real', they had produced a distinctly Québecois cinema which simultaneously engendered the idea of reality and acknowledged their national self. These film-makers have since sought to develop a more aesthetically and individually-driven work, which responded to global narratives, urban experiences and personal (rather then collective) political beliefs and notions of national identity.

Into this cinematic space, Lepage has brought fictionalised identities and a plurality of possible existences, lives full of overlapping and often colliding worlds, and a subjective view on personal and collective myths and memories. Nick Mansfield points out that

> our interior lives inevitably seem to involve other people, either as objects of need, desire and interest or as necessary sharers of common experience. In

this way, the subject is always linked to something outside of it – an idea or principle or the society of other subjects. It is this linkage that the word subject insists upon. (2000: 3)

Lepage constructs the subjective experience of his characters through their involvement with the outside world, but this is a world that extends far beyond the local and familiar. At the same time, Lepage's film characters never fully depart from their local environment, nor do they forget their past. The pertinent question for Lepage, then, is how will the past be relevant for the present moment?

Narrative as myth and memory can be reordered according to the present moment, selected and edited based on personal as well as collective needs to tell a story in a particular way. Lepage points out that Pierre Falardeau's film *15 fevrier 1839* (2001), about the Patriots' Rebellion in Lower-Canada (now Québec), received most of the available funds from government in 2001, thus preventing the funding of other film projects. The narrative of this film was fundamentally dealing, as Lepage points out, with 'remembering the past in a certain way' and 'correcting the history' (2002). The film was very well received by Québecois audiences, which suggests that an obsession with the past is pertinent in present-day Québec.

The contradiction and tension in Québec between new and old world; modernity and postmodernity, localism and internationalism, personal and collective, is all too apparent in Lepage's work. Taking up these themes, Bill Marshall's seminal book, *Québec National Cinema* (2001), offers a valuable explanation of the relationship between Québec's cinema and its national identity. His study ends with an examination of memory and *Le Confessionnal*, stating that 'memory is not within us as individuals; rather, we are within memory, of the nation and of the world' (2001: 312). Lepage is interested in communicating these experiences and connecting to the world, in exploring what it is that makes us similar and different, expressing the problematic, and never fully resolving characters' feelings and conflicts.

So what is the place of Lepage's cinema of personalised visual imagery and poetics of memory in the context of Québecois cinema? How does the 'personal' in his films work in combination with the social and cultural pressures for commercial success and the representation of national identity? His cultural milieu is rooted in the contradictions of contemporary Canada and Québec. Québec (as geographically part of North America) is, indeed, in postmodern terms, culturally and nationally unstable terrain, made of a set of social contracts where the need to preserve the past collides with a pragmatic present, where a plurality of perspectives and multi-disciplinary forms thrive alongside modernity, protectionism and nationalism. These conflicting forces are a complex of influences that shape the conception and reception of film narrative.

Lepage's work has to be considered against the outside influences shaping Québecois cinema. His film narratives give presence to Québec cinema within the context of the global film industry dominated by Hollywood and to lesser extent Europe. It is a significant problem for any national cinema attempting to find a space for the representation of its own authentic voice – from the use of English as a world cinema language to the adoption of specific filming styles, stories and themes. Increased dominance by US cultural models and the ownership of cinemas by American corporations have affected Québecois society, no less than any other regional society: in multiplex cinemas and on cable television, 'the same cultural products are shown across the continent' (Dickinson & Young 2003: 365).

Critical context: performance, technology and media

Historically, film theory has been dominated by two central concerns: the establishment of film as an art form, and the exploration of its social and cultural function. Motivated by the desire to elevate the status of film theory, using films as a visual text that can be recorded and analysed from a theoretical perspective, theorists have attempted to incorporate the dominant relevant discourse of the day. There is a tendency in film criticism to interpret films using methodologies employed by other disciplines: literature, psychoanalysis, politics, cultural studies, sociology, feminism, to name but a few. In order to understand Lepage's creative process it is important to look at his film-making within the context of performance theory and practice. Considering his work as an auteur, this book will examine how theatre performance techniques, in particular Ann Halprin's RSVP Cycles – a creative process for dance theatre – and Alan Knapp's devised performance techniques, are used in transforming theatricality, character and *mise-en-scène* to create a film text.

As with his work in theatre, opera, rock concert and television, Lepage is a creator of film texts who uses the specific technology of a medium to tell a story, as an instrument of narration. Nick James's observation that North America's 'most creatively fertile cinemas' are at a point of change, with an uncertain future due to new digital and internet technology, helps us to understand the context in which Lepage operates:

> It is thus a timely opportunity to consider the shifting parameters of the contemporary North American film industry, and illuminate the variety of currently working film-makers ... auteurs, movie brats, studio hacks and independent artists. It may very well be that, as cheaper movie-making technology enables more people to be included in directing such as this, the cinema will become richer and stranger. (2002: xix)

Cinema began as a technological device, a bastard child of photography and live performance, incorporating elements of theatre, painting and literature. Popular use of digital technology in film and theatre making will, in all likelihood, allow a change in the way film and theatre are made and perceived. Lepage points out that there may now be emerging a form of art located somewhere in the middle, between theatre and film:

I really think that there's not a lot of hope for theatre as it is today and there's not a lot of hope for cinema in the direction it's going right now … And there's a place in the middle I think, and there's a form of art and I don't know what it looks like and I don't know what's going to happen … but I am sure it's going to happen and that's what I'm interested in. (2002)

Lepage did not come out of the film industry, nor did his personal creativity follow industrialised production methods. Rather, his film-making process is suggestive of theatrical collective creation and collaboration. Lepage's cinema cannot be viewed separately from his efforts as a multi-disciplinary artist; his films are adaptations of other film and theatre texts. He works as a renaissance artist, freely engaging with other art forms essential to his self-expression, and unafraid to enter into group collaboration where art is produced in the workshop. It is not surprising that throughout the history of film, works external to the cinematic canon of the time, such as Orson Welles' *Citizen Kane* (1941) and Alain Resnais' *Hiroshima Mon Amour* (1959), succeeded in extending the vocabulary of film as a medium by bringing a new set of references borrowed from other disciplines. Welles came from theatre and placed the camera as a spectator in different perspectives, and Resnais, drawing on new avant-garde literature, displaced the chronological order of plot with subjective recollections.

Lepage is an important auteur not only because of the quality of his films, but also because of the manner in which he works. He is engaged in the analysis of the nature of cinema itself and the exploration of the medium, seeking to move cinema further into the area where film and theatre merge. Like other film artists entering cinema from a variety of other disciplines, Lepage brings with him a creative vocabulary developed in live performance as actor, director and writer. Coming to film from theatre thus freed Lepage from the burdens of a heritage of film theory and practice, having neither formal training nor experience in the film industry. He has therefore attempted to use film solely as a medium, exploring its potentials and shortfalls.

Prior to working in film, Lepage spent 15 years with his Québec-based theatre group. Every one of his films comes out of, or is related to, a theatre production. This way of working in theatre was thus transported into film narrative and these performance influences will be closely examined in chapter one. Some of the actors from the theatre group also worked on Lepage's films. These and Lepage's other collaborators were more than colleagues; they were long-standing friends, part of an extended family. They include: Marie Brassard, Marie Gignac, Patrick Goyette, Richard Fréchette, and Normand Bissonette among others. The composers Robert Caux (*Le Polygraphe*) and Michel Coté (*Nô*) composed the original music for Lepage's films as well as for his theatre productions. At his studio base in La Caserne in the rue Dalhousie in Québec City, where most of the interior shots for *Nô* were filmed, Lepage controlled all aspects of the work, by having his collaborators on site, with offices facing the central studio space. La Caserne has also been used for theatre production rehearsals; it is a generic performance space for multi-media productions.

In his studio Lepage experiments with both theatre and film, exploring the technology of these media.

Central to Lepage's cinema is the adaptation of narratives and working methods taken from his theatre practice. These exchanges between media merit close scrutiny and will also be examined in chapter one. Like Jean Cocteau, Mike Leigh or Woody Allen, Lepage is an artist who works with his group of actors around very personal themes. Similarly to that of Mike Leigh, Lepage's devising process places character at the centre of the creative process basing development of the story on the actor/co-creator. Lepage creates his cinematic imagery primarily through engagement with Québec's social and cultural milieu. Film narratives are symbolically related to the loss of space of Québec's national identity, and the social, political and cultural factors that shape such film narrative will be considered in chapter two.

Lepage's film debut, *Le Confessionnal*, was the result of an invitation to direct a film that would bear the creative signature of his theatre work. He did not bring with him any inherited clichés of the cinematic medium, or concrete ideas of how films should be made. He was relatively 'innocent' and convention-free from the craftsmanship of the medium. As a consequence, his films create personal worlds made of poetic and visual images that favour a subjective position over 'group thought'. With *Le Confessionnal* Lepage discovered that it was his own ideas and impulses that were critically acclaimed. After this experience, he wanted to learn more about film by just doing it. 'So, that's how I was pushed into this thing. Now that I'm in it, I'm trying to learn how to do it. That's why now I'm doing these little improv things with a DV camera, and I'm trying to do my own school and to learn how to understand the medium' (Lepage 2002). With each new film, he continues to educate himself in order to discover something new and relevant about contemporary life.

Lepage's theatre has frequently displayed his interest in science, in particular the relationship between human biology and identity in terms of genetic coding and its influence over behaviour. His films reflect this fascination with nature and the information we receive from our biological setting rather than conventional social and psychological framing of the subject. The most overt reference to science is in *Possible Worlds*, where the central image is the human brain on a life-support system and the narrative collages of multiple realities created by the brain. However, in each of his three previous films, Lepage uses biological factors as an important reference point. In *Le Confessionnal*, there are consciously repeated pointers to signs of diabetes and blindness used as proof of parenthood. In *Le Polygraphe*, the central image is a lie detector, questioning the nature of truth and the imperfection of personal memory. In *Nô*, the main character discovers that she is pregnant but is unsure who the real father is.

Lepage relies heavily on his own recurring themes in communicating through 'universal' images that relate to the spectator in the manner of Jungian archetypes. Trusting the work to show itself, looking for hidden connections and similarities, using personal and collective memories and playing with them, following intuition and freely associating ideas – these are the essential aspects of Lepage's poetics of memory. Thus, this work has to consider the sources from which these ways of working are formed and attempt to rationally explain an aestheticism that fundamentally privileges the irrational, fantasy and imagination.

The poetic interpretation of memory has a thematic and structural presence in Lepage's film narrative. His characters are in emotional states of being, responding to a set of outside influences; they are trying to understand their past and present selves in situations of grief, loss, doubt, anxiety, loneliness, displacement and personal chaos. Chapters three, four, five and six examine his films individually and pose key questions central to his engagement with memory. An exclusive interview with Robert Lepage is included as an appendix, offering a first-hand insight into the director's work.

I very much hope that this book will be of interest to readers in film studies and contemporary performance studies, multi-media, postmodernism, and those interested in cultural and personal memory. It should also attract those concerned with Québecois and Canadian national cinema in the representation of personal and collective identities. Finally, I hope that the reader will find my attempts to engage with Lepage's life and cinema on the crossroads of the poetic and the real, the personal and the collective, the national and the international, both stimulating and provocative.

CHAPTER ONE

Film Narrative as Myth and Memory

The Politics of Language as Identity

As a film and theatre director, Robert Lepage is both proud and critical of his Francophone and Anglophone cultural background. In his film and theatre work, he employs various languages, particularly a mix of French and English, to present bilingual tensions in Canada. Additionally, he makes reference to other languages (Japanese, Chinese, German) in order to view Québec not only as the projection of a cultural-political terrain of Canada but also as a terrain of the world. The politics of language, which dominates Québec's national identity, is generally characterised by instability and a constant searching. Into this sphere, Lepage's work introduces a new awareness: an identity constructed as a combination of local and global references. His films attempt to confront localism and the enclosure of Québec's narrative of national identity by, often ironically, contrasting internationalism and direct engagement with the outside world. These interactions between cultures and worlds are as much an answer to a problem as a problem in themselves, and this duality is well represented in his film narratives through characters whose driving force does not come from the external actions of the plot but their own need to understand themselves and the world around them.

Another pertinent aspect of Lepage's politics of identity is the rejection of purity and coherence of national culture, understanding that in a postmodern sense, the concept of national identity is very unstable. His films pose an important question about human identity, in an age where multi-national corporations are replacing nations, and life works moment to moment, revolving around the 'now' and over-riding the traditions of the past. Such all-pervasive concepts as consumerism and capitalism, through logos and public icons, impact upon patterns of individual behaviour, ultimately erasing differences and choice. In the twenty-first century we may consider how relevant are fixed, national-personal ideals that addressed an assumed collective identity, and what is the trauma of the loss of shared national and cultural space?

In his film narratives Lepage strives to achieve authenticity by telling stories about the life he knows. He sees the authenticity of his work as its main appeal to international audiences. He cites playwright Michel Tremblay as an important influence, particularly Tremblay's assertion that in order to touch the whole world one must be aware of one's own self (Lepage 1999a). Lepage's cinematic language is the result of a need to be recognised, to share individual experience with the outside group. His storytelling is, fundamentally, a process of collective identification not only with national space but also the global community.

Theatre and film have been central to the exportability of Québec's culture. The language obstacles it suffered from actually served as its creative stimuli; a provocation to invent a new artistic language in order to be recognised.[1] Responding to a collective 'need to be understood', Lepage's theatre and films mix languages and the respective art forms, in order to create communication that is not limited by linguistic or cultural obstacles and misunderstandings. Socio-linguists accept that 'human languages fulfil two social functions: identity and communication' (Bovet 2000: 3). The first function is fulfilled through the 'identity tongue'. This refers to the language used during childhood, which is very close to intimacy and personal emotions. In a uni-lingual environment, all communicators share the same 'identity tongue'. However, in a multi-lingual context the communication requires only one identity tongue, which inevitably gives an advantage to one communicator over the other. It is also possible that communicators in a multi-lingual context adopt a new language, which is not their own, but which combines a number of languages (for instance, combining French and English or Spanish and English).

Multi-lingualism in Lepage's work often proves to be the cause of farcical misunderstanding, suggesting that the verbal language can be incapable of establishing real communication. He explores 'communication media' through his theatre and film work, in order to find a new theatrical and cinematic language that can speak to the world. As Jeanne Bovet suggests, verbal language is 'being replaced by other non-verbal languages: the language of the body and the language of art' (2000: 4).

A multi-cultural history

Robert Lepage was born into a working-class French-Canadian family in Québec City in 1957. His mother was a housewife and a member of CWAC (Canadian Women's Army Corps) who lived in London during the Second World War. His father, a cab driver, participated in the war in the Navy. Both of Lepage's parents therefore lived under the Commonwealth's command, and it was during this time that both became fluent in English. Lepage explains that 'even if they were French-Canadians at that time they developed and brought to Québec an English personality' (2002). Desiring children but unable to conceive, Lepage's parents adopted two English-speaking children. Some years after the adoption, Robert and Lynda were born. As a result he grew up in a house of mixed languages. His family was, as he often likes to point out, 'a cultural metaphor for Canada' (2002).

However, this cultural metaphor was as much about unification as it was about conflict. Families in Québec preserve the essence of cultural identity in their community, which, according to Lepage, 'has survived because of family and because of blood connections' (2002). Multi-lingual families were uncommon in Québec, and the family environment in which Lepage grew up was extremely different from other 'typical' Québecois households – some children were adopted and some were birth children; some had French as first language and others had English. Lepage points to tensions existing in such a family mix; 'to have every night the same conflict about "Do we watch the news in English or do we watch the news in French", "Do we watch the sports in French or do we watch the sports in English?"' (2002). Although Lepage saw the bi-cultural diversity of his family as an advantage, it also meant that he was marginalised because of his family otherness. Bilingual upbringing was an exception in a predominantly Francophone cultural environment that did not look favourably on any differences, particularly the English language, which was seen as the language of oppression.

When Lepage was growing up, in the 1960s and 1970s, Québec was still influenced by clerical control over the government. Traditionally there was a division and tension between Québec City and Montréal. Québec City was an old city, a strong nationalist centre, where national identity meant being Catholic, white and French; while Montréal, due to immigration during the post-war years, had a plurality of cultures informing its national identity through linguistic and ethnic tensions. The Anglophone minority, mainly centred in Montréal and the Eastern Townships, was in a better financial and social position than that of the Francophone majority, particularly the French working class that upheld nationalist causes. Moreover, up to World War Two, Montréal had been Canada's main business centre, a position it lost after the war to Toronto, which housed the most American controlled companies.

The relationship between Francophone and Anglophone Québec is a complex one. The history of Québec evolved from its origins as a French colony, New France, first settled by Europeans throughout the sixteenth century. From 1663, the French monarchy took direct control over the colony. Following six years of war between the French and English, the area was re-colonised in 1760 by the British Empire, becoming known as Lower Canada. English colonial rule in Québec has all the usual colonial characteristics of segregated society: religious separation, different education systems and colonial exploitation of economic resources. After the English conquest, the rights of Catholics and natives were not guaranteed. Destruction of the colonial élite in New France meant that French-Canadians lost their dominance over Québec's economy, forcing them to turn to a rural life and agriculture and away from economic and political influence. Anglophone merchants with strong ties to British firms and capital were able to monopolise the economy and industrial sector, driving out other, smaller, mainly Francophone businesses. Due to British colonial oppression, French-Canadian society was not afforded the opportunity to create its own 'nation-state' throughout much of the eighteenth and nineteenth centuries. The conquest became the root of Québecois nationalism for the next three centuries. When the Canadian Confederation was first established in 1867, Québecers retreated within their own cultural boundaries, informed by clerical nationalism and cultural protectionism. The rise of nationalism and separatism can also be seen in the light of post-colonial discourse, as a response to the dominant centre that imposed its social hierarchy, marginalising the Francophone population.

Until the late 1950s, the dominance over Québec by the Anglophone business class maintained its prevalence, which only served to reinforce the desire of Québecois nationalists for a separate state. While English was seen as the language of the empowered minority, French was equated with a language of the disempowered majority. This heritage of economic impoverishment and political disempowerment resulted in Québecers' desire for 'recognition', which equally presented itself in Québec's political life, culture and arts. This need to gain control over its own national identity was extended into theatre and film as a way of establishing and maintaining Québec's national and collective self.

From the 1950s onwards, however, the influence of French culture on Québec's identity began to give way to the increasing influence of 'Americanisation'. The supremacy of this process worked mainly through its economic dominance of cultural models – as the major holder of resources, the United States increasingly set the dominant cultural narrative. The main political, social and cultural change in Québec started following the death of Maurice Duplessis in September 1959 and the election of Jean Lessang's Liberals in 1960. During this period, a societal shift from the religious towards the technological brought the state closer to private life. The state influenced all aspects of society and culture; it separated from the Catholic Church, built a support system for mass education, and demanded a welfare state. Most importantly, the state intervened in defence of the French language which became the essence of national identity, replacing the role of the Church. This period became known as the Quiet Revolution, a period of transition towards finding a whole new identity, where a new national identity was not yet fully developed and the old traditions were still embedded in social interactions.

The dependency of Québec on North America, and its close links with France, made its national project problematic and unstable. As William Roseberry indicates, the process of Americanisation necessarily involves culture, history and politics, leading to a 'variety of experiences of dependence and incorporation' (1989: 82). The failed 1995 referendum on Québec's separation from Canada created a new awareness of Québec's national political project. Is the distinctiveness of Québec's national identity only to be expressed through the (French) past, (Catholic) religion and (white) race? Or can it be equated to English language (or any other minority language) as a means of communication, diverse religions and races that embody the existence of contemporary Québec?

The characters in Lepage's films have the need to come out of the 'protective' surroundings which often they are not part of, going out and telling their story by entering into a relationship with the outside world, escaping the confinements of their location. This feature can be directly traced to Lepage's childhood:

> My life or my career reflects my childhood a little in the fact that I had French-speaking friends, but because I also spoke English, I would hang out with the English-speaking kids too. So my best friend was Anglophone but I was brought up French and I went to a French school and my family were French … Today it is the same thing. I mean the Québecois cultural milieu is very incestuous and you know I feel a bit of an outsider because I am interested in working with people from England, Australia, Italy… (2002)

This position ultimately invites a different interpretation of Anglo-French duality within Canada. Lepage's engagement with redefining Québec's identity, by including rather then excluding English Canada, firstly, and then the whole world, places Lepage in the tradition of the first Québecois film auteur, Claude Jutra. Jutra's *A tout prandre* (1963) was considered controversial for its time for its style of filming: fast camera movements, montage, zoom, freeze-frame and slow-motion. Jutra's national and international acceptance as a great Canadian film-maker came with his film about a search for identity, *Mon Oncle Antoine* (1971), which was considered by critics to be the greatest Canadian film of all time. The film mobilises, as Bill Marshall explains, 'collective, national discourses as well as individual and "universal" ones' (2001: 141). Lepage's position is similar: his film narratives (as quest for identity) are 'mobilising' national as well as international readings, where central characters are looking at Québecois themes from a distance, as if observing the inside world from the outside, trying to understand the present moment and their place within it.

Québecers' love/hate relationship with English Canada is relevant to both artists: after 1973, Jutra left Québec for a self-imposed exile in English Canada, finding it easier to work as a film-maker there. Like Jutra, Lepage is also an international Québecois film-maker who includes English Canada as an important part of what Québec is and is not about. Lepage emphasises that, by understanding what English Canada had to offer (since he worked more in English Canada than in Québec), he gained insight into the question of separatism, understanding the side that opposes it. Informing themselves about English Canada, 'Québecers can form their own opinions about whether or not to be in the union' (Lepage 2002).

Politically, Lepage does not promote federalism, but responds to – as Jutra did before him – a cultural protectionism as a defensive force against Anglophones. National cinema in Québec went 'against the grain', not only socially and culturally, but also historically, with the legacy of colonialism. Traditionally Québec's film-makers had to engage in a conflict that Réal La Rochelle and Gilbert Maggi call 'the problem of the existence of a national cinema in a colonized country' (1971: 53).

'Le direct' and collective creation

Crucial for Québecois film was to find a distinct cinematic language that could communicate stories dealing with Québec's reality whereby a spectator observing Québec, not via a French or American perspective but through its own authentic frame of reference, could 'understand' Québec. The development of national narratives in theatre and film relate to a need to tell personal stories. Historically, the development of Québecois film narrative can be observed in the attempts to capture a moment in time through black and white documentaries. Capturing life straight on camera, recording it, became known as *le direct*, taking the short documentary *Les Raquetteurs* (1958), directed by Michel Brault and Gilles Groulx, as a starting point for the new aesthetics. The theme and characters in this documentary reflect Québecois life, a festival based on rural customs in Sherbrook, showing landscape and human faces, as the camera enters the crowd.

Le direct is a form of filming that sought to establish direct communication between the film-maker and the subject of the film, attempting to minimise the mediation of the camera, striving to reject the conventions of classic Hollywood practices. Technological changes, mainly the portable lighter cameras with simultaneous sound recording, and artistic developments in France, had direct impact on this mode of film-making. *Le direct* (or *cinéma vérité*, as it was also known) placed the observation of reality at the centre of its creative focus. It was used to capture the 'real' as much as is possible, presenting the 'truth' of life. This was an important departure, a shift of focus from the melodramas and romanticised stories dominant in the previous period (mid-1940s and 1950s).

Discovering a 'personal story' is particularly linked with Québec's theatre, where performance-language was used as a political forum for exploring and solidifying national identity. Theatre was seen as a medium where Québec's language could be created and defended. Working as a theatre performer on collective creations, Lepage encountered the Québecois discourse on national narrative for the first time. It is thus important to contextually explain the new Québecois theatre, which had an impact on Lepage's work and whose traditions he incorporated into his film work.

The arrival of the 'nouveau théâtre Québecois' in the 1960s – namely with playwrights Michel Tremblay, Jean-Claude Germain and Jean Barbeau – marked a radical shift from their predecessors through their use of Québecois dialects in plays. Popular speech on stage liberated theatre to use domestic influences, giving voice to the Québecois way of life. For the first time, Québecois subject matter and familiar settings were presented on stage, and the popular dialect 'joual' (Montréal's working-class French) was used.

Québecois culture/theatre was supported in the 1970s by the independent political movement *Parti Québécois*. The 'new Québécoise dramaturgy', as it has been called, 'pointedly rejected foreign influences, especially French, and served as a cure for alienation as well as an impetus for collective affirmation' (Hébert 1995: 29). Language in theatre and film became reflective of the conditions in Québec, having an ideological function as a medium, representing an awareness of identity. Mike Schudson explains that language had an important role in integrating national societies:

> Language evolves and a common language comes to be shared in a social group without explicit political directives. But in the modern age, the nation-state has increasingly played a central role in turning language to use for societal integration. (1994: 27)

Lepage came to film from a background of collective creations in theatre. Collective creation was a form of cultural resistance that started to develop in theatre in the 1960s against the mainstream social and cultural structures. By replacing individual ownership over creation, analogous to the capitalist-patriarchal model, with a collective-communal model, theatre groups sought to reform the production and organisational nature of artistic creation. Lepage's film *Nô* makes abundant references to the duality existing between Québec's theatrical collective creation and colonial-bourgeois French theatre. Collective creation conceived its own narrative that empowered people's theatre, giving voice to their own stories, outside the narrative of the dominant centre. In Québec, collective and experimental theatre became a very popular trend.

After graduating as an actor in 1978 from the Conservatoire d'Art Dramatique de Québec, in Québec City, Lepage was involved in a number of small experimental theatre groups on collective creations. Unable to find work in official mainstream theatre or film, he was considered by his professors at the academy to be a sort of 'Jack of all trades', able to do most things well, but excelling in none. Lepage had a natural gift for games and excelled in improvisation events and performances that were, similar to sports, unpredictable and offered no defined outcome. He was never good at official, mainstream theatre and film. He never saw himself as an actor but rather as a player, improviser and author, a performer who does not rely on traditional verbal language but utilises the language of a medium as a main communicational device. This approach led to his multi-disciplinary and multi-cultural theatre work that extended into his films.

In the same year that he graduated, he founded Théâtre Hummm… with his colleague from the Conservatoire Richard Fréchette, working as a director and adapting plays for a small group touring schools and local arts venues. In 1980, he was asked to direct a play for Théâtre Repère, a collective group that was already well established. In 1982, Théâtre Hummm… was invited to join Théâtre Repère, which would become his main theatre company throughout the 1980s. With Théâtre

Repère, Lepage developed his own approach to devising stories, using the methods of work explored by Jacques Lessard. Throughout the decade, Lepage was in charge of developing new projects with the company and their international touring, looking for a market outside Québec for experimental new work. Using fundamentally Québecois stories but developing an artistic language that communicated these stories to an international audience created experiences that Lepage would later import into his films. Simple stories were narrated through influences taken from popular references; cinema, rock concerts, television, visual and physical imagery, intercultural and interdisciplinary arts, and multi-lingualism. Borrowing from cinema vocabulary in the creation of his theatre performances, employing elements from both media, became pertinent to his solo shows, notably *Needles and Opium* (1992–95) and *Elsinore* (1995–96),[2] whose *mise-en-scène* is a collage of live performance, film and visual projections.

In the late 1980s, the orientation shifted from a collective method of work to a collaborative approach to production. The reason for the change was to transfer creative responsibility from the actor/writer to the director and designer, using the word 'collaborative' instead of 'collective methodology' to describe the new work (Filewood 1988). The practice of playwrights directing their own work penetrated mainstream theatre in Québec. Furthermore, the theatrical organisation, as a production company, used the collaborative approach between the playwright, director and designer, radically re-writing the text as a production team.

Lepage points out that the political function of spoken language in Montréal and Québec City had a strong impact on the language used in arts: the language of theatre and film. The struggle for identity meant redefining language and finding new ideological support for the separatist cause by having a Québecois language – a voice that is distinctively representative of Québec.

Personal and Cultural Memory – *Je Me Souviens*

Making stories from personal and collective memory is an essential aspect in Lepage's theatre and film work. He explains that in order to write, one has to be a mythomaniac:

> You have to be able to amplify the stories you hear, give a larger dimension to the stories you invent. This is how you transform them into legends and myths. So there's a very close connection between mythology and mythomania, a connection that has a lot to do with the world of storytelling and memory. Mythology is linked to the handing down of shared stories from generation to generation. (Quoted in Charest 1997: 19)

This is particularly revealing about storytelling in Lepage's childhood. He often talks about his childhood fascination with the family car trips organised by his father who was apparently a skilful storyteller. This was Lepage's greatest opportunity to see the world that existed beyond Québec City. His father would earn extra money by driving tourists in his taxi and telling stories about Québec City. The imperfections of his mother's recollection of war stories and his fascination with the world outside Québec, impacted on Lepage's understanding of storytelling, not as an exact account of events but rather as a result of the narrator's personal memory. Furthermore, the stories about Québec that his father improvised for the tourists during a voyage are similar to the position of narrator in Lepage's films regarding the spectator. The reception of the stories depend on the subject; thus narration invites them into a world of film by establishing a familiar frame of reference that the subject can relate to; discovery of the unknown and the need for international audiences to recognise the authenticity of the story.

Viewing Lepage's films, it becomes clear that narrating is a means to personalise national or local mythology and memory; film is the storytelling device of a personal journey. His work supports the idea that stories in literature, theatre and film show a movement of actions not as a factual recollection of event but rather personal reflections: 'It's not so important if a fishing story is true or not. What really counts is how we transform events through the distorting lens of memory. It's the blurred, invented aspects of storytelling that give it its beauty and greatness' (in Charest 1997: 20). Like avant-garde or counter-cinema (as opposed to mainstream cinema), Lepage emphasises the subject and focuses on the relationships between spectator and text. The individual experience is detached from a sense of the 'real', distrusting the mystifications and ideology of fiction as it is used in traditional cinema, and favouring pulp or popular fiction used in a postmodern context as quotation and fragmented recollections of plural narratives that are interwoven together. More importantly, this approach to narrative could place Lepage in the international context of 'Cinema et exil' alongside film directors such as Andrei Tarkovsky, Theo Angelopolous, Atom Egoyan, Raúl Ruiz, Fernando Solanas, Léa Pool and Michka Saäl among others (see *24 Images* 2001).

Fundamentally, this narrative of *mise-à-distance* looks at the conflict and contra-diction experienced by individuals who broke from their past and roots. The narrative is organised around themes that are relevant to time. The central preoccupation is on capturing and preserving time, which is embodied in the image of a place – a 'non-location' which is simultaneously fantasised, even fetished, invented and remembered. This place is the key to triggering and re-living emotional contents stored in the characters' subconscious that allow the characters to relive a sense of self that is at a loss at the present moment. Memory is 'alive' and constructs the characters' environment through the involuntary re-enactment of the past, as in Raúl Ruiz's film *Le temps retrouvé* (1999), an adaptation of Marcel Proust's novel. Likewise, Lepage's *Le Confessional* and *Possible Worlds* use involuntary recollection or what Edward Branigan calls 'unauthored flashback', where 'the past is simply made present' (1992: 173).

However, remembrance is an important cultural process in Québec. In terms of the representation of national identity in film, it is a most crucial, political concept that invites the spectator, as a subject, to be in the process of perpetual remembrance. A car as a film object is often utilised in Lepage's film narrative as a signifier for time. In *Le Confessional* a car indicates in a single continuous shot the time that has passed between two periods, the 1950s and 1980s. Or it signals a non-location as in *Possible Worlds*, where a car with no plates creates a contra-sign, preventing the spectator from equating location with identity. An invitation, or a reminder to remember, is perhaps best epitomised by the sign on the car licence plates in Québec. Each Canadian province has a written logo on their car plates; Québec's used to be 'La Belle Province'. Sometime after the October Crisis in 1970, when Québec nationalism, through the Front Libération de Québec (FLQ), attempted unsuccessfully to resolve their quest for the independence through militant action, car license plates in the province were exchanged for 'Je me souviens' (I remember), reflecting clearly the sentiments of the Francophone population towards remembering as a political action.

But what exactly does Québec pledge to remember? Lepage observes that

> this is a spooky question where nobody knows exactly what 'Je me Souviens' means, what it refers to. Is it the past? Is it a vengeance? Is it Québec saying 'I will remember what has been done to me'? Does it mean, Je me Souviens in the sense, 'I remember that I am different, I remember my language; I'm in a society where its cultural expression, its first cultural expression which is French, is being forgotten'? So, do I have to be reminded that I have to not forget this language'? It means many things, Je me Souviens. It is about solving the past. There is a very interesting film-maker who has made many documentaries here, Pierre Perrault, whom I respect a lot. He was very active at the National Film Board in the 1960s and 1970s. He said that all the referendums and the cultural clashes in Québec and the separatist movement were not a project for the future. We don't want to have a better future; it's something that we want to solve in the past. So, much of Québec is about remembering, about Je me Souviens ... that's why Québec cinema is very much a cinema of remembering. (2002)

Québec's dilemma about remembering its past and accepting their differences whilst moving forward is indicative in Lepage's explanation of the meaning behind 'Je me Souviens'. Likewise, his films reflect similar tension and ambiguity, contradictions of collective identity captured between the national and global politics of cultural, social, political and economic forces. Lepage further points out that, 'the nature of cinema is recording. It's about leaving traces and it's about remembering how things were and what they meant' (2002).

Using film to record time and embody existence at a given moment, making it immortal by stopping time, is fundamentally different from the ephemeral liveliness of theatre. Lepage's way of working utilises time to workshop material, which means that the development of the narrative depends on time. Transformation of narrative through theatre performance takes two to three years of working in order for narrative to 'mature', to be discovered and come to fruition. From a film-making perspective, theatre becomes a workshop in which a film narrative can be explored and experimented. Since film necessitates fixed time frame, defined rehearsal and a precise shooting schedule, involving greater financial resources, theatre becomes a much more flexible art form in which to search for the narrative. However, once the film narrative is completed, the factor of external time becomes irrelevant and Lepage's theatre continues to transform through productions. The notion of time is central to Lepage's perception of film structure. His deliberate distortion of time within the film narrative – similar to the treatment of time in avant-garde and non-linear cinema – is to reflect the subjectivity of the interpretation of time. Lepage disrupts temporal and spatial continuity through jump-cuts, flash-forwards and particularly flash-backs (the cinematic representation of memory), creating transitions through continuous shots into another temporal and spatial reality.

There are temporal limitations of film – its dependency on a specific time frame, the ability only to reflect life at a specific moment – whereas theatre performance has the ability to evolve with time. Simultaneously undertaking theatre and film projects would seem to imply that by the time his film emerged, Lepage would be engaged on another project, that the film could only reflect the ideas captured at the time of film-making, relevant to that moment. However, for Lepage, film is not only relevant to the past, but can also point towards future developments, as he discovered by chance when he was in Berlin a few years after he filmed *Le Confessionnal*:

> I met this woman who directs a film conservatory, and by coincidence she was teaching *Le Confessionnal*. I was interested to hear how people analyse the movie, but frankly I was a little embarrassed. It's like this old thing that I did and I just wanted to excuse it, 'yeah, it was my first film'. She showed up after a performance with a few students who had prepared questions on *Le Confessionnal*. They had this whole theory about the way I had used colour in the film, the order in which the colours of the wall go from yellowish to red to green and blue. They said, 'Have you been a Buddhist for long?' I said, 'What are you talking about?' Well I've been in a Buddhist environment for the past six years of my life. I met a guy from Chicago – he's my boyfriend – who's a Buddhist; I started working with a lot of people who are Buddhists. I did a one-man show for which Laurie Anderson wrote the music and when I went to meet her at her apartment I saw she had a Buddhist shrine. And there's Lou Reed ... a lot of people I know now, or who I've collaborated with are Buddhists, and I've become interested. But at the time I shot *Le Confessionnal*, there was none of that around. So for me it was so interesting: they had this whole theory that was logical and that worked, but I wasn't aware of any of

this when I made the film. It made me realise these things are there, and film – something that's locked and canned – can actually have its virtues. It can actually tell you, 'Stop running away from what you are. This is what this film is about, this is what you were about, and what you were bound to become.' So I shouldn't be embarrassed by these films after two years. I should accept what they become, that they mean something else with time. That they morph along with you, and all your possible worlds. (quoted in *Take One* 2000)

Cinema as a Medium for Remembrance

For Lepage, film in Québec is always about dealing with the past; remembering and engaging with the political trauma of lost territory and integrity. He does not want his films to be tools for looking at the past, re-writing it or solving it as films generally do in Québec, but to deal with the present moment. His position is similar to that of another Québec film auteur, Michka Saäl, who came to Québec as an immigrant. She claims that 'memory is there not so much to remember but mainly to interrogate the present by tracing the past' (2001: 28–9).

Film for Lepage is an extremely personal medium, where subjective experience is part of his unconscious self and can be materialised and shown through cinematic images. Each of Lepage's four films relate to the main character's personal quests, which are in fact Lepage's own obsessions: to discover something about their 'self' that is linked with the process of remembering. Where do I come from? Who am I? Where am I going? However, Lepage makes spectators the real subjects of this journey of discovery, not his film's characters, who are never fully aware of the circumstances that surround them. These questions, that connect the narrative, are relevant to Québec's perpetual investigation of collective identity, but even more so to the universal quest of individuals in the struggle to find meaning and explanation for the life that surrounds them.

Characters searching for answers but not finding them in satisfying ways reflects a more problematic vision of life where personality is dispossessed of cultural traditions and individualism, and possessed by the values of a globalised, late-capitalist society – consumerism, branding, commodity and depersonalisation. Thus, memory becomes a place of refuge, a way of understanding the present and seeing the future but searching for answers in the past. However, his film characters do not voluntarily control memories. Their actions depend more on biological 'making', a conditioning of the body memory, than conventions taken from social and psychological environment.

Le Confessionnal shows brothers Marc and Pierre engaged in the question, 'Where do I come from?' Pierre returns from his studies in China to Québec City where he is to attend his father's funeral and wants to help Marc, his adoptive brother, find his biological father. Influenced by Buddhism, Pierre wants to unlock the past so that he can give life to the present and free himself from illusion. The protagonists

Figure 1 *Le Confessional*: 1950s Québec City audience watch the première of Hitchcock's *I Confess*.

go on a journey that develops through various locations, organised around two main sub-narratives, one set in the past, the other in the present. However, in order to understand the narrative of the present, the past has to be rediscovered/remembered and the answer to the main question about identity is in a hereditary illness. *Le Polygraphe* develops from a premise that poses the questions, 'Who am I?' and 'What is my truth?' François' girlfriend is murdered, rendering him a main suspect for two years. He doubts himself and his own understanding of reality, and questions his past in order to explain his present position. His body tricks the polygraph machine and although not guilty his results are inconclusive. Throughout the film, his fantasies intersect with reality; what his body wants and what he wants are not the same, making him powerless to define his own life.

Both films directly reflect Sophocles' play *Oedipus Rex* and Oedipus' quest to solve a problem from the past, which consequently will resolve the present crisis. Revelation comes with understanding that we carry the past within us. However, like Oedipus, once the box containing uncertainties from the past is opened, anything and everything may surface. The ending of the film suggests the implicit possibility that it would have been better if the box of the past had never been opened in the first place. In other words, knowledge will not ultimately change the characters' lives for the good; it can add another layer of burden.

Lepage's introspective creative cycle moved on from questioning the past and present to questioning the future. The protagonists in his third film, *Nô*, Sophie and

Michel, respond to the question, 'Where am I going?' Both have to make a decision regarding their future: Sophie whether to continue her pregnancy and have a child or not, and Michel on the cause of his political action in planning a bomb attack on the government during the FLQ crisis.

Lepage's fourth film, *Possible Worlds*, was re-worked from a theatre text into a film synopsis in collaboration with the original author, John Mighton. However, the themes and characters' intentions remain very close to Lepage's own interests. The questions that George, the protagonist, unsuccessfully attempts to answer throughout the film are 'What is my reality?' and 'Where do I exist?' We see the life of George, or rather the images that his brain constructs, as his own reality. However, since George lives multiple realities, his own existence is questioned. He can only exist if he can keep remembering the circumstances of the situation he is in.

RSVP Cycles

Lepage's way of creating narrative, as noted previously, is inherited from theatre. However his 'method' in making theatre was based on the heritage of dance performance, a creative process called RSVP Cycles that he learned with Théâtre Repère. RSVP Cycles can be adapted to any human creative process and therefore, as a material, can be adapted to theatre or film.

In the 1960s, Ann Halprin started a San Francisco dance theatre company in California and used scores as a way of recording and developing performance with her dancers. Halprin and her husband Lawrence elaborated their experiences in a book in 1968 on the RSVP Cycles that used scores as a way to embody the human creative process; Ann's with dance theatre and Lawrence's with environmental design. Scores are not the final product but the recording of a creative process that can exist in a number of different media and can have various applications. RSVP Scores are structures that evolve in a cyclical manner making all structures flexible to change and open to transformation. Throughout the 1970s people from different disciplines came to do workshops with Ann Halprin, incorporating RSVP Cycles into their field of work. One of them was Jacques Lessard, founder of Théâtre Repère, which Lepage joined in 1982.

In devising performances, creating narrative utilises material that derives from the unconsciousness, either of the individual or of the group. Lepage's devised narrative develops from myths and memories in a cyclical form, perpetually changing. They are not an outcome of ideology, where ideology is seen as a conscious construct, or as Louis Althusser defines it, 'the imaginary relation of individual to their real conditions of existence' (1971: 153), but rather as a personal expression of the world that surrounds him/her as a creator. Therefore, Lepage's theatre and film cannot be seen only within the political reading as an application of ideology, but rather as a way of using narratives as a language that 'secrets a mythology', in Nietzsche's context. Furthermore, Lepage's films can be viewed within the boundaries of Jacques Lacan's concept of language as constitutive, an elaboration of 'the idea that neither words nor images transmitted neutrally a pre-given reality, but offered a perspective through which reality was constituted' (Lapsley & Westlake 1988: 37).

Like his theatre, Lepage's films aim to discover, through a personal interpretation of reality, the secrets of mythology that are hidden behind the surface of life and the poetry of existence. These objectives do not necessarily relate well to film as an industry and can result in failed experiments, such as the film *Le Polygraphe*. In this case Lepage used a play as an artistic resource from which to develop a new creative cycle, thus importing the RSVP Cycles' way of working into the making of his film narrative. RSVP Cycles are rooted in the American performance tradition of John Cage (music) and Marce Cunningham (dance), which broke away from conceptualisation, emphasising the personal and chance. The essential elements of this way of working are founded on collective work, spontaneous playfulness, accidental discovery, free association, impropriations from resources, simulations, multiple actions, absence of narrative structure and character. Therefore, RSVP Cycles allow personal freedom in restructuring material that is in the process of creation – or translation into another medium.

'RSVP' consists of four parts: 'Resource' (motivation/material), 'Score' (process), 'Valuaction' (selection) and 'Performance' (presentation in progress). Lessard turned these fundamentally dance-oriented processes into a model that can be used in the theatre devising process – Re (resource), Pé (partiture experimental and partiture synthesis) and Re (representation). Lepage learned this way of working from Lessard and brought to it his own intuitive method of spontaneous creativity. He explains that in Théâtre Repère, 'for each of us, though, the Cycles represented something quite different and produced different results' (in Charest 1997: 140).

The RSVP method is not arranged as an indicator of implied structure or hierarchy, but because it represents a communicational idea suggesting audience responses. The parts are flexible and can be used in any given order. The arrangement of the letters into RSVP stands for 'Répondez s'il vous plait' – please respond. Each part of the creative process is independent from the other and can be central in making a new creative Cycle. His view on RSVP Scores is embedded in his theatre and film narrative in the way he creates his visual language through free association, multi-disciplinary *mise-en-scène*, hybridity, marginality of forms and global references.

The Cycles deal with personal fantasies and imagination, which use the self – the artist's own experiences – as creative material. They are a generic method for liberating personal or group creativity employed in dance performance that could have applications in disciplines different from theatre such as psychology, business, education and politics. Creating narrative through Cycles by shifting between inner-personal and outer-group can be seen, following Lacan, as an extension of one's own subjectivity; self into an ousted world. The subject, as Nick Mansfield points out, 'only gets a sense of its own definition from the outside, specifically from an image of itself returned to it from the world. The subject does not define itself. Instead, it is defined by something other then itself. Put in Lacanian terms, the subject is the discourse of the other' (2000: 43).

Carl Jung (1971) points out that fantasy as a 'continually creative act' combines all of the compasses of the psyche and joins the inner and outer world in a living union. Therefore, RSVP Cycles are concerned with using fantasy as an artistic impulse for translating it into an artistic work. Working from intuition rather than intellectual analysis, Lepage as a director/author conceives his film narrative as a subjective experience, where fantasies are the very element that thematically fuels his work.

The 'Resource' can be either human or physical, and its purpose is to provide the starting point for the exploration of the scores. 'Resource' includes the motivations and aims of the individual working within the group setting, which remain individually defined by the performer rather than by the director. The text is written by the actor from inside, or in the case of Lepage, who is fundamentally an actor-creator, he writes his text simultaneously from inside the group, as an actor, and from outside the group, as a director.

His approach to film narrative is fundamentally theatrical, so Lepage does not offer a singular plot-driven narrative, but plural and simultaneous narratives organised around themes. The plurality of narratives is the outcome of RSVP Cycles and the theatrical devising process. He narrates from within the film, as an actor-creator: he puts himself in the story without using a conventional first-person narrative but by offering a very subjective interpretation of the events, often ironic, where the observer is distant from the material s/he is observing. In collective creations the actor is an author of the text as well as the director – the actor is a total artist behind the creative process. Through theatrical devising processes, Lepage learned to develop his own ways of interpreting narrative, which would have a strong impact on his film narrative and the ways in which it was constructed.

The Cycles are thus dealing with the creative process rather than the final artistic product, with what the impulses are that the individual artist has and wants to express rather than how to achieve this. A perpetual process of re-discovery and transformation of narrative is part of the search for self expression and communication with the spectator until the 'final' version of narrative is defined, becoming a part of collective consciousness.

The influence of Cocteau

Lepage has said that Jean Cocteau trained his 'soul to be an acrobat', to achieve a clear view by living a convention-free life (see Carlson 1996). Lepage's shifts between forms of presentation are similar to Cocteau's fascination with the transformation of form (theatre, poetry, film, paintings) – from the application of 'popular' entertainment (melodrama, vaudeville) in his poetic work, to changing one object into another. 'The metamorphosis of a wallet into a flower (the final image in his last film, *Le Testament d'Orphée*) is, for Cocteau, an idea potentially as poetic as the legendary metamorphoses in classical myth' (Buss 1994: 9). Lepage 'inherited' from Cocteau a desire to pursue a transforming artistic expression in film, seeing film as a poetic transition from one image to another. Lepage explains that

> compared to any other way of a telling a story, film has a possibility to go from one reality to another. In Jean Cocteau's *Orpheus*, he always challenges you, he always says, 'Well we're here in this room and now if we want to go into the world of death, or something, we have to go through the mirror'. But he can't go through the mirror the same way; every time he has to find a different way. If you look at the film there's seven different ways that he uses the idea of going through a mirror, there's not one single repeat. So it's also about transitioning, it's always about going from one place to another and how you get there, and it's the way you get there that gives the language to the film. (2002)

Edward Freeman explains the results of Cocteau's artistic style as an outcome of eclectic mixture, stating:

> This ability to juxtapose and merge disparate artistic forms into a dramatic equivalent of the collage technique is one of the most distinctive features of Cocteau's style. The result is a slightly different work each time but the principle is the same. All of Cocteau's plays and films are experiments in stylisation. (1992: 16)

Cocteau viewed film as a vehicle for poetry – that it can show what is not possible to say and objectify all the abstractions that are highly subjective (La Rochelle 2001: 6). He used any form of expression available to him and his work. Cocteau's creative process continued to live in a number of different media: painting, dance-theatre performance, writing plays, novels, scripts, poetry, directing in film and theatre. He used cyclical narratives, which are similar to RSVP Scores, rather than more traditional linear plot structures. Poetic transformation of events within a film is a cinematic device that Lepage likes to use and credits to Jean Cocteau.

Like Cocteau, the introspective nature of Lepage's theatre and film reflects autobiographical elements. Cocteau used film (*The Cycle of Orpheus*, *The Blood of a Poet* (1930)) to explore a fantastic alternative inner world, making film narrative symbolic rather than realist, as a metaphor for human desires. For both artists, the theatricality of their private lives found in film and theatre an alternative reality in which they could hide and live many different existences. This need for inner escape and to find a form to materialise this escape influenced the content of their work. Their artistic style, the form through which they contextualise their 'dreams', is the result of exploring the potential effects of a medium. The film *Possible Worlds* is rich in surreal imagery, exposed in its dream sequences. It is significant that Surrealism as a movement sought in film a new medium capable of presenting all that is hidden from the surface of life. Through the Surrealists, film's capacity for presenting 'reality' was established alongside its ability to present 'fantasy'.

In the early period of his artistic search, Cocteau established the overall theme, which he constantly repeated in various art forms and endeavours: the quest of finding his identity as a 'poet' – a person whose own humanity is defined through an external form (poem, painting, theatre, film and so on). In the context of Cocteau's creative opus, the term 'poet' can include many different arts with which he engaged during his long artistic life: poet, novelist, dramatist, film director, portraitist, designer of posters and many more. Like Cocteau, Lepage's multi-faceted and multi-disciplinary work is concerned with poetry in expression, regardless of the form in which it will take place. The term 'poetic', which Lepage often uses to explain his work, points to simultaneous occurrences and metaphors where meaning functions on multiple and separate levels. Although Lepage is changing his media of expression, to date he has remained faithful to his personal thematic and visual obsessions throughout his work. He communicates his personal visions and feelings by using contemporary 'myths' and figures such as Hiroshima, the Holocaust, AIDS, drugs, identity, cross-culturalism, divisions, Leonardo da Vinci, Hamlet, Jean Cocteau, and the jazz musician Miles Davis.

The repetition and recurrence of themes in Robert Lepage's work is reminiscent of Cocteau's use of personal mythology. One of the recurring themes to surface in two of Lepage's projects is that of lost and found brothers. *The Seven Streams of the River Ota* (1993–96) and the movie *Le Confessionnal* were created during the same period and share the common theme of a missing brother. Marie Brassard, writing in the theatre programme, points out:

> Actually this whole idea of the two Jeffreys (the second brother) comes from Robert. I think that it's just something very personal to him, and that is the thing that you find in the 'Confessionnal'. I could say that it comes from his personal history. He has a brother, Dave, who was adopted and was English-speaking, and he was French-speaking. Dave is a photographer. They have been raised in both languages.

Another recurring theme for Lepage is the figure of the missing father. In the theatre performance *The Seven Streams of the River Ota* we only see the back of the character of the father, and he is absent in the life of Japanese Jeffrey. In the movie *Le Confessionnal*, the father is at the centre of intrigue but has an ambiguous presence. For example, we do not know who Marc's father is until the end, after Marc has killed himself. In the theatre play *The Dragon's Trilogy* (1986–89), a foster father is presented, while the real father remains a fantasy. Often in Lepage's productions, the father figure is not the natural father, but someone who assumes this position.

Running parallel to these themes is the recurring preoccupation with the loss or death of a loved one. Since the suicide of Cocteau's father during his childhood, he was exposed to numerous abrupt disappearances of people he cared about (in the early years Roland Garros, Guillaume Apollinaire and Raymond Radiguet). Edward Freeman points to Cocteau's personal experience of death as crucial to forming this concern; the idea of violent death, in particular, is one of the principal qualities of the director's work.

The atmosphere created by Cocteau in the Orphée *ménage* in both the play and the film is more than just a *jeu d'esprit* in the manner of, say, Giraudoux. More than one commentator has observed that fathers appear rarely in Cocteau's work, and that when they do, they appear, as Francis Steegmuller has it, 'ingloriously' (1970: 35). The material comfort of Cocteau's early life masks an emotional void, which explains in no small measure the sexual ambivalence of so much of his work (Freeman 1992: x)

A more direct connection between autobiographical events and Cocteau's work is evident in the immediate creations following a stressful period of his life, after the death of Raymond Radiguet, his young lover-poet. Radiguet's death inspired him to write the poem *L'Ange Heurtebise,* which was later used as a source to write the play *Orpheus.* The poem, the result of an opium fantasy, is 'a description of the painful process by which it was itself created', or on a deeper level, a 'beautiful and spiritual fantasy of passive love' (Steegmuller 1970: 35). The poem provided the influential theme for the play *Orpheus.* The play follows the poem closely, using an angel who works for the underworld, as a representative of 'someone else' who influences the actions of the other characters' 'alter ego'.

Likewise, Lepage's preoccupation with death and loss of love is directly elaborated as the main theme in *Needles and Opium.* The film *Le Confessional* came after the death of his father and the film has strong autobiographical references. His most recent solo show, *The Far Side of the Moon* (2000), followed the death of his mother and reflects on the loss of roots, place and grounding. The actual and accidental death of Lepage's actress colleague, which was investigated by the police, was used as the starting point for *Le Polygraphe.* In *Possible Worlds,* a man is physically dead, but his mind remains alive. The process of gradually dying is shown through different stories in which this man loses his beloved. Death is thus the state of being unloved.

The influence of Cocteau in liberating the form of presentation from the conceptually-defined content – in finding an adequate mode of presentation – is important in any contextualisation of Lepage's approach to film. The meaning of the film narrative is in its structure and form. Cocteau's notion that the form of presentation – the poetry of images – has the same integrity as the poetry in language is crucial for Lepage's development of cinematic vocabulary.

Towards a synergy of styles

Before Lepage began to make films, cinematography inspired his theatre. In time, the theatre would serve as a laboratory to explore and develop the next level of expression in a new creative cycle – a film narrative. For Lepage, working on film represents yet another cycle, a creative phase of work, and another narrative as a part of RSVP Cycles. The departure into a different medium places the existing form of art as a ripe resource, one that can then be developed into another form. Apart from performing in theatre, since 1990 Lepage became increasingly interested in multiple artistic disciplines. He directed opera (*Bluebeard's Castle, Erwartung, Faust*), rock spectacle (Peter Gabriel's *Secret World Tour*), films and museology (*Métissage*). He used the vocabulary of cinema as a valuable creative resource in his solo shows. *Elsinore* was widely considered to be cinematic theatre, or rather a play more similar to film than theatre, using film projections both live and recorded combined with live stage performance. The theatre-devised performance *Tectonic Plates* (1988–91) resulted in a television film version that was developed by another director, Peter Mettler, who followed the rehearsal process. In the film *Nô*, which resulted from the development of one of the seven segments of *The Seven Streams of the River Ota,* the theatre production was used as a resource to create a new phase. This was filmed in La Caserne, and the whole building was transformed to become a film studio for the occasion.

Lepage's films cast light on a specific creative process that combines various media, particularly the crossover between film and live-art forms. Generally, commentators would refer to his theatre as a point of critical comparison for his films; when reviewing his theatre, critics have tended to borrow from 'cinematic' vocabulary to describe his visual language of images and fragmented multiple narratives. Lepage confesses that his theatre has taken from film 'rules and ways of telling story' (in Hauer 1992). He believes that theatre usually borrows the wrong concepts from film, namely naturalism and the 'fourth wall' presentation of reality. He views cinema as liberating, that it helps to set theatre free from the conventions of the traditional presentation of reality (Lepage 1999a). Theatre is a medium for collective dreams, a presentation of a total picture, while film is a medium for the personal, which gives a subjective representation of external realities. Lepage's film narratives evolve around local references and themes directly and indirectly relevant to Québec locations and events, while his theatre plays are conceptualised within international locations and themes. As an artist, he is perpetually on a journey between art forms, both in theatre and cinema. He shares the belief with other contemporary multimedia artists that if film and theatre do not evolve further then they have little hope in the future. The synergy between media and incorporation of new technologies would create a new place in the middle, perhaps a new form of art:

> I think that I've been borrowing a lot from the cinema to do a different style of theatre and that seems to interest people and it moves people and they're interested and so I go, 'Oh, well maybe I should push it further' and I was hoping that I could do the same thing in the other direction, but it's too big of a system in cinema, cinema's like a huge empire and it's all about money, so I think there's something in the middle. Anyway the audience wants that, the audience is bored by theatre that doesn't offer what film has to offer and is,

I think, bored from cinema that doesn't give you the live experience that live events or concerts give you. (2002)

Theatre performance can be edited and reworked constantly, while film, once put together, cannot be altered. The tension between film as a static product and theatre's transformability provokes Lepage to think of the new possibilities for cinema; he tends to avoid creating a conventionally 'well made' film that would satisfy established cinema conventions.

Like a number of other film-makers who came from a theatre background into film, most notably Jean Cocteau, Peter Brook, Ingmar Bergman, Mike Leigh, Patrice Chéreau and Andrzej Wajda, Lepage has benefited from a plurality of artistic references to import into his films. However, the story of Robert Lepage, the film-maker, is not only a crossover between theatre and cinema but also, through his film narratives, an account of a process of transformation. Through a process of mixing reality with memories, Lepage creates a hybrid work that exists on the margins of forms, contents, cultures and genre. In fact, the tension between various traditions – artistic and cultural, media and realities – forms the nexus of Lepage's creative force. Furthermore, he has placed himself in a unique position, working in each of the art forms simultaneously and separately, as an actor, stage and film director, involved in each of these disciplines independently.

In London, *Possible Worlds* opened to generally favourable reviews at the same time that he was performing his solo show *The Far Side of the Moon* at the Royal National Theatre, which was voted by critics to be the best production of the season. Both projects had been developed simultaneously. In December 1999, in Québec City, while editing *Possible Worlds*, Lepage rehearsed *The Far Side of the Moon*. He was also developing tours for the collective production, *Zulu Time*, which incorporates acting, dance, robots as puppets, new and old technologies. Working on several projects concurrently keeps Lepage artistically stimulated. He feeds from the energy of one project and brings the experience of working in one medium to another. This is reflected within the overlaps that exist between his various narratives and methods of work. In shifting from cinematography to theatricality and vice-versa, Lepage not only crosses artistic boundaries but also those of geographical, cultural and social and political distinction.

CHAPTER TWO

The Representation of Québecois Society and Culture in Film

The Formation of Boundaries: French Colonialism, Americanisation and the National Project

The question of identity has dominated Québec's public sphere so intensely and for such a long period that the question 'who are we?' has become central to the narrative of Québec and is reflected in every aspect of contemporary Québecois life. The search for a national identity thus became a pivotal point for Québec's cinematic culture and national cinema developed as an arena where Québecers could debate and reinforce their ideas, needs, and desires for recognition of their cultural/national self.

Robert Lepage contributed to opening up the question of identity to international influences, redefining Québec's identity by juxtaposing it with other cultures. In the mid-1990s, when he entered the clearly defined space of Québec's film industry, it was dominated by a range of factors, including Americanisation in the form of the Hollywood machine and its commercialism. Alongside these American influences, Québec's French heritage and neo-colonial attitude existed in a state of tension with Anglophone cultural élitism and presumed supremacy. In this milieu, Québec's film criticism and establishment raised their respective ideals of what national cinema should be. Meanwhile, Québec's society struggled to accommodate the process of transition from a modern to a postmodern culture. This chapter will examine the implications of this situation – the forces that exist within the boundaries of Québec's national cinema and the influences of social and cultural aspects on Lepage's film narrative.

The struggle with hegemony

Lepage is very aware of the concept of global cultural hegemony, chiefly exemplified by the contemporary global narrative based on US-produced English-language products that dominate other cultures. The struggles and contradictions in Québecois culture may be seen through Antonio Gramsci's concept of hegemony as constituting not only political and economic power, but also the ability to project the way of seeing the world, to impose an interpretation on those who are subordinate and who accept that vision as 'common sense'. Lepage is also well aware of the colonial legacy present in Québec culture: 'For a long time anybody in English Canada who was an artistic director of a big theatre company had a British accent, and in Québec those people had a French accent' (in Huxley & Witts 1996: 238). The use of film as a public sphere in which to debate a national fictionalised selfhood, a social text that projects hidden collective needs and desires, can be explained as a response to the colonial past (that never really left Québec) as well as present global cultural hegemony.

The movement for expression of the authentic national and cultural self, both in Québec's theatre and film, is motivated by events as recent as the 1960s – the protests of 1968, the Vietnam war, political struggle against the bourgeoisie and so on – that gave the new generation the impulse to stake their 'territory' against hegemony. Before film, theatre was used as a public sphere to negotiate the national self, and up to the middle of the twentieth century, the structure and themes of plays made in Canada were constructed to mirror the latest offerings in Paris and London; theatre artists – mainly performers – would often come from these cities. Following this, film came under the direct influence of the USA and Europe, and Québec was a market for their cultural products. In this way, theatre and film expressed and enacted cultural colonialism, and were seen as a cultural reminder to Canadian audiences of the proud empires of which they were a part. Mike Schudson, reiterating Gramsci, outlines the process by which the 'donor' culture imposes cultural hegemony:

> The 'centre' is not so much a set of values commonly taken to have sacred significance but the home of a dominant class that promotes a world-view to the population at large that serves its own interests at the expense of others. This world-view comes to be accepted by subordinate groups as common sense, and so they conspire in their own subordination, accepting beliefs and values that justify the unequal distribution of power and rewards in society. (1994: 26)

Québec has a reputation for having one of the most developed national cinema cultures in the world. However, once the national film is exported to the outside world, the fictional national identity embedded within the narrative is confronted with the existing global narrative. The narrative is read differently, informed by perceptions of the wider world. As Lepage observes:

It is difficult to make Québecers see the faces of the province that aren't the face of the majority, to make clear to them the image that the rest of the world has of us. Québec defines itself in relation to English-Canada, to the United States, to France, and, much more than we would like to admit, in relation to England, but beyond these countries, its utter darkness. (in Charest 1997: 51)

It is not surprising, then, that theatre and film in Canada are related to national and political identity, and that the social 'centre' and dominant culture assert control over them. The different readings and interpretations of the past are important factors in understanding identity and can cause social and cultural tensions. Lepage distances himself from the traditional reading of the past by subverting the question 'who are we?' and suggesting in his films that the real questions are 'who do we want to be seen as?' and 'how do we want our past to be interpreted/remembered?' Lepage explains that 'when you do a film of the past in other cultures, it seems, it's an aesthetic choice, it's a dramaturgical choice, but in Québec it's writing the past, it's solving the past, it's remembering the past in a certain way' (2002). To protect and preserve Québec's individuality, certain defence mechanisms were put in place, namely, to preserve the experience of selfhood amidst the influences of Americanisation, English Canada, France, and immigrants who are neither Anglophone nor Francophone. Each of these factors have a considerable cultural influence on Québec, the development of Québec's society and culture, and consequently on the development of cinematic culture.

As the prevailing film industry, Hollywood constructs the global narrative of influence, creating a dominant narrative with social and cultural implications. As an industry of mass culture, it is the most popular of our time, and as the study of popular culture shows, the terrain of cultural interaction is one of perpetual struggle, where the various social groups compete with each other for dominance in an ongoing competition, in Gramscian terms, of a hegemonic struggle (Stacey & Kuhn 1998: 41). At the core of Québec's identity is a continuous resistance towards oppression – from colonialism, hegemony and capitalism – in order to preserve and continue its sense of national self (French language, Catholic religion, historical contexts). Thus, Québec's identity, as that of any culture bordering other powerful cultures, has an unstable relationship with its surrounding environment (America, France, English Canada). As a result, it is constituted through its opposition to these external forces. From this grows cultural protectionism and preservation and, inevitably, nationalism.

The role of Catholicism

Ever since the English conquest of Québec in 1760, Catholicism, strong family values and rural life were seen to be at the core of Québecois identity. These symbols and preservers of core identity survived pressures both from the outer, Anglophone culture and from the Francophone bourgeoisie. Catholic and Francophone Montréal

Figure 2 *I Confess*: Hitchcock's representation of Québec City, an image dominated by Catholicism

developed throughout the period of industrial capitalism (1890-1930) as a financial and manufacturing centre.

Though from a Catholic family, Lepage does not claim to be a Catholic by belief. Nevertheless, his film characters struggle with the questions of personal guilt and moral responsibility. His first film, in particular, elaborates on the impact of the clergy on everyday life – the strong influence of the Catholic Church's institutions on Québecois society. One of the reasons for *Le Polygraphe*'s confused narrative is the unreadability of the main character's personal conflict regarding his own guilt and responsibility. From the mid-nineteenth century, the Catholic Church in Québec had an essential role in managing the state with the elected government of the time, running both the educational and health care systems. Political leaders from mayors to premiers all wished to maintain a positive relationship with church officials. Church and state, as Scott MacKenzie points out, 'were quite inseparable when it came to laws that mandated the policing of the "public good". Both institutions used legalistic and discursive means in an attempt to limit the effects of urbanisation and modernity in Québec, in general, and Montréal in particular' (2000: 184).

The Church tried to suppress and control cinema in Québec because it was perceived to be a threat to the established order. Cinema offered a space within the public sphere where fictionalised reality could bring large groups of people together outside of the church environment. By setting *Le Confessionnal* in 1952, Lepage deliberately chose a moment in time when film-going was at its peak in Québec; cinema was a sensation and an alternative reality that fictionalised an imaginary life removed from 'Duplessiste' Québec.

'Duplessiste' Québec was the period from the 1930s up to 1960, often referred as the *Grande noirceur*. It was a period of clerical nationalism, conservative ideology that emphasised agriculture and traditional values that profoundly marked twentieth-century Québec; it was used as a social background in *Le Confessionnal*. Maurice Duplessis was a leader of Québec's Conservative Party from 1933; joining with Action Liberal National under the name Union National, he won the 1935 election. He became the premier of the province in 1936 as a leader of the Union National party and remained a significant political force up to his death in 1959. He was against communism, the labour party, syndicalism, internationalism of any sort, and his political values were founded on the support of the rural areas. He enjoyed great support from the Catholic Church to whom he gave control over education and health. Clericalism had significant control over the public consciousness and social sphere, a space that cinema would normally appropriate and claim as its own. Lepage's cinema is very much aware of that period and its impact on the formation of social and political views. It was a time when state clericalism was challenged but had not yet been replaced by the set of values brought into Québec society during the Quiet Revolution, a period of extensive social, political and cultural change in the early 1960s.[1]

It was during this period that the case of the Duplessis Orphans took place, widely recognised as the largest case of institution-based youth abuse in Canadian history, and which informs the plot development and the main conflict in *Le Confessional*. Survivors claim that while institutionalised they suffered horrendous treatment and, in many cases, sexual abuse. It is believed that most of the orphans were in fact children born to unmarried parents; during the 1930s, 1940s and 1950s, these children were left in the care of religious orders that operated orphanages. Because local politicians could secure more federal funds for health care facilities than for schools and orphanages, political manoeuvring transformed these establishments into health care facilities. As a result, many children were labelled mentally deficient and moved from orphanages to hospitals, also run by religious orders.

Exposing the underbelly of one of Canada's most beautiful cities motivated Lepage to relate the stories of his city to the outside world. The Duplessis period is an important signpost for Québec. It marks the turning point from a closed society into a more internationally aware and culturally open society. Lepage highlights the changing face of Québecois society over time, through temporal shifts in his narratives. His first application of contrasting time periods was in 1985 with his theatre production *The Dragons' Trilogy*, which traced the plight of Chinese immigrants in Québec throughout the twentieth century. His films continued this playfulness, becoming increasingly complex in their manipulation of time.

French cinematic influences

Between the mid-1940s and the mid-1950s there were approximately 15 films made in the French language in Québec, indicating the peak of cinema attendance. In the late 1950s the medium for exploration of Québecois identity changed. In Québec, as elsewhere, popular culture encapsulated in mass media, especially television, had a particularly important role in the formation of national communities that extended beyond the immediate contact of individuals within a specific geographical location. Commenting on the role of visual media, Bill Marshall observes that 'early film in Québec offered its audience a place to negotiate their national (if not nationalist) identity, to re-imagine their history, and to envision an egalitarian future' (2001: 184).

Traditionally, popular culture in Québec revolves around references to French culture, either emulating it or acting in opposition to it. France and French culture became a concept, an idea from which to ask and aim to solve the question, 'who are we?' Lepage suggests that Québec's insularity, its position as a conduit for foreign influence, yet unwilling to explore these influences beyond its own borders, lies at the very heart of its search for identity:

> We are here and we are asking ourselves who we are. But we don't know who we are as long as we don't leave. This is why I find Montréal and Québec so incestuous. We are a small family and we are all trying to explain in a different way our identity and what we should be doing. If the seven million of Québec paid a little visit to Australia or to Japan, or to wherever, on their return we would know who we are. (Quoted in Féral 2001: 162)

For Lepage, Québecers' identity is constructed largely in terms of what they are not as a way of finding out who they are. Traditionally, the idea of identity in Québec is positioned *vis-à-vis* various entities (the Church, America, France) that serve as a focus for a binary opposition in the process of definition. The emphasis is not on the similarity with, but rather on an awareness of difference from, the majority. Such reasoning has lead Lepage to confront the shifting tensions between individuality and the need to be accepted by others – family, friends, a conflict between independent film-making and the established film industry, English and French Canada, localism and internationalism – even if it means adopting a value system that is not necessarily his own.

In the context of Québecois cinema, as suggested by Marshall, France becomes a cipher used in different ways, whose meaning is constantly changing (2001: 75). France is significant as a film co-producer, in the construction of a transatlantic film audience and in the cultural translation of film-making practices such as auteurism. By co-producing films with France, or looking at French films for stylistic inspiration and influence, post-Duplessiste film-makers hoped to access the world's French speaking audience and align themselves with France's cultural domain (at the same time, Québec and Canada in general were seen as a natural resource for Hollywood, who took advantage of cheaper labour and production costs). On the other hand, in order to find an audience outside the region, independent film-makers in Québec had to develop an adequate cinematic language. The path pointed to influences received from France.

The French *Nouvelle Vague* of the 1950s had an important impact on national Québec cinema. However, there is a substantial cultural difference between Québec and France in relation to the audience and towards Hollywood. The movement's appearance in France came about from the need to reach new audiences by expanding the film narrative and making it relevant to a diverse society. In Québec, its influence was more on maintaining audience presence through new and exciting trends, since there was a lack of interest in Québec's national film. The existence of an established national cinema in France was seen as capable of providing a counter-balance to the commercialism of Hollywood 'ideology' that flooded French national cinema. Unfortunately this was not the case in Québec. The dominating influence of the USA on Canada and Québec was enormous. This, combined with geographical proximity to America – and consequent issues of economics, distribution and access – resulted in Hollywood's hegemony over not only Québec's film space, but also the Canadian audience in general. Consequently, the popular audience tended to watch American films.

The dilemma of independent cinema

Hollywood defines the global film narrative that has to be followed by small national cinemas, such as Québec, if they are to have financial success. These differences lay the ground for tension between popular audience taste for American films and art houses' inspiration found in European and in particular French films.

This polarity prevailed throughout the 1980s and 1990s and continues to shape the contemporary Québec film industry, a dominant influence on Québecois film-makers. If film is to be popular, it has to follow American film conventions. If it is to be artistically accountable, it draws from French models. If it is to be funded, film has to engage with elusive debates on national identity. Such tensions profoundly influence Lepage's film-making; as an independent film-maker, he depends on government funding and support given by national cultural organisations as much as he depends on co-producers.

A further tension exists between the perception of film as a local, regional forum for expression and its place in a complex industry which requires a wide audience in order to be financially valid and, ultimately, to exist. Film as a form, regardless of its artistic potential, can survive only if it reaches an audience. Therefore, the industry is an intricate web of relations between social, cultural, political and economic factors that mediate between the film and its audience.[2] It could be said that film has to find its own audience before being disseminated through the distribution and exhibition chain. The film narrative is subject to the same market laws and regulations as any other business would be, with the year's top-selling titles relating to popular success and higher accessibility to spectatorship.

Québec's national cinema, like Canadian films in general, has enjoyed limited commercial success. The question of national context has been traditionally disputed in Canadian film criticism. The clichéd debate about the Canadian audience's preference for films produced elsewhere questions the validity of national cinema. There is an expectation that the audience have to support such cinema for patriotic reasons, even if it happens to be boring, trivial and highly predictable, because it refers to a national cinematic code of regional language and place. However, having no commercial success is not necessarily a sign of decay. This can liberate film from expectations built by the industry regarding profits, allowing film to explore its visual language and narrative more personally, making it more relevant to its own cultural contexts. This can also be seen as a way of finding a culturally specific visual film language that differs from the one dictated by mainstream America.

The film industry is not only shaped by economic forces, there are also profound political influences that use film as an ideological tool. In late-capitalism, the global narrative that coincides with the social and cultural mind-set is governed by economic interest, which derives from the need to create a successful box-office hit. Political agendas imposed on film narrative are not necessarily the outcome of ideological motivation or moral censorship, but a response to economic conditions that dictate the film narrative's capacity for mass marketing, and thus its appeal to popular beliefs, dreams and desires. Therefore film, as an 'opium for the masses' (even replacing religion), is a relatively cheap escapism into identification with a world where anything is possible. This can explain why Hollywood film formulae have resulted in the strongest film industry worldwide. Distributors and exhibitors make an initial selection based on what they believe the audience would choose to see, thereby facilitating a box-office hit: 'Thus the politics of distribution, after those of production, constrain and order the very possibility of any particular film becoming a box-office hit' (Stacey & Kuhn 1998: 48).

The result of this tension between global and film narrative can be seen in the projects of independent producers, who reach venues outside of the industry's matrix in order to create the possibility of viewing their own narrative. This could also be true of smaller national cinemas where the internationalisation of film narrative is an important financial and political factor influencing the film-making process. In making an international film, one can be creating a film narrative that has the ability to transcend its cultural boundaries and references. Debating the state of French cinema in the 1950s, Eric Rohmer observed that 'what should be deplored is not so much that French cinema isn't producing worthwhile work, but that its work is shut off – I mean it doesn't influence work in other countries' (quoted in Dormachi & Doniol-Valcrozer 1985: 65).

This belief is relevant to films within the context of smaller national cinemas that respond to the international platform by attempting to present their narrative in a way that can be widely relevant, and make reference relevant to other cultures. The difficulty with developing a national cinema for international audiences, as Lepage is well aware, is that it has to work against the patterns already set up by the Hollywood industry, against the dominant narratives that create the frame of reference within which one has to operate.

Next to geographical location, demographic structure is of equal relevance to the historical and political circumstances of Québec's film culture. In economic terms within the film industry in Québec, the film audience consists of a small portion of the 7 million people (the population of the Province of Québec). The limitation of resources available, in terms of funds and actual quantity of films being made, implies that external funds either by government or international co-producers are necessary for a film to be produced. Both provincial and federal funding agencies, in particular the National Film Board of Canada (NFB), have a crucial role in Québecois national cinema. Although the original mission of the NFB was to develop documentary and animation in opposition to the commercialism of the Hollywood film industry, the mission statement embraced the promotion and distribution of films about Canadians, with an intention to interpret Canada both nationally and internationally.[3]

In 1967, the creation of the Canadian Film Development Corporation (CFDC) increased the production of features films in Québec. Being a market of only 7 million people has advantages and disadvantages. It is small enough to be centralised and controlled by a dominant group that imposes itself as the cultural 'gate-keeper' (Schudson 1994), yet because of language differences and pressure from the outside (Anglophone culture) there is much work needed to keep the local culture vibrant and alive. As Marshall demonstrates, of the total box office receipts in Québec for 1997, the share for Québecois films was 3–4 per cent, compared to the 84 per cent share for American films. Evidently, Québec national cinema has a marginal share 'of a market massively dominated by Hollywood' (2002: 15).

Most of the films produced in Canada have little exposure nationally and even less internationally. From the 1970s onwards, Canadian films that were imitating Hollywood and conventional action – goal-oriented narrative, with characters as specific types, and happy endings – were favoured by funding boards, suggesting a possibility for the internationalisation of Canadian film. Contemporary Québecois film negotiates between the position of the auteur and commercial preoccupations. The attempts of Québecois popular cinema to survive severe competition from the American film industry, and the attempts of art films to find funding positioned the relationship with America at the centre – Hollywood-style films were seen as both a measure of success and a negative influence. Art films in Québec, while struggling to preserve their own identity, had to accomplish international recognition at the film festivals and with influential critics in the media.

Tensions within: modernism and postmodernism

Douglas Kellner observed that Jean Baudrillard described the emergence of a new postmodern society as a world made of 'dramatic implosion, in which classes, genders, political differences, and once autonomous realms of society and culture imploded into each other, erasing boundaries and differences in a postmodern kaleidoscope' (1995: 295). Thus, postmodernism can be seen as an artistic style, a particular response to contemporary society. As a film auteur, Lepage is 'a child of his country' and inevitably continues the established traditions of auteurism, and alternative and independent Québecois film-making. His films are stylistically part of the established cinematic tradition of representing Québec's postmodern society.

This tradition could be traced back to Claude Jutra, one of the first Québecois film auteurs. Jim Leach situates Jutra's films 'in the context of postmodernist theories on subjectivity and culture' (1999: 29). The main tendencies in Jutra's work that reappear in Lepage's film narratives are: instability of identity; mockery of convictions that are fixed and final; parody and irony that comes out of the characters' unwillingness/inability to make decisions. Both auteurs share an acceptance of Jean-François Lyotard's notion that the meaning comes out of 'language games' rather than from 'grand narratives'. Interestingly, it was the Québec government that commissioned Lyotard to write his famous *Le Condition Postmodern*. These features in the work of Jutra and Lepage reflect such prevailing Québecois characteristics as frustration with political engagement and a preference for avoiding a Hollywood 'happy ending' as an optimistic resolution of problems, suggesting happiness in the future. Although these elements are present in all of Lepage's films, they are particularly relevant to *Le Confessionnal*, which has the strongest postmodern 'feeling'.

In the mid-1990s, Lepage's work was generally viewed as a case study for postmodern film. Rightly or wrongly, *Le Confessionnal* and the solo show *Elsinore* have been criticised for their overtly postmodern disregard of traditional values of narrative and character emotion. When asked to give his opinion on postmodern drama, Heiner Müller, widely considered among the foremost of the postmodernist playwrights, said 'the only postmodernist I know was August Stramm, a modernist who worked in a post office' (Huxley & Witts 1996: 19). Müller continues to dismiss any labelling of contemporary film and theatre art, explaining that the stylised approach to classicism in East Germany and naturalism in West Germany are the result of the cultural climate and a response to the conditions of the outside world. In other words, postmodernism can be seen as a subjective response to the existing reality that uses a plurality of references for its expression. This interpretation is close to the way Lepage's cinema responds to postmodern society, as a reflection on the plurality of cultural references, information, sensations, superficiality and a visually constructed reality.

Postmodernism, for Lepage, is only relevant as a response to society, as a recording of life in a particular moment; as an artistic style that reflects what is outside in the world, in Müller's notion, the result of the cultural climate. The characters In *Le Confessionnal* and *Nô* respond to Québec's social context with the instability of their personal identities and mockery of definite and fixed values, such as family or state. Norman K. Denzin explains what impact social context has on cinema in the postmodern moment:

Contemporary cinema perpetuates modernist impulses (auteurism, social realism, genre-driven productions such as comedies, cop-mystery thrillers, musicals, westerns, biographies) punctuated by periodic postmodern breaks with the past ... This invokes nostalgia for earlier films while presenting a mix of pastiche and parody of those productions ... Films locate the viewer in a perpetual present, where the signifiers from the past circulate alongside advanced technologies, and modern conveniences ... These films mock contemporary social formations and myths (family, signs, love, intimacy, the middle-class) by confronting the viewer with 'inseparable' violent images of sexuality and urban decay. (1991: 10)

Lepage's first three films – *Le Confessionnal, Le Polygraphe* and *Nô* – attest to this description. They have strong ironic representation of Québec's self-obsession with national identity and the implicit frictions between Anglo and Franco duality, which are seen against the backdrop of other cultures or form the international perspective. For example, the parody of a character that is unable to decide is implicit in *Nô*.

Lepage's films are not mere postmodern constructs but rather observations and personal accounts of his reality. The ambiguity in his work suggests a postmodern style that is actually an observation on Canadian and Québecois reality. Reality in his films reflects the social fabric of Canada, a country some commentators suggest is the first postmodern state. The term 'Canada' can be defined as an 'agreed-on set of distinctive policies and institutional arrangements' (Marshall 2001: 287), and as such can dispense with the usual trappings of a unified national identity.

While this separation of culture from politics has obvious benefits, it makes some commentators uneasy, fearing crisis and fragmentation. The absence of common historical and traditional grand narrative, a necessity to define the new territory in its own right within North America, meant that cultural space and notions of what constitute national identity were constructed through a set of contracts by various groups or individuals, agreements based on particular interest, protection and pragmatic considerations. This suggests that there are no absolute obligations, but rather a group of individuals collectively agree to uphold certain principles if they are suitable for them and secure economic means. Linda Hutcheon argues that Canada, because of its unstable cultural identity, has 'a privileged place in postmodernism' as it calls into question 'the possibility of a centred, coherent subjectivity' (1988: 174). However, the concept of 'coherent subjectivity' is replaced by personalised interpretation of dominant narratives where, as Stuart Hall observes, 'identity is formed at the unstable point where the *unspeakable* stories of a subjectivity met the narrative of history, of a culture' (1987: 44). It is in the space between the inability to have a coherent subjective centre and the existence of multiple perspectives of individual readings that the characters in Lepage's films inhabit. This friction is the fertile ground for his humour and satire: small people and their limited abilities with big ambitions and views on the world.

Lepage positions his characters in a situation in which they need to make an important decision to then go on a journey of self-discovery. They find themselves in unusual situations, which play in opposition to their own experiences. His films are about characters that encounter their own place, but see it from a different perspective. In *Le Confessionnal*, Pierre's experience in China redefines his home in Québec City. In *Nô*, Sophie, through her performance in Japan, gains a new understanding of cultural politics in Québec. Lepage brings the spectators into a location that is familiar to them, and then reveals to them the world that can now be discovered differently.

Lepage's film narrative is not a traditional plot-driven narrative, but rather a story told through sequences of images and multiple narratives. Cinematic image as language has an important place in Lepage's representation of postmodern Québecois society; the visual signification of images that are made of a combination of multiple references to other media, cultures and art traditions are essential to his creative expression. The presence of other media within film has a physical impact on the action; the film itself becomes a response to outside events that are directly brought into its 'reality' by quoting sources from other media. The visual quality that envelops the life of the characters in Lepage's films can thus be linked to postmodern sensibility – where the modern way of living is spent in front of screens and video cameras.

Nicholas Mirzoeff (1999) stipulates that the visual experience in postmodern culture can be observed as a unification of visual disciplines (film, paintings, pop videos, internet, advertising) into visual culture. Since postmodernism has often been defined as the crisis of modernism, Mirzoeff suggests that the failure of modern culture to confront its own strategy of visualising led to this crisis: 'it is the visual crisis of culture that creates postmodernity, not its textuality' (1999: 3). Mirzoeff's statement implies that visual culture has its own language, which is different from textual language. This is particularly important for Lepage's work, because, as discussed in chapter one, his visual language arose from the need to develop a mode of communication that could overcome the political and cultural limitations of textual language.

Postmodernism reconsidered: Jesus of Montréal

The portal through which Lepage entered into the perpetual negotiation between modernity and postmodernity, as found in Québec cinema, was his work with the internationally acclaimed Québecois director Denys Arcand. Lepage's first real film experience was as an actor in Arcand's *Jésus de Montréal* (1989). Throughout the 1960s, 1970s and 1980s, Québec film existed in an invented space that responded to a collective fantasy of national identity, self-obsessed with the creation of a cultural refuge from the existing hegemony and dominance of the Anglophone majority. Québec national cinema did not export well into the world of cinema, mostly because it did not want to depart from its own cultural heritage by introducing mainstream formulas set by the Hollywood film industry. With the national and international success of Arcand's films, *Le déclin de l'empire Américain* (1986) and *Jésus de Montréal*,

Figure 3 *Jésus de Montréal*: The performance prohibited by Montréal police

these conditions changed. A novel understanding of cinema was inaugurated from the perspective 'of a Québec inserted in global flows of culture and communication' (Marshall 2001: 283).

Jésus de Montréal followed on the back of the international success of *Le déclin de l'empire Américain*, which won the Jury Prize and the Ecumenical Prize at Cannes as well as a nomination for Best Foreign Film at the Academy Awards. It presented Lepage with an example of a cinematic medium capable of communicating with the world, not just Québecois audiences. This was in direct opposition to the localism and cultural protectionism that narrowly looked only inwards, offering little shared experience in comparison to the advanced and sophisticated international world of film.

The starting point for *Jésus de Montréal* came from an anecdote. During the auditions for *Le déclin de l'empire Américain*, Arcand was taken by the irony of the situation of an actor who had a beard because he was playing Jesus in the Passion Play whilst auditioning for commercials during the day. Arcand observes that 'consumerism may be the legacy of the 1980s but there has got to be more to life than that. *Jésus de Montréal* is about a yearning for something else, a search for a sort of meaning' (in Burnett 1990).

Lepage played a supporting role in *Jésus de Montréal* as an actor, René, hired to play Pontius Pilate in the staging of a theatre play, *The Passion*, in the famous Montréal basilica. René is one of a group of unemployed actors who was cast by the local priest to rewrite the Passion Play since the old version, after being a success for more than

Figure 4 *Jésus de Montréal*: Robert Lepage (right) rehearsing the role of Pilate, playing with Oriental theatrical styles

forty years, has become old-fashioned and does not relate to a modern audience. Most of the actors have experience of collective creation and group work in alternative Québecois theatre and manage to create a play that is good theatre, but fails in term of public relations, offering an unorthodox reading of the Gospel story. Despite good reviews and audience response, the chief authorities order the play to be toned down so as not to offend the establishment. The conflict in the film is evident: theatrical and cinematic representations are at odds with clerical vision and dominance over the most important narrative (and through that the social sphere or social space).

Daniel (Lothaire Bluteau) is the actor who plays Christ. Throughout the film, he discovers that his own life is taking on aspects of Christ's, and by the end of the film, the reality of life and the reality of theatre have merged so the Crucifixion scene from the Passion Play is actually played out in real life. Despite legal and religious pressure, the actors find the courage to confront the authorities and persist in presenting the play. At the end of the film, Jesus of Montréal (Daniel) dies and his eyes and heart are donated for a transplant. Commentators suggested that the end of the film suggests that protest and struggle always continue and life's cycle continues.

The main conflict in the film is between commercialism and spiritual values. Arcand's film eroded the boundaries that create the nexus of Québec's identity, exposing the ownership of media and social space that plays a diabolical part in the complexity of Jesus/Daniel's role. Individuality has been fractured within a multi-referential society, where ownership of public space is clearly demarked by those who have financial, clerical or legal power. The end of the film can also indicate a final commodification of Daniel; in late-capitalism everything is open for purchase, money buys any affiliations and moral principals.

According to Ron Burnett (1990), it was difficult for Arcand to explain the film's domestic and international success as well as the audience's emotional response to the story. The film was able to communicate a universally accepted narrative that came out of the fundamental struggle of one individual with the media, with an over-powering plurality of references, and with a superficial, eclectic and disenfranchised reality. With this film, Arcand defined Québec's postmodernity as a world in transition between old and new, where new has a tendency to negate individuality and authenticity in favour of a globalised and commercialised world. By doing that, Arcand merged Québec's narrative with the international narrative.

However, working with Arcand misled Lepage about the nature of film work. *Jésus de Montréal* was, according to Lepage, the Québecois film with the biggest budget to date. The film had all the resources that Lepage would not have for his own productions:

> We had a lot of money so we could take our time to do things and do them well and try out various options. And secondly, Arcand has a vision of what cinema should be. It is something that is extremely written. Because the film is so scripted Arcand does not feel that he is looking for his film when he shoots it. For him, it is done. (2002)

Whilst working on his own films, Lepage does not write and structure in a form that may prevent him from improvising on set. Still, Arcand proved to be a strong thematic influence on him. The representation of Québec society captured in the clash between modernity and postmodernity, in a transition between the new and old world, is a theme from *Jésus de Montréal* which is echoed in Lepage's film work.

This tension which exists between modernity and postmodernity in the early 1990s is embedded in Lepage's *Le Confessionnal*; a transition point between Arcand's global position of pessimism and national mission, towards individual displacement in a non-place as presented in *Possible Worlds*. Lepage continues the existence of that duality, responding to a collage of received stimuli arriving from the tensions and frictions between the new and the old.

Escaping boundaries: internationalism and acculturation

Postmodern theorising is increasingly preoccupied by the visual society and the cultural logics that present new aspects of individual problems such as drug addiction, AIDS, homelessness, recession, depression (personal and national), unemployment, domestic violence, exile and national identity. Lepage's films are referential to the combination of twentieth-century theatre and film practice, quotations and montage of different styles and art forms, and various cultures. Apart from using his theatre work as a new creative cycle, he freely 'quotes' from different cultures and artistic contexts, ranging from Asian traditional theatre, to Hitchcock's classic film *I Confess* (1953). Charles Jencks explains:

> The influence of the international media, so emphasised as a defining aspect of the post-industrial society, has made these movements cross over national boundaries. Postmodern art, like architecture, is influenced by the 'world village' and the sensibility that comes with this: an iconic cosmopolitanism. (1989: 22)

In Lepage's visualisation, 'iconic cosmopolitanism' is expressed through locations that form a global reference: Québec City, Montréal, Osaka, Berlin. In *Possible Worlds,* iconic cosmopolitanism is replaced by actual existence in a non-place. This visualisation is possible because Lepage's film structure is deliberately fragmented; each location co-exists in a parallel way with another. His films thus resist the traditional narrative of psychological wholeness.

Deconstructing narratives and replacing them with a number of subplots that have their own location and are alive in a dreamlike form is also a way of using film to dismantle the ideology of the dominant cinema. One established narrative or understanding is reinterpreted from different angles. Noel Carrol points out that 'deconstructionism answers the call for content, supposedly, by dismantling dominant cinema through supplying spectators with the knowledge necessary to see through its artifice' (1998: 312). Lepage's cinematic work reflects this collage and collision of narratives, which co-exist and intertwine. His films could be interpreted as deconstruction of the dominant visual narrative (Hollywood films, Québec television) exposing the story of the centre to a different set of references associated with transition, non-place, marginality and otherness. Important media events like the presence of Hollywood stars in Québec City in the 1950s, Tiananmen Square, the FLQ crisis in Québec, and the fall of the Berlin Wall are seen through small-time characters and interpreted through their own specific local set of references.

Lepage's film narrative also has an 'iconic cosmopolitanism' in the way it juxtaposes the local and distinctively Québecois to international and intercultural exchanges. Lepage states that the 'meetings and exchanges I have abroad enrich my work and the work of my company, work that remains profoundly Québecois' (in Charest 1997: 50). He continues to explain that a Québecois living in China is closer to an understanding of Québec than one living in Québec, who may have never left the country. Distance provides an inside-outside view of one's culture, and in order to understand one's own culture, it is necessary to be exposed to influences from other cultures, to be in contact with the rest of the world. Lepage acknowledges that Québec needs to open up to the influences of other cultures: 'Our traditional reflex of cultural protectionism in Québec has made us a little xenophobic' (ibid.). Although Lepage declares himself to be a nationalist, his version of nationalism is more of an internationalist with a national agenda at heart.

As a film-maker, Lepage uses Québec's national obsession with both national and personal identity and its past as a creative resource, and subverts national narrative to a representation of people whose sentiments and words are stronger than their actions and decisions. By representing Québec's inability to deal with questions of its own identity through personalised stories, and the characters' individual struggle to make choices in a world that is giving them less and less space to do so, his films respond to overt consumerism, fragmented sensations and enforced concepts of doing, acquiring and achieving goals in a late-capitalist society. His film personas are therefore motivated by self-understanding, reflection or discovery of their own identity.

Exiles and Non-place

The survival of Québecois identity lies in Québecers' ability to turn to the wider world and engage with relevant processes. This is the political position that underpins Lepage's film ouevre. His narratives feature an outsider, an exile (a self-imposed exile), who is marginalised or becomes a displaced person, separated from his place or from his body. Lepage's cinema reflects Québec's own collective and individual identities, constructed through constant processes of remembrance and de-territorialisation. Like Québec itself, Lepage's characteristic narrative seems to be perpetually losing and finding its place. After all, everyone in Québec (except the indigenous community) is an immigrant at some point, a transitional entity.

As pointed out in chapter one, memory and remembrance are central to Québec's reading of its own selfhood. Since memory serves as a way of inventing, interpreting or personalising national narrative, memory is closer to the fantasy of a national identity than to factual reality. The national reality is not one of unified factors, but rather 'the nation is unfixed, not one reference point, not a refuge of stability faced with globalisation, but a very mobile spiral' (Marshall 2001: 3). It is a terrain of struggle and tensions, exchanges and negotiations, transitions and transgressions. In Lepage's film narrative, this terrain of transition and transgression becomes a non-place, an invented location in-between worlds. As Paul Ricoeur suggests, the re-enactment of the past happens through personal imagination and not through actual reliving of the events that happened: 'Rethinking (the past) contains the critical moment that requires us to detour by way of the historical imagination' (1988: 148). The main characters escape their own territory by finding a refuge in an invented space, an imagined past, in a reality founded on the unknown, within a different context, and cut-off from their original circumstances. The characters are on a journey to search for their own identity, and are able to find themselves by engaging with their memory and asking questions about their past, present and future. The position of characters in-between worlds, either between past and present like in *Le Confessionnal*, inside and outside as in *Le Polygraphe*, in different geographical locations in *Nô*, or reality and fantasy in *Possible Worlds*, will be looked at in more detail in the following chapters as fundamental to Lepage's creative compulsion.

Although his film narrative is fundamentally based on Québecois themes, relevant to national cinema, he does break away from the nostalgic vision of the idealised Québecois and Canadian national cinema. The neo-romantic cinematic representation of a Québec that needs to liberate itself from 'oppression' and solve its past had to be redefined after the failed 1995 second referendum on separatism. This period coincides with Lepage's first film and his engagement with the internationalisation of Québec's cultural politics, internationally promoting and supporting Québec's bid for separatism. Lepage explains that for him this referendum was not just about Québec, it was about Canada. It was about defining the whole federation. He points out, 'It was about saying "Québec wants out" and saying "Who are you English Canadians?" And I became more comfortable speaking openly about my political position because I was more involved and I was working more in English Canada' (2002). Incidentally, this 'opening-up' coincides with themes of personal and national identity questioned in *Le Confessionnal*. The questions, 'Who am I?' and 'What is my past?', were posed in the film and are directly relevant to the second referendum. In this period, Lepage returned to Québec City in order to find a more permanent base after years of working abroad. He found a 'home' for his company Ex Machina in La Caserne in the old part port of Québec City. Lepage's return to Québec, the beginning of his film-making, and his engagement in cultural politics were simultaneous events whose outcome was his re-definition of the boundaries of national cinema and of the representation of Québec's identity.

Lepage being very much in self-imposed exile, the journey of the characters in his films tends to reflect his own. His films have a discernible root in his experiences, as a director who has never been forced into exile, but has chosen to live in-between worlds – in-between North America and Europe, West and East. (Living and working outside of Canada actually caused Lepage to temporarily lose residence at one point in Québec.) In fact, being positioned on the outside relates not only to his Québecois identity, but also to his Québecois working-class roots and bilingual family, his sexually ambiguous identity, and his status as an actor afflicted with a condition affecting his appearance (he suffered from alopecia from an early age). Rather than growing up as part of the mainstream culture, he developed in opposition to the accepted existing principles, in a position of marginality and displacement. All of these factors – linguistic, cultural and personal – contributed to his status as an outsider, perceiving himself as a rebel who did not associate with conventional social pressures and roles.

Lepage points out that, as a Québecois artist, outside Canada he receives media attention not always given to political figures. Without any real political connections, he is given space on the front pages of leading journals to express his opinion in interviews. As a result of international exposure, he is now seen as a political tool to promote Québec: 'We the artists have more impact than politicians outside of our country. We are able to discuss the role that culture has on our own society and collectivist' (in Féral 2001: 176).

However, in his films, Lepage treats the 'hot topics' of Québec's identity indirectly. His films are more about an individual search and displacement, which are projected onto the background of Québecois society. This could explain the international acceptance of his films: they are local, but thematically transcend localism and open up to a widespread reading of human displacement, confusion and search for self. The main characters in Lepage's films are in an unstable position; they are on the move and exist in a non-place. Socially, these characters are marginalised. They are artists, actors, unemployed, students and prostitutes. Their identity depends on forces that exist outside them: family, politicians, group of friends, religion, technology, or science. This position is relevant to Québec, captured as it is between past and present, between Europe and America, existing in a place of transition. Québec's problematisation of identity constitutes, in fact, an identity crisis.

Lepage is not alone in his preference for transcending boundaries. In contemporary Québecois film-making there is a general tendency to approach national identity through universalism. Georges Privet identifies universalism as a trend in the work of contemporary Québecois film-makers such as Denys Arcand, François Girard, André Forcier, Richard Ciupka and Robert Lepage, among others:

> Québecers are never more themselves than when they are abroad: from the USA in *La Florida* to France in *Boys II*. Why? Because to be universal, today's Québecois film-makers seem to believe that they have to go elsewhere; it does not matter where, but elsewhere... (2001: 15)

The implication that Québecers are more themselves outside of Québec is not only relevant to issues surrounding Québecois identity, but it can also be equated to the general position of finding one's own identity once surrounded with differences.

The traditional experience of first-generation immigrants attests to that shifting feeling of otherness. Indeed, my own observation of immigrant communities in Canada indicates that the first and second generation of Serbian immigrants feel Serbian in the host country, but when they go back to their place of origin, they feel Canadian. This is symptomatic of the conscious association with the permanent position of otherness to the centre. The socio-cultural position of an 'immigrant' requires he/she to be placed in subordination to the 'centre', with his/her own 'otherness' defined in terms of constructed or fantasised personal and national identity. The immigrants (foreign cultures) are contextualised by the social 'centre' (host culture) into a position of perpetual 'otherness' that only allows them to invent their identities if they favourably respond to existing hegemony, by embracing set boundaries imposed by the centre. Therefore, history/past as a notion of personal and national identity has been removed and the existence is only verified in present terms defined by the dominant 'centre'.

This erasure leads to acculturation. William Roseberry explains that acculturation has to be viewed from the position of political power and neo-colonial concepts and not only from the relevancy of cultural equality or inequality between the culture of the donor and receptor. He argues that the important problem in cultural pluralism is 'the denial of history to at least one of the cultures. What acculturationists called the donor culture – the colonial power or dominant centre – might been seen to have a history ... But we might have much less to say about the so-called receptor' (1989: 86).

As Privet observes, in the 1990s, the characters in Québecois films are going abroad in search of themselves, whereas in the 1980s they were locked in existential anguish in their lofts, and in the 1970s they went to the countryside in search of answers. He attributes this tendency to present characters as going elsewhere to a number of factors: a legitimate but naïve attempt to 'open-up to the world' (2001: 15); a desire to solve in one stroke the double problem of exportability and co-production; but especially the abandonment of the very notion of country as being passé and old-fashioned, reactionary and non-existent, after two failed referendums. Representation of life in today's Québecois cinema has become a vague zone, uncertain and unknowable, that has to be avoided. What is this saying about Québec, if not that it is becoming a non-place? Most of Québecois cinema is aiming to be like Hollywood, attempting to conform to typical commercial values mainly for practical reasons: transportability and access to funds. The question of identity becomes secondary to notions of being accepted into the dominant cinematic main frame.

Lepage's cinema presents Québec's society and culture through a set of oppositions – including the confrontation of 'Québecness' with other or foreign cultures. 'Other' cultures are seen as useful in providing a mirror in which one society can view itself. One of the first mirrors for Lepage was the East that helped him understand the West by providing an opposition to the known value system (Charest 1997: 36).

The aesthetic, philosophical journeys of Lepage juxtapose Québec to Berlin in *Le Polygraphe*, and Montréal to Osaka in *Nô*. In film narrative, departing from Québec yet not reaching stasis – a point of permanency – outside Québec whilst continuing to have a perpetual relationship with Québec, locates the character in a non-place, a position in between two worlds. Lepage is cinematically exploring the process in which Québecers are currently engaged. After two failed referendums, for Lepage the answer to Québec's identity is being sought in the context of internationalisation and globalisation. It appears that, as a society, Québec has matured enough to take on the world and its complexities. There is an understanding that the multicultural nature of its society means that Québec can be seen as a microcosm of the world at large and not only as a construct of French colonialism and American capitalist dominance. Although film is a chronicle of its own time, the reality represented in the film thus reflects the film-makers 'truth' and is more of a response to existing reality than simply a recording. Lepage's film narratives are therefore willing to internationalise the space of Québec national cinema, but the real issue is the uncertain and ongoing contradiction between past and present in the construction of Québec's identity. Will the willingness of Québec's audiences and the cultural politics of funding continue in a more lasting manner to embrace identity, as constructed within global narratives? Or will it support narratives of its own past, dominated by the need to control national mythology and memory?

Universalising the insider-outsider perspective

Cross-cultural reading in Lepage's films results in the alignment with the position of the spectator to his own as a film auteur, simultaneously aware of the significance of the material within and outside of its cultural context. The characters in Lepage's films bring with them a different cultural position into Québec's milieu, a cultural perspective acquired whilst being outside. This creates a difference between the local Québecois perspective and the international perspective: the inside view is now challenged by elements from the outside that threaten to expose Québec's inbuilt cultural attitude as ridiculous or petty, relevant only to its own momentum.

What makes Lepage's work different from that of other film authors in Québec is that his subjective reading of film narrative is in-between worlds: simultaneously on the outside looking in and on the inside looking out. This peculiar position of dual perception is a result of both Lepage's upbringing and his theatre work. As pointed out in chapter one, the experience of growing up in Québec in a bilingual and bicultural family gave him a valuable insight into being simultaneously an insider and outsider. By developing his performances in Québec and then taking them on international tours, he acquired the ability to transpose one cultural understanding into another. Arnold Hauser, who developed the traditional approach to sociology of culture, states that:

> Every artistic means of expression contains national characteristics. Not one uses a universal, nationally indifferent language, but not one of them is from the beginning confined within the borders of one nation. Every art, not just literature, expresses itself in a national idiom. (1985: 109)

The main accomplishment of Lepage's film narrative is the ability to translate 'national idiom' into an internationally understood and relevant narrative. He does not 'offer' the audience a fixed product, nor does he relate his narrative to the international audience as if they were a homogeneous entity. His narrative is open to a plurality of readings according to the range of perspectives in which audiences engage with the work. Lepage's films develop from his theatre productions, and embody that understanding of international cultures and multiple perspectives. His theatre narrative is unfixed and perpetually transformative. It is a work in progress that feeds from the cultural specificities of the different locations where it is performed. Each culture where Lepage performs contributes something to the narrative and leaves an imprint on the *mise-en-scène*. Richard Schechner, who initially used the term inter-culturalism in the mid-1970s as exchange between cultures has stated:

I felt that the real exchange of importance to artists was not that among nations, which really suggests official exchanges and artificial kinds of boundaries, but the exchange among cultures, something which could be done by individuals or by non-official grouping. (1996: 42)

Lepage's international cultural exchange does not mimic a culture aiming for its naturalistic representation; rather he personalises and appropriates a culture as an artistic resource that has an experiential value and can be communicated to the international audience outside the original cultural boundaries.

This internationalism is not only bound to the narrative; Lepage's cinematography also utilises his own intercultural experience. His long-term infatuation with Asian arts and cultural traditions is evident in the way his films treat time, space, colour and the relation between the personal/public, rhythm and structure. Lepage's poetics of memory consist of these intercultural influences, various overlaps of meanings, multilayered imagery, multiple perceptions and simultaneous readings. These will be explored in greater detail within the context of his individual works in the following chapters.

CHAPTER THREE

Le Confessionnal: Where do I come from?

Exploration of Cinematic Resources

For many, *Le Confessionnal* (1995) is Lepage's benchmark film. It certainly made his cinematic reputation when it first appeared and received Genie Awards for best picture, best art director and best director. The Academy of Canadian Cinema and Television also gave Lepage the prestigious Claude Jutra Award for direction of a first feature film. The award recognises the unique vision and creativity of emerging film-makers, and was an important recognition at the beginning of Lepage's film career.

Lepage wanted to make a film about his family, about representation of memory and how the past affects the present. The film successfully contrasts two epochs separated by the changes that took place during Québec's Quiet Revolution: the clerical Québec of the 1950s and international Québec at the beginning of the 1990s. The film narrative is a metaphorical bridge (the 'bridge' over the St. Lawrence River is also physically represented, serving as an opening and closing shot) between 'then' and 'now'. The time period that separates these two events is an important divide between clerical, secretive, hypocritical, mission-ridden Québec and the internationally informed modern Québec, with fragmented values, fake touristy cosmopolitanism and an atmosphere of hedonistic superficiality.

Lepage points out that '*Le Confessionnal* was, from the start, a film project. I was longing to tell this story on film' (in Dossier 1995a: 28). His interest in the poetics of cinematic language made film the perfect medium for self-confession. However, Lepage was not used to composing alone, but rather as part of a collaborative group. This was the first time that he wrote alone, and he worked on the film narrative for

Le Confessionnal as he would for his solo theatre performances, using a set of outside resources and personalising them. In this way Lepage offers his own private reading of the past, and presents this personalised, codified representation of the past as functional for the preservation of Québec's national identity. In *Le Confessionnal*, Lepage's engagement with personal and collective memory and discovery, or even re-construction of the past by using personal material, is relevant to a postmodern representation of culture and expands on the work of Denys Arcand. For Bill Marshall, Lepage's work responds to the postmodern tensions regarding past and identity: 'It is necessary to ask in what ways the new emphasis on space, the perpetual present, and the loss of historical grand narrative might be transforming cinema's representation of memory and the past' (2001: 305).

The overall question that Lepage asks in his first film is 'Where do I come from?' This question is the connecting device for a number of sub-narratives. It is also a personal response to Lepage's own dilemma: what are the impacts that personal and collective readings of the past have on the understanding of self in the present moment? What is particularly important in *Le Confessionnal* is the relationship of the collective past, remembered as well as reinvented, with the individual identity. As such, this chapter will analyse the film in a similar manner to Lepage's use of resources within the RSVP Cycle method to create his narrative.

Resources are relevant to an author's individuality – they are personal and subjective, and represent units from which the author engages in the process of human creativity. A story or an object can become a resource only if they establish a relation with the author. Anything can become a resource if it can provide personal content and is rich enough in meaning to inspire those engaged in the creative process. Resources are not a narrative but only creative stimuli, giving freedom for the structure to be found during the process of exploration. The use of resources in the creative process is a way of working that Lepage borrowed from the RSVP Cycles where, as previously explained, the 'R' stands for 'Resource', the term 'Resource' coming out of the tradition of dance theatre/environmental design in which anything can become a resource if the author or the performer is able to engage with it. The resources are emotional – as personal and collective memories, and material – as in the use of objects and space in aiding the re-discovery of location and its past, in order to find the truth about the characters' present. Resources are also relevant to the aesthetic qualities of the film narrative, in particular those based on intercultural influences relating to Buddhism, and the use of technology in terms of the tracking shot, light and colour. These elements not only pertain to *Le Confessionnal*, but to the way Lepage creates a plurality of the narratives and *mise-en-scène* in all his films.

The examination of cinematic resources as part of the RSVP Cycle of creating narrative is relevant to the way film is created, but not necessarily to the interpretation of the narrative as a finished product. Resources should not be confused with semiotics and signifiers or psychoanalytical symbols; RSVP Cycles are not goal-oriented psychological analyses of the finished work.

As pointed out in chapter one, Lepage used RSVP Cycles initially in theatre, and then translated them to cinema as part of his development within a new artistic form. This is not a new or unusual way of working; Mike Leigh made his international film reputation through transposing theatrical modes to the creation of film narrative (see Carney & Quart 2000). The resources serve as an inspiration and as connecting devices between material and creators (actors, director, writer and so on); a material from which the film narrative will be developed. Lepage observes that the resource has to be 'like a juicy fruit'; it has to be inspirational:

> You come up to someone or to a group and you say let's do a show about Hiroshima, and you can see that everybody has their own thing, it is very very rich. So resource is just that, it's just a provocation. It could be a word, a song, an object, something that you feel electricity for and of course you have to channel it in the right direction. It runs errant sometimes in all directions, and you wonder what are you doing. The resource is a trigger, is something that you feel is rich and you know that if you say that word or bring that object people will connect. (1999b)

Le Confessionnal is Lepage's own confessional, where he brings his own family references into the film narrative. In the same way, the film's main character, Pierre, confesses his family's past to the audience. The film was dedicated to the memory of Lepage's father, a cab driver like the character of the father in the *Le Confessionnal*. The main intrigue revolves around the search for the identity of the father of the main character's adopted brother – Lepage himself has an adopted brother. In fact, the script underwent a number of changes since its first version, which was so autobiographical that Lepage's sister and manager had to prevent him from making a film that would severely expose his own family. Cinematically, confession was represented in the film through the confession box, the church, and the sacramental elements of water and blood.

Le Confessionnal did not start with a script but with an offer from producers to Lepage to make his first film. The starting point for the film was Lepage himself, his personal world, and also his name and international reputation. Having an internationally recognisable name and reputation, and being the most prominent Canadian 'cultural export', as pointed out by Canadian Minister of International Affairs, Lloyd Axworthy, in the mid-1990s, implied that Lepage could sell the film and achieve success at international festivals and at the box office. Like many other art films in Québec, this film was a Canadian-British-French co-production, and the producers expected the film to have access to the international market.

Although *Le Confessionnal* is rooted in Québecois culture, the continuous referencing to Hitchcock's *I Confess* makes that film a major cinematic resource. *I Confess* is the material Lepage imports into his personal story, as a resource to demarcate the past and give familiarity to his story, making narrative recognisable for the audience. Lepage's use of *I Confess* and Hitchcock himself is multi-referential: he sets his work against a totality of ideological contexts that Hitchcock evokes as a cultural icon and a popular symbol. However, the references to Hitchcock are not only metaphorical, but also a starting resource and a reference point, a tool borrowed from Lepage's creative process in theatre, to personalise the material and make it more accessible to himself. Hitchcock was also a point of intervention into the cinematic medium that helped Lepage overcome his theatrical way of thinking.

> What I write is either too theatrical or uninformed of the cinematic medium. So the thing that helped me is that in my story there was an Alfred Hitchcock reference. So I could at least go and see a lot of Hitchcock films and some dramaturgical recipes and say 'OK, well then I could invite that into my film because there's also a little bit about Hitchcock in the film.' (2002)

By using a Hitchcock film within his own, Lepage brings the idea of the Hollywood 'dream machine' into 1952 Québec City, the year in which the main character Pierre Lamontagne was born. At the beginning, Pierre tells us that this year was important for the introduction of television into Québec, for the re-election of Maurice Duplessis and for Hitchcock's filming in Québec City, three events that played a vital role in Québec society. Television as a medium provided a space and unifying frame of reference for national identity; the Duplessis phenomenon had a political and social impact on Québec from the Great Depression in the 1930s up to the Quiet Revolution in the 1960s; and the increasing importance of American corporations and capital on Québec was represented through the making of *I Confess* and the business negotiations conducted by Hitchcock's entrepreneurial assistant.

Henry R. Garrity states that *Le Confessionnal* as 'a metaphor for Québec's quest for national identity represents no less than a meta-text, an alternative scenario of *I Confess*' (2000: 96). However, *I Confess* is an important resource but it is not an alternative scenario, it is rather a social text for Lepage's representation of Québec in the 1950s. *Le Confessionnal* is a family drama that uses Hitchcock's film as a resource, transporting into it his own personal material; when deconstructed, *I Confess* is a resource that uses Hitchcock's recognisable world to talk about Lepage's personal stories. Lepage explains that the starting point in *Le Confessionnal* was the identity of people once exposed to a new, influential, overpowering reality. He explains that the film is

> about people who live in a typical French-Canadian reality, but who suddenly find themselves faced with a sort of mythological, Hollywoodian reality, filled with stars – naturally – but with a massive presence of Americanism. I thought it would be a good way to question identity. It is a film about the search for identity, which also looks into the game of truth. It seems to me today that the world is obsessed with the idea of truth and knowledge. The knowledge of

Figure 4 *Le Confessionnal*: Throughout the film Lepage makes visual references to Hitchcock iconic presence

truth and secrets, and the refusal of concealment. Also, it seems to me that very few people can stand the truth, and I thought it would be an interesting idea to develop. This is why the whole structure of the film is built around a concealed secret, a truth never spoken. All in all, I believe the fate of these characters would have been deeply changed had they known the truth in the first place. (in Dossier 1995b: 30)

Narrative of 'Le Confessionnal'

The film narrative uses events from 1952 to represent the past that Pierre Lamontagne (Lothaire Bluteau) is searching for, in the process unveiling previously undisclosed memories, but maintaining the suspense and secrecy of the identity of Marc's father until the end of the film. After Pierre's return from China to Québec, to attend his father Paul-Emile's (François Papineau) funeral, he attempts to piece his life together. By chance, he encounters his adopted brother, Marc (Patrick Goyette), leaving a client's hotel room. Pierre finds the family home dilapidated so he decides to renovate. He finds work as a porter through his cousin André (Richard Fréchette) and begins to rebuild his life. Pierre and Marc find that in order to do this, they need to decipher their past to thus know where they are going.

The film narrative is constructed through fragments of time and space, not allowing the audience access to the truth, so that they are always at the same level of awareness as Pierre, enveloped in the mystery. The film narrative follows a basic narrative pattern; a character is searching through the past in order to solve his present

Figure 5 *Le Confessionnal*: Marc in a gay sauna seen from above; the grille is suggestive of the confessional box

conditions of angst and sense of displacement, to find his own way to the future. Resolving the past and journeying towards finding oneself is also a dominant driving force for the characters in Lepage's theatre productions, the motivation behind their actions, and the explanation of why they embark on these physical journeys.

The family story spans four decades and involves a marriage triangle. In the early 1950s a typical Québecois couple, Françoise (Marie Gignac) and Paul-Emile, are trying to conceive a child. Rachel (Françoise's 16-year-old sister) becomes pregnant after a secret affair with Paul-Emile. She gives birth to Marc. This birth is surrounded with intrigue and mystery as the father's identity is kept a secret. Rachel only confides the truth surrounding her pregnancy to one person, the priest Father Massicotte (Jean-Louis Millette), who is bound by the confessional vow of silence. When accused of fathering Rachel's child, the priest is unable to defend himself by revealing the identity of the child's father. Subsequently he is defrocked and ousted from the church. Unable to cope with her situation, Rachel commits suicide, leaving Marc's upbringing to Françoise and Paul-Emile. Marc's adoption by the Lamontagne's is the official story told to the young Pierre in order to avoid all the social and religious implications of a Catholic mother who committed suicide after producing a child out of wedlock and with an unknown man. It was a clean start, a 'concealed secret, a truth never spoken'. Until Paul-Emile's death and Pierre's return to Québec, Marc's adoption had never been questioned. However, in 1989 Pierre finds himself wanting to save his brother by helping him find his father.

The connecting figure in both periods is Massicotte, who in 1952 was a young priest and, in 1989, as Marc's lover and father figure, is now a politician, a prominent Québecois diplomat. He knows who Marc's father is since his mother confessed to him. Unlike the priest in *I Confess*, who was able to save himself and continue to be a priest, Massicotte has had to endure the full spectrum of condemnation and shame by having to leave the priesthood. Ousted from the Church and having abandoned his own faith, he remains obedient to the Church's rule of silence. Through Massicotte, Lepage plays on the impact of destiny on human life. Massicotte, once accused of fathering Marc, later becomes Marc's father figure, as a lover from whom Marc is desperate to escape but to whom he always returns. Marc displays suicidal tendencies, which Lepage uses as a hereditary link to connect with Rachel's suicide. In Japan, Marc, like his mother, commits suicide. It is left open as to whether Marc discovered who his real father was, and whether that was the final straw that led to his suicide. In both cases, the deaths revolve around Massicotte. He remains a power figure: in clerical Québec he is a priest and in contemporary cosmopolitan Québec, he is a politician.

Pierre takes charge of Marc's son, allowing Massicotte to give money for their silence regarding his involvement in Marc's death. We may see Pierre's motivation for involvement in resolving Marc's past as stemming from his own need for family identity. The mystery in the film revolves around the necessity to define personal identity, and to negotiate the external powers of church, state and society, embodied in the character of Massicotte, who represents clerical, political and paternal authority. The global narrative of *Le Confessionnal* works with Québec's space/time context as well as with the perpetual search for individual identity and the empowerment to express the self.

Enter Hitchcock's 'I Confess'

The decision to choose Québec City as a location, for Hitchcock as for Lepage, was influenced by the strong presence of national clericalism in the city in the 1950s. Hitchcock used the location in order to contemporise the story from 1902, because Québec was seen at the time to be a relatively old-fashioned. As Martin Lefebvre states:

> There can be no question that in choosing Québec City to shoot a French play written in 1902, Hitchcock was aiming at a particular chronotope: that of a backward society not fully in tune – or in time, should I say – with the rest of the industrial world, still clinging to old world values. Had Hitchcock wanted to shoot the film elsewhere, say in an equally urban environment in Europe for example, he most certainly would have had to make this a period or costume film. Duplessis-era Québec City was the perfect site for *I Confess*. (1998: 92)

If the interpretation of generic films depends on the audience's generic expectation, as Rick Altman (1999) argues, then genre for Lepage is a vehicle to represent a given time period. In *Le Confessionnal*, the past was represented through Hitchcock's film, not so much as a film narrative but as a social representation and cultural event: the filming of a dramatic and atmospheric thriller. Susan Hayward gives a general definition of the thriller as a film that relies on 'intricacy of plot to create fear and apprehension in the audience. It plays on our own fears by drawing on our infantile and therefore mostly repressed fantasies that are voyeuristic and sexual in nature' (2000: 440). Hitchcock's narrative revolves around basic themes, re-working traditional conflicts over duty and love or money and faith. He constructs a simple film narrative that is effective in manipulating its audience, absorbing them within the film's world. He achieved this by giving the audience clues – by pre-empting the forthcoming actions – therefore leaving them in suspense, waiting for the inevitable to happen. Hayward points out that thriller films are sadomasochistic, setting up a binary opposition between the victim and the aggressor. If Hitchcock puts the audience in the position of aggressor, Lepage positions the audience as victims. Lepage aligns the audience with the main characters in this respect, unaware throughout the film of the central intrigue.

I Confess uses all the essential stylistic elements of Hitchcock's film narrative. The storyline of *I Confess* centres on a mystery, the murder of a lawyer, Villiette, by Keller, the lay caretaker of a parish church. Keller, dressed as a priest, draws suspicion onto Father Logan. Two girls saw a priest leaving the murder scene. Keller confesses the crime to Father Logan in order to receive absolution, and possibly to frame him. Inspector Laurrue suspects Logan, as he has seen him outside Villiette's apartment with a mysterious woman, Ruth. Villiette was blackmailing Ruth, now the wife of a respectable politician who had an affair with the then un-ordained priest Logan. This has led Ruth to Logan looking for help. Their affair is revealed and Logan becomes the prime suspect in Villiete's murder. Having to keep his vow of silence, Logan is unable to defend himself and reveal who the real killer is. After going to trial, Logan is found not guilty, but on leaving the court is attacked by the crowd. Alma, Keller's wife, goes to help him and wants to reveal that Father Logan is not a killer, but Keller kills her. In the chase and shooting with the police, Keller is fatally wounded. He dies in Father Logan's arms, confessing Logan's innocence and receiving forgiveness from him.

Unlike the cause-and-effect plot of *I Confess*, *Le Confessionnal* has a non-linear structure that interweaves past and present, fact and fiction into four branches that together compose the film narrative: a) the filming and the premiere screening of *I Confess* b) Paul-Emile's family situation in 1952 c) Pierre's discoveries in 1989 d) the circumstances of Marc's life. These sub-narratives are connected by Pierre Lamontagne's search for the father of his adopted brother Marc. The past is revealed to us, as it is to him, through his journey.

The film's narratives develop through flashbacks and juxtapositions of two time periods: 1952 – the time of Hitchcock's filming of *I Confess* in Québec City, and 1989 – when Pierre has returned from China to Québec City.

The auteur on auteurism

I Confess not only has a social function as a text revealing Québec, but also represents a comment on aestheticism, namely on film auteurism. *Le Confessionnal* makes direct references to Hitchcock as a film auteur by quoting his scenes and locations, by references to 'stars' and the influence of Catholicism and personal guilt. Indeed Hitchcock was one of the key film-makers upon whose work auteur criticism was based, listing stylistic and thematic elements that can be found in his films, constituting a recognisable and consistent directorial signature. Claude Chabrol has identified the stylistic and thematic integrity of Hitchcock's work, which revolves around shared guilt and Catholicism. He points out that Hitchcock creates a whole universe, which is founded on the form: 'In Hitchcock's work, form does not embellish content, it creates it' (1979: 152). Hitchcock's artistic integrity as well as his presence in the public sphere, casts him as a cultural icon, a resource with multi-layered and global references.

The concept of *la politique des auteurs* (the author policy), formulated by the members of the French *nouvelle vague* in the mid-1950s, included critics who later became well-known film-makers, such as Jean-Luc Godard, François Truffaut, Jacques Rivette, Eric Rohmer and Claude Chabrol. Auteurism perceives film as the outcome of a specific individual artistic vision and personal expression. It is an artist-centred explanation of film as an artwork that reflects a personal approach to the creation of a work. In the mid-1950s Truffaut published an essay, *A Certain Tendency of the French Cinema*, where he presented a manifesto for new wave films using the term 'auteur', distinguishing between director as an artist and director as a technician, the latter remaining faithful to literary scenarios whilst transposing them into film. Looking at American cinema to set an example for the role of new French cinema, 'auteur' critics recognise directors such as Fritz Lang, Hitchcock, Howard Hawks and Nicholas Ray as the 'authors' of their films. This was necessary in order to form a canon, to create a classical cinematic art-form to which new French cinema could respond. Gerald Mast proclaimed that 'just as there is only one poet per pen, one painter per canvas, there can be only one creator of a movie' (1976: 3).

Lepage quotes Hitchcock's locations and events; however, he places them in a deliberately different context, making his film very un-Hitchcockian. Showing the filming of *I Confess* and its premiere in Québec – the use of Québecois extras and their auditions, and the relationship to French language as secondary nuisance that only causes problems in communications with the American film company – signifies the past in which Québec is entrenched. The collision of American entrepreneurship and the Hollywood version of Catholic Québec, with its dominant clericalism and provincial insularity, prescribing and codifying all that is hidden and revealed in family life, is personified through Pierre's search for the father of his adoptive brother Marc.

At both the beginning and end of the film, Hitchcock frames the film narrative within a wide-angle shot of Chateau Frontenac, Québec's most famous tourist landmark. He skilfully relies on editing to illustrate various points of view as well as to cut off the whole picture, so that the spectators are only aware of part of the scene. In *I Confess*, Hitchcock expresses the closeness and confinement of the oldest city in North America by editing fragments of buildings, street signs, walls and alleyways. Hitchcock's major influences, gained from German Expressionism and Eisenstein's theory on montage, can best be illustrated in the number of shots he used to screen one event (the shower scene in *Psycho* (1960) took 34 shots for 25 seconds of footage). In *I Confess,* the introductory scene consists of a large number of short shots, detailing the church, the streets and some of the main characters, pointing towards the murder on which the film centres. It is common to find in Hitchcock's work a high number of 'point of view' shots. These shots represent the visual perspective of a character and the direction in which he/she is looking. They act as a stream of consciousness, giving the audience an insight into the character's thoughts.

Lepage's cinema, on the other hand, organises its visual images within the shot itself, drawing upon his theatrical experience in manipulating space to create an exchange between past and present and to define our point of view as audience. Unlike Hitchcock's cross cutting and fast editing of a number of shots, Lepage mainly employs tracking shot techniques. Compared to Hitchcock, Lepage takes time; he is an epic storyteller. By using plan-séquence in one continuous shot, the camera tracks from one side to another an event that takes place in 1952 and transforms into 1989. The locations are the same: church, apartment, exterior of a house, bridge, and events from the past become alive, merging in the same location: the present is coming out of the past and the past is coming out of the present. In this way, memory makes the present moment, as much as the present moment defines memory. This is particularly relevant to the presentation of the family apartment, where the camera shows a room and hallway in the 1950s and as the camera moves to the next room we are in 1989, where Pierre is refurbishing his flat.

Manipulation of perceptions and dramatic irony

In *I Confess*, the audience is aware that specific characters are vulnerable and helpless, either as a result of their past experiences or as part of their position in society, making them participants in a sadomasochistic relationship between the film and the audience. In this way, the audience participates in a sadomasochistic scenario and through voyeurism 'derive pleasure from re-experiencing our primitive and infantile desires' as Hayward describes. This is not only relevant to Hitchcock's thrillers, but to the stage in general. Theatre performances as well as films tend to exert social pressures and conventions, often focusing on the downfall of a protagonist (generally with social status) for the audience and cast to ridicule by making the audience aware of what that protagonist does not know. This dramatic device, whereby the audience is placed in a privileged position of 'knowing' more than the characters, is usually referred to as dramatic irony. Lepage makes extensive use of it both in his stage work and in his films. Likewise, intrigue, gossip and tabloid material feed into a need to witness disgrace, a downfall, preferably of someone who occupies a social role and who embodies social rules, moral or judicial. The thriller is like a ritual of collective and personal purification, and like Greek tragedy in Classical times, it reinforces and challenges norms. In *I Confess* it is a priest as a fictional murderer and lover, while in *Le Confessionnal* this figure becomes a fictionalised father/lover to his 'son'. On a fictional level, thrillers reproduce the experience of degradation of a character's social position that results in a temporary liberation from the social rules of engagement.

In *I Confess*, Hitchcock subjects Ruth, a young woman married to an up-and-coming politician, to the audience's subliminal voyeuristic/sadomasochistic pleasures by making her helpless. In her past, Ruth had an affair that her husband was not aware of with a man who then became a priest. The public knowledge, exposing this intrigue, is the main motivation behind her helplessness. Likewise, Father Logan, a young priest, is also subjected to disgrace, not only being socially ridiculed as a priest who had an affair with a married woman, but also accused of murder. In this manner, theatre and film often employ carnivalesque revelry, creating relationships and imagery that would be liberating to the individual and private self by suspending temporarily the order and freeing oneself from the dominant social rules.

Through Pierre's search for Marc we look at the objects and people of the gay sexual underworld in a voyeuristic way. Marc's humiliation and need for self-punishment and Pierre's unsuccessful attempts to save Marc from 'imprisonment' by his lover Massicotte, clearly a father figure to him, leads after prolonged suffering and anxiety to Marc's suicide. We are observing Marc's demise. Like Hitchcock's Ruth, Marc is a victim as a gay (bisexual) man, but he is also doomed and will die as a punishment for his real father's 'sins' committed in the past. Although Lepage does not associate himself with any categorisation such as that of gay film-maker, his openness about his homosexuality and fundamentally gay models and theme can place *Le Confessionnal* within New Queer Cinema. However, the consideration for a mainstream audience prevailed. Marc's sexual relation with a much older man is placed in a context of prostitution and self-punishment, something imposed on him rather then the outcome of his individual free choice.

The manipulation of perceptions in *Le Confessionnal* is reminiscent of the post-structuralists' tendencies in terms of auteur theory. Lepage includes all relevant discourses (social, political, aesthetic, historical) around and within the film text. From the point of view of new auteurism theory, Lepage is consciously playing on auteurial inter-textuality. Duplessiste Québec of the 1950s, Catholicism as a vital force, Hitchcook's iconography and his filming in Québec City, *I Confess*, Oedipus, Lepage's autobiography and the fictional story of *Le Confessionnal* are just some of the different 'texts' around and within the film that are shown as having an effect upon one another. Thus, the perception is manipulated from these different positions. As Hayward points out, 'the auteur is a figure constructed out of her or his film;

for although there exist authorial signs within a film that make it ostensibly that of a certain film-maker, none the less that authorial text is also influenced by those others' (2000: 362). The subject is the author-spectator relation and the protagonist is the vehicle for the author's voice to reach the audience for whom he/she is directly narrating and walking through the process of his own discovery. Lepage maintains the mystery throughout the film by revealing to the audience just as much as the protagonist is able to discover on his quest.

By quoting Hitchcock's film and making visual references to Hitchcock's character in *Le Confessionnal*, Lepage points to the cultural iconography of auteur cinema transposed into different social and cultural codes relevant to the contemporary spectator. Furthermore, by casting the British actress, Kristin Scott Thomas, in the role of Hitchcock's assistant, an aspiring blond starlet and Hollywood star look-alike from that period, Lepage's irony becomes sharper. He is commenting on the film industry's commercial values, Americans coming to Québec to do a little bit of business. Hitchcock as a film auteur had his own stylistic considerations, which included awareness of the necessity to have a 'star' present in order to succeed at the box office. In the public consciousness, recognition of a film is achieved largely through the audience demanding to 'see' a star, whereby the star becomes a symbol through which the identification process with the circumstances of the film narrative occurs. The star serves as the vehicle of acceptance of the film narrative by the audience.

Lepage's resistance to the clichéd concept of synergy between star and story is evident in his use of his stock group of performers – theatre actors, with whom he works on collectively-devised performances. From film's position, working with unknown actors who have no links with mass-media entertainment provides authenticity in the creative style and offers a fresh look at stories and characters. At the same time, however, Lepage uses for the main roles not stars in a strict sense but up-and-coming actors that have a certain reputation within the film industry, such as Kristin Scott Thomas, Lothaire Bluteau and Peter Stalbot.

Collective and Personal Memories

The emotional resources in *Le Confessionnal* are stories, anecdotes and myths upon which a score of narratives are developed: Lepage's family, Hitchcock's filming of *I Confess*, the myth of Oedipus and religious references (Catholicism, Buddhism). Bruce Kirkland in the review in *Toronto Star* observes:

> The story is set both in 1989 and 1952 and Lepage fluidly mines the territory between those years for insights into how dramatically Québec society has changed. He does so through the lives of individuals, not through dreary political or social documentation. (1995: C5)

Lepage's subjective vision of Québec, seen through the imperfection of personal memory comes to us via a film persona, his own alter ego, Pierre Lamontagne. Offering a subjective account of the director's life and inviting us on a journey into his city recalls another film auteur who narrates tales from his city, Woody Allen. Lepage not only admires Allen's work, he also uses it as a resource. Like Allen's stock stand-up comedy character, who is fundamentally the same in all his films, Pierre Lamontagne serves as a connecting device within the narratives, linking together the past with the present, a vehicle or the catalyst of the truth, which is revealed to the spectator through his actions. Lepage explains:

> He is all-purpose because he is relatively young and an artist, which allows us to place him anywhere, in almost any circumstances. He is a very flexible, very mobile character – a blank character, in a way. He provides the link between the story and the audience ... in *Le Confessionnal* he is not aware of his family's secrets or of those behind the filming of Alfred Hitchcock's *I Confess*. Through his curiosity and the discoveries he makes, such a character becomes a doorway or, better yet, a key for the audience, who therefore identify more easily with him and can use him to gain access to the play's core. (in Charest 1997: 34)

Lepage's own psychoanalysis sessions, Jung's ideas and the RSVP Cycles – his theatre work as preoccupation with his own fantasies and obsessions – resulted in a particular way of working where he invents a character as a means to personalise and make direct reference to his material. He integrates the personal into his work by becoming one of the characters within the story. He developed this approach through his solo shows which he writes, performs and directs. However, he does not act in his films. Yet this is something he wants to do, like Allen does; to narrate from within his films, embodied within the frame, as an actor, having a visible presence. Lepage explains that what he likes about Allen is that

> he's not as obsessed by what the film looks like as much as what it feels like. And I think I would be a better actor, director, better writer ... if I was in the middle of my film and I haven't had the courage to do that yet. (2002)

The key similarity between Allen's work and Lepage's is the presence of a narrating persona. Allen's film persona is fundamentally a type of character that has been present in popular farce throughout the centuries, from Ancient Roman comedy, to Renaissance Italian Commedia del Arte, silent film and stand-up comedy routines built on contradictions. Allen's on-screen alter ego is a self-obsessed loudmouth, but also a coward: lustful towards women, but insecure; nervous and unable to have relations, but full of opinions and 'wisdom'. Allen's film narrative operates through set types of farcical characters, who transform throughout the story because of outside experience, often caught in unusual situations that are bigger than they are, an observable lack or absence in their life. Allen's characters are mostly limited to a specific location that he knows well. As he himself observes, 'They're mostly New Yorkers, kind of upper-class, educated, neurotic. It's almost the only thing I ever write about, because it's almost the only thing I know' (in Björkman 1995: 46). Lepage creates his film narratives from a similar position: the localism of Québecois, authenticity, and use of farce, dissatisfied characters in search of a solution, existential uncertainty, fractured and fragmented lives, and a sense of difference from others. In *Le Confessionnal*, Pierre searches for his own past by wanting to resolve a mystery: who is the father of his adopted brother Marc. This is in fact Lepage's personal engagement with his family and life in Québec City.

Lepage uses location – especially specific countries and cities – as an important resource for creating film narrative. This is taken from intercultural references dominant in his work. Pierre, an art student in China, brings with him a different mindset, which is directly linked to the Oriental influences he has experienced. Pierre's use of colours, the renovation of his apartment – which is minimised in terms of objects but maximised in terms of space – his cuisine, his use of chopsticks and his studies of calligraphy all reflect the physical and mental attitude that he brought with him from China. Furthermore, the constant references to the Tiananmen Square events, present throughout the film in the form of televised news footage and voice-overs, emphasise the effects that China continues to exert on his present circumstances. When Pierre is not engaged in the search for the identity of Marc's father, he is working on the family apartment and following the current events in China. It could be said that the material resources relevant to the Orient assist actor Lothaire Bluteau to create a personal resource for Pierre's character. We may also see China as a visual resource providing rich symbols and imagery for Lepage's cinematic expression.

Cinematically, much as the events of 1952 in Québec City are informed by Catholicism and claustrophobically regulated by social codification, the year 1989 is characterised by the changes Pierre wishes to bring about. In order to create his own personal space, Pierre has to clear out the remnants of his past. In the same way that he is clearing his apartment, Pierre is also re-ordering his family past. The journey between the embedded Catholicism of Québec City and the multiculturally referenced Orient in Lepage's work was previously used in his theatre production *The Dragon's Trilogy*. The story takes place over 75 years, between the passage of two Halley comets. *The Dragon's Trilogy* moves through Chinese communities in Canada, from the beginning of the twentieth century in Québec City to Toronto in the 1940s and 1950s, ending with Vancouver's multicultural milieu at the end of the millennium, a journey that defines the key events of cultural integration in Canada. We follow the life span of two women, Jeanne and Françoise, from their childhood to maturity and death, including the lives of their children. This production, as with *Le Confessionnal*, portrays Québec City as a small, oppressed and stifling community in order to demonstrate a progression throughout the play, where, under the influence of Oriental references characters achieve openness, enlightenment and personal freedom.

The filming of *I Confess* represents a social milieu, a backdrop against which the personal history of the Lamontagne family is played out. Unlike *I Confess*, which uses the characters' voluntary memory in the form of flashbacks, memory in *Le Confessionnal* is involuntary; it is imprinted on the present day. The past imposes itself on the present, literally coming out of the walls, whereby 1952 lives alongside 1989. Choosing the moment when Hollywood visited Québec City serves as a valuable counterpoint to a small-minded way of life, represented by an incestuous family situation.

The incest in the story of Oedipus was an important emotional resource that counterbalanced Hitchcock's anecdote. The spatial confinement of a world where life evolved around one's place of birth, which usually was also the place of one's death, found resonance in Lepage's story. The contrast between these two resources, Hollywood and Oedipus, is represented through two different characters – Rachel and Hitchcock's assistant – and their positions as women in society. The Lamontagne family's secret, Rachel's pregnancy and suicide, and the preparation for Hitchcock's filming, conducted mainly by a nameless character played by Kristin Scott Thomas, present two different readings of women. Early on, the audience are shown Hitchcock's assistant, an efficient Hollywood blonde who, with the assistance of Father Massicotte, explains the plot structure of the film and the reasoning behind Hitchcock's choice of film location. The only other woman in this scene is Rachel, a device for drawing a total contrast between the social reality of Québec and the one recreated for them by Hollywood. The assistant explains to Massicotte and the Bishop that 'Mr Hitchcock feels that this story is universal' and ends her attempt to persuade the two men by stating: 'Besides, your church is so photogenic.' Throughout the film narrative, the character of the assistant is used to depict the Americanisation of Québec, orchestrating the events surrounding the filming.

In 1989, Pierre is trying to find the truth that has never been spoken and is concealed in the past. What happened to Rachel was concealed by the veil of family secrecy which Pierre is now uncovering in his pursuit to find Marc's father. Like Oedipus, Pierre is set on-course to resolve the past in order to set the course right in the present moment. The Oedipal quest to resolve the deeds of the past is very much the connecting element of *Le Confessionnal*'s film narrative. The character of Oedipus provides a resource for three characters in the film's narrative. First, Marc is the one who without knowing, almost as if by the hand of fate, maintains a sexual relationship with the man accused of being his father at the time of his birth. Second, throughout the film, Pierre is concerned with the search for an answer, leaving the possibility of who Marc's real father is open until the end. Third, Paul-Emile embodies relationships with two sisters and suffers the fate of Oedipus, becoming blind. Moreover, Paul-Emile passes all the suffering onto his children.

Unlike the Greek myth, the characters of *Le Confessionnal* have personal freedom but they believe that if they discover their past, their whole understanding of themselves will be altered. As an emotional resource this is echoed throughout the film, where Pierre's search for the past is the only way he knows to define himself. The ending of the film is very suggestive of an ambiguous uncertainty, which could easily question the need for knowledge. This brings us back to Lepage's observation that the world at present is obsessed with truth and knowledge and the question: are our lives that much better for knowing what was concealed, was never meant to be found? The end of the film reflects the ambiguity in interpreting the future. In the last shot of the film, Pierre and Marc's son walk over the bridge into the future after receiving a cheque from Massicotte to secure the child's prospects. However, Marc's son is shown walking on the rails of the bridge with Pierre holding his hand. The cliché of a happy ending, getting the money and going into the future, is subverted by a long shot of crossing a bridge. Where are they going? Will money be able to divert the inevitable natural process and influence of heredity by which Marc's son has diabetes? What would happen if Pierre did not get the money?

Diabetes is an important theme connecting two time periods, a proof of heredity, and a metaphorical indication of blindness, relevant to King Oedipus' blindness, brought about at the end of Sophocles' play. Paul-Emile, suggests a suspense story to Hitchcock as he sits in the rear of his cab, which in fact details his affair with Rachel and Marc's birth. Hitchcock states: That's not a suspense story … it's a Greek tragedy. Asking 'what happens to the man?' Paul-Emile responds, 'Well he just can't bring himself to love this child and so when he sees all the suffering he has caused he blacks his eyes out.' Oedipus himself gouges out his eyes, so tormented by his past that he cannot bear to see the suffering he has caused to his family. Likewise, Paul-Emile suggests this as a suitable punishment for himself, having passed on diabetes through the family line. It is emphasised throughout the film that Marc refuses to be tested for diabetes despite his son's condition. In this way, diabetes is used as a family link that Massicotte divulges as a clue to Pierre in finding Marc's real father.

The emotional resources of the past as embodied in Hitchcock's filming, and of the present as relevant to an Oedipal search, are complemented by careful use of language signification: the social, political and cultural role of the English language in Québec. Language as a resource works as an inverted representation of the actor by which the secondary and subservient language, French in Hitchcock's *I Confess*, becomes English in Lepage's *Le Confessionnal*. Through the use of English language, *Le Confessionnal* creates an atmosphere in which the cultural consciousness of Québec is palpable. The only other time that Lepage refers to English language throughout the film, apart from Kristin Scott Thomas's lines which are translated, is in the scenes involving the topless dancer 'Mowse'[1] and her dance co-partner, 'Moose', in the seedy motel next to a railroad track. 'Moose', a Native Canadian, is the only other character who is completely Anglophone. The underworld that Marc's ex-girlfriend and child inhabit is presented as socially and economically deprived, and enveloped by the English language. This is in sharp contrast to the world of 1952, where English is associated with glamour, style and prestige. The political context of the English language in *Le Confessionnal* is clearly demarcated between these two time frames, where English, represented in the 1950s, is the language of empowerment, associated with a higher status and wealth, whereas in 1989 and the 1990s suggests disempowerment, associated with the lower social class and cheap motels. Between these two time frames, Anglophones are equated to indigenous people in Québec, in the same way as Native Canadians are marginalised as the underdogs in society.

The use of the English language in *Le Confessionnal* reflects a reversal of attitude from the one that Hitchcock has in *I Confess*, where the film narrative is in English, using French for the maids, servants and the background *mise-en-scène*. Rachel's pregnancy is more than a device to generate the main conflict in the film narrative; it is a valuable emotional resource, given Québec's agricultural social milieu, which emphasises the dominance of reproduction as a rebirth necessary for survival of the agrarian social structure. Pregnancy functions as a resource that can generate dramatic conflict on individual and collective levels – colliding with religion, social expectations and personal understanding.

Objects and Locations

The material resources are physical objects and space; locations that can trigger narrative contents and have a visual and material presence in the film's *mise-en-scène*. In *Le Confessionnal* locations as resources embody memory. The family apartment has preserved life of the past; it serves as evidence that the past is still real. Stories 'hidden' in the walls – family photos, objects, furniture and colours – trigger memory, keeping the past present. Pierre's re-occurring painting of the apartment represents an attempt to escape from the past by transforming the location. In *Le Confessionnal* the material resources are photographs, taxis, the church, confession boxes, the Lamontagne apartment, the walls of the apartment, Hotel Chateau Frontenac, the motel, Oriental symbols, water, wine, blood and paint. A number of the material resources are used to create visual images that are central to scenes. The photographs become a symbol of the past and a way to find the answer. The walls of the Lamontagne's apartment are strewn with family photos framed on the wall. The frames have been removed from the walls but the stains remain. Throughout the film Pierre tries to paint the walls to cover the stains and symbolically take control over the present; however, the empty spaces still show through as a sign of the past's presence. Later in the film, Marc and Pierre go on a quest to find the family photograph album, which Marc gave to his ex-girlfriend stripper, so that they might see Marc's christening photograph to identify those that attended the ceremony, and to decide whether, once recognised, they would be able to shed light on his father's identity.

A taxi is used as another material resource, a device connecting the past with the present. It is also a device that depicts the passing of time. At the beginning of *Le Confessionnal*, the audience is watching the premiere of *I Confess*; this image cuts and the audience is transported to 1989 as a red taxi pulls up outside the Lamontagne apartment. A few moments later, Pierre is in the garage and we see the black, 1950s taxi that belonged to his father. Not only are we shown the cars of two different eras, but Lepage shows them to us in the same era and then later introduces us to Paul-Emile's taxi when it was new. Once they have mended it in 1989, Pierre and Marc use the old taxi to find the photograph album. At the beginning of the film, while Pierre talks to us about his city and family, visually we are in 1950s Québec. A transformation to the 1980s is made within a single frame with a fixed shot in which the exterior of the Lamontagne's home is seen. The location is transformed by the passage of two models of cars, one from the 1950s and the other from the 1980s, announcing the different periods.

The actual church is an important material resource, a signpost in the film action towards a place that keeps secrets of the past. The presence of the church as a space dominates the narrative of the 1950s more than that of 1989. Indeed in the part of the narrative which deals with 1989, the church as a location and resource is only used twice; once for the funeral of Paul-Emile and then when Pierre re-visits the priest who held the ceremony to discuss the church records to find out who baptised Marc. On the other hand, the narrative involving the early 1950s uses the church as a crucial location that embodies the key developments of the film, serving as a place of personal and social interactions. The church for the 1950s strand of narrative is a location of stability and a model of the way life should be lived. The audience sees Hitchcock's assistant placating the priests in the church; it is also used as a location for filming scenes from Hitchcock's *I Confess*; it is shown to be the place where Rachel works and is fired from; the young priest Massicotte is shown working there and berated for his alleged affair with Rachel which ultimately sends him into exile; it is the place where Françoise visits to find solace and where both she and Rachel go to confess their 'sins'. In fact, the church holds the truth about Pierre and Marc's past and maintains the secrecy, protected by the sacred vow of the confessional. It is intriguing that Lepage resorts to the church as a keeper of the past and of identity, which on many levels informs contemporary Québec's position towards its Catholic past, where religion dominated all aspects of political and social life. The stability of the church is replaced with the 1989 instability of locations and transitional spaces, temporary places such as hotels, sleazy motels, and sauna clubs, where old men are soliciting young partners.

The confessional box is another important resource that embodies the idea in the title of the film – confession. As a resource it has symbolic value, recurring throughout the film in numerous forms, namely in the visual signification of the confessional screen separating the priest from the confessor. The screens are mirrored by the presence of slatted shutters at Pierre's family home (which we see him open very early in the film suggesting a future of truth), and by the window at Pierre's house; when Marc first visits Pierre the audience see him through a multi-paned window, fragmented by his own confessional screen – his fractured personality. When Father Massicotte visits the Lamontagne home, under the guise of seeing Françoise, it is Rachel who goes to the door. Between the two characters there is a pane of etched glass, the only thing that separates them. Massicotte is trying to coax Rachel into telling the church her secret so that he will not be ousted. Terrified by the prospect of destroying her family, Rachel breaks down into tears and falls against the glass repeatedly asking Massicotte to go away. The use of frosted glass, with its opacity, is reminiscent of the confessional screen, through which only small fragments of the face can be seen.

This suggestion of the constant presence of the confessional screen is repeated in the décor of Massicotte's Japanese style apartment, particularly in the bathroom where Marc finally commits suicide. It could be said that the symmetry used between objects, locations and people within the film reflects the layout of the confessional box. If in a two-person mid-shot a screen was placed between the two people, one would automatically see a confessional box scenario; indeed in the symmetry consistently used between the two houses, the alleyway is suggestive of the screen. For the most part, Lepage's *mise-en-scène* is interior; the action in the film, apart from a few transitional scenes, takes place within the walls of an enclosed space. Aside of the obvious link to Lepage's stage experience, this conscious way of filming within an enclosed environment arises from the confessional box as a starting resource.

Another important physical resource that functions throughout the film as polyvalent symbolism is water. Lepage employs blood, water (bath, sauna, jacuzzi, river, aquarium), paint and wine. He likes to use water as an element that can be transformed into various different visual signifiers. In *Tectonic Plates* (his first theatre production to be remodelled into a television film), a swimming pool onto which various images are projected represents Venice, changing water into a canvas. Likewise, in *Le Confessionnal*, the transformation of water plays an important visual role. For instance, after a friendly water-fight with Françoise, Paul-Emile ends up in the bath with her. After mid-shots of the two of them looking down into the water, the camera, following on from a wide-angle of the two of them in the bath, tracks over the side of the tub revealing the water to have changed to red. A downwards shot of the bath reveals Françoise searching in the blood-red water. Her hand is brought out of the bath and the audience are led to assume that she has miscarried as she falls forward towards Paul-Emile. This shot is held, as if in tableau, to maximise the effect of the colour against the white of the bath.

Lepage uses water to simultaneously present two key scenes of suicide. Marc is seen in the bathroom of Massicotte's Japanese apartment. This is inter-cut with Rachel leaving the family home and running along the bridge over the river. Using a downwards shot of the entire bath, the audience see Marc standing up in the bath, holding a cut-throat razor to his wrist. He pulls the blades across and as he does so, sinks down face up into the water. Very quickly, the water becomes a solid block of red colour. Within seconds, the body of Rachel surfaces, face down in the same water. The idea of suicide is planted early on in the film, connecting the suicides of Marc and his mother when Rachel is seen removing a cut-throat razor from the family bathroom cabinet. The audience know her despair and when a downwards camera shot into the bathroom sink shows a swirling red liquid they believe she has drawn the knife across

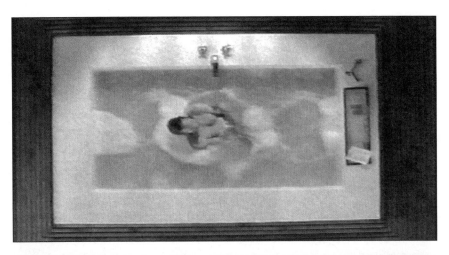

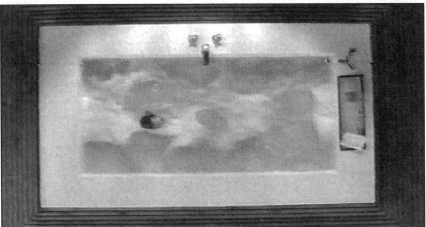

Figure 6 *Le Confessionnal*: Marc's suicide and the transformation of water into blood

her wrists. However, within seconds it is revealed that it is Pierre washing his brush having painted a wall of the apartment in red. In this case the red paint signified the blood that would later be shed. There are, of course, strong religious implications, for instance, the image of water turning to blood. The use of water is a significant symbol of life, and the use of liquid is highly important as an aid to the aesthetic outlook and the overall narrative of *Le Confessionnal.*

The use of light

Lepage's approach to film-making, similarly to his theatre work, begins with light, light that comes in and gives birth to the image. The clash between theatrical and cinematic media was apparent during the filming of *Le Confessionnal*, with Lepage wanting to experiment with light and colour much more than he was able to and he did not have control over the work in the same way as he did in theatre. According to his own recollection, half of his ideas were rejected or found objectionable by people working with him, since they challenged established cinema techniques. As this was his first film as director, his demands were regarded with suspicion and rejected, coming as they did from someone who was cinematically uninformed. Lepage explains that everybody from the cinema establishment who was working on the film was saying, '"No, you can't do that, or you don't do this in cinema" and that the ideas that were considered aesthetically interesting were the ones he was insisting upon' (2002).

The use of light has an important place in Lepage's work, both theatrically and cinematically. On stage, he creates space as a visual image through manipulation of lights. Transposing and adapting this technique to film, Lepage manipulates light and space to represent time through organisation of the frame and elements within the frame. The *mise-en-scène* in *Le Confessionnal* displays theatrical qualities in the way it uses lighting, emphasising colour, atmosphere, emotional context and subjective experience. However, light is essential for the medium of cinema as much as space is essential for theatre. Lighting plays an important part in shaping the objects and the emotional qualities they represent for the viewer. Moreover, it also creates atmosphere, and thus assumes an important role in narrative structure. In this respect, film uses light to create its illusion, to create its art form.

The use of light in cinema has been thoroughly investigated in its technological, practical and ideological aspects. Classical Hollywood cinema dictates strict rules on the use of dramatic lighting, in which lighting should fit the situation and never work against it. At the same time, lighting should not become intrusive (Hayward 2000: 210).[2]

Light, therefore, can be deliberately used to distort the characters, offering a variety of interpretations, from subjective viewing to expressionistic disfiguration. Lepage is aware of this effect of light on *mise-en-scène* because of his theatrical experience. Light in *Le Confessionnal* is subjective and has an emotional function. The reality Lepage constructs cinematically combines past and present as one unity within a space, using light – and particularly colours – to give specific visual qualities to each period. By transforming space through tracking shots, Lepage transcends time between Québec in the 1950s and in 1989. As a connecting device between these times, he used colours and shapes of objects and the level of their illumination. For instance, he takes the same location where action commences in two different time frames.

Theorising colour

Theorising black and white film, Rudolf Arnheim points to the limitations of film technology in creating a realistic illusion: 'The absence of colour, of three-dimensional depth, by being sharply limited by the margins of the screen, and so forth, film is most satisfactorily denuded of its realism' (1958: 31). Nevertheless, these are not deterrents for accepting film as a true depiction of reality. Arnheim asserts that particularly the absence of colour is a fundamental 'divergence from nature':

> The reduction of all colours to black and white, which does not leave even the brightness value untouched (the reds, for instance, may come too dark or too light, depending on the emulsion), very considerably modifies the picture of the actual world yet everyone who goes to see a film accepts the screen world as being true to nature. (1958: 22)

Arnheim explains this set of conventions as a phenomenon of 'partial illusion'. In that respect, Eisenstein's use of colour to construct a meaning coincides with Arnheim's notes on the absence of colour, in the way that the author constructs a reality for the audience. It is the author's/director's reality that the audience witnesses.

Lepage creates a cinematic reality that establishes its own reality through connections with colour and light. To create this reality Lepage manipulates colour in the same way that Hitchcock manipulates low-key lighting. At the opening of *I Confess*, Hitchcock creates the atmosphere of suspense in which a murder is revealed. He creates this atmospheric level by using multiple short takes. Throughout *Le Confessionnal* the atmospheric level is constructed through the manipulation of colours. Lepage uses blazing colours, influenced by Japanese and Chinese culture and possibly Hong Kong film-making. Cinematic use of colours not only creates a visual metaphor, but points to the influence of Buddhist philosophy on the film narrative, which, as previously mentioned, may have played a more sub-conscious role upon Lepage's stylistic decisions.

Throughout, colour has an important function in creating dynamic visual effects and connecting a number of plot strands. Colours very often dominate the screen rather than simply forming the background. The use of the colour red governs the scene in which Madame Lamontagne has a miscarriage in the bathtub. Pierre Lamontagne is seen painting the apartment of his birth, having returned from China to find his home derelict. The image we see is of an entire wall painted blood red. At one point we see him throw the bucket of paint at the wall. Because the use of colour is so symbolic in expressing meaning and creating atmosphere, Lepage employs a stationary camera and longer takes. Colour serves Lepage's purpose, replacing the use of light and short takes which Hitchcock used to create atmosphere. It is both an important narrative device and a defining stylistic element. For Lepage, as for Hitchcock, style is of utmost importance as a storytelling device; for example, the wall in the Lamontagne's house has stains from the old photos that will not go away regardless of Pierre's painting, which suggest that the past informs present and future life and is destined to remain until the past's riddles are finally revealed and laid to rest. The narrator of the film uses the colour red to cover the past, which is coming out of the walls. Red is used as a narrative link, symbolising blood and the sacraments.

The use of colour to demarcate time can be seen in the example of the wide-angle shot of the building containing the Lamontagne apartment, featuring a black 1950s cab driving past the building, giving the overall tonal quality of a sepia image. In the same take, the audience see a brightly coloured 1980s car pass by the apartment tenement reflecting Lepage's shift to 1989. The overall effect of having a bright colour introduced into the shot gives the building a lighter and more contemporary look. By using a stationary camera and having cars pass one after the other, Lepage achieves the shift in time.

Another example can be seen when Pierre is looking at the brightly coloured red wall which transforms itself into the same wall of forty years earlier, revealing a scene from his family past. Lepage focuses the camera onto the wall, drawing the audience's attention to its transformation. The marks of the old pictures that previously hung are visible through the red paint. The red dissolves away revealing the original pictures of the 1950s. The camera then pulls back and the action continues. The use of contrast between colour and black and white is edited in the scene depicting the premiere of *I Confess* in Québec. The audience are shown in a very plush and vibrantly coloured cinema foyer, which has a rich red carpet and gilt décor. This contrasts sharply with the original black and white footage of *I Confess* that Lepage uses to show the on-screen audience watching. Even the audience's clothes are vibrant, to the point that it appears as if the celluloid was retouched to enhance the colours.

In addition to its stylistic and narrative functions, then, the colours have a strong psychological function, offering the audience an insight into the characters' state of mind. 'Undesirable' thoughts, which are repressed from consciousness, are projected through symbols in which colours and transformation of events play a significant part. The instance where Rachel takes a cut-throat razor from the bathroom cabinet is spliced with a view of the bathroom sink. The audience sees red liquid spiralling down the plug-hole, the camera pulls back and then Pierre is seen to be washing his paint brush. With this inter-cutting of images, the audience witness Rachel's distress and suicidal struggle. The image of Pierre 'rescues' the audience away from a potentially tragic act by replacing it with a mundane duty. Nevertheless, for Pierre, painting serves the purpose of escapism, just as playing with a razor suggests a possible exit out of Rachel's neurosis. Throughout the film, colour is used as a transformative device between events serving also as a tool in evoking memory, device of remembrance and connection with the past.

Robert Lepage cannot be interpreted simply through traditional film auteur discourse. As noted previously, the *new auteurism* does not separate the impact of individual auteur genius from the political, social and cultural conditions influencing the formation of a film narrative. Lepage's film narrative not only derives from his personal position as a writer and director (his internal creative cycle), but through a set of engagements relevant to the external creative cycle that have an impact on the narrative: economic, social, cultural, technological, intellectual, national and international factors. These factors compose a matrix that collectively impacts upon the reading of the film narrative. *Le Confessionnal* entered this terrain of struggle. The film narrative is a discovery of an intricate and secretive family history, revolving around unknown parenthood, religion, culture and identity. *Le Confessionnal* is simultaneously a search for the past and an escape from it, showing the abilities or inabilities of characters to deal with their own history.

CHAPTER FOUR

Le Polygraphe: What is truth?

The Process of Narrative Selection

In 1995, soon after the success of *Le Confessionnal*, Lepage and his long-time collaborator, Marie Brassard, reworked their devised performance *Le Polygraphe* (1989) into a screenplay. The theatre play became a resource for a new narrative cycle – the film *Le Polygraphe* (1996). Not wanting to write alone, as he did in *Le Confessionnal*, and following his experience with performance collective creation, the film scenario for *Le Polygraphe* was collaboratively developed. Apart from Lepage and Brassard, other collaborators included screenwriter Michael MacKenzie and actor Patrick Goyette, who also played the central character of François in the film. This time, Lepage wanted to have full artistic independence during the process so he decided to set up a production company with Bruno Jobin, In Extremes. Subsequently, all of Lepage's film projects have been produced by In Extremes in collaboration with other national and international producers. Due to his international theatre touring experience, Lepage was used to adjusting the story to fit the space available and thus did not have problems finding locations for *Le Polygraphe*. During the winter of 1996, *Le Polygraphe* was filmed on locations throughout Québec City and Montréal with a team of actors largely composed of members of his theatre group.

It had a limited success and did not build greatly on Lepage's reputation as a film-maker. It is perhaps Lepage's least accomplished film, coming across more as a filmed play rather than as a piece of cinema. However, *Le Polygraphe* was essential for Lepage in terms of understanding the craft of film-making and looking for ways to personalise the medium by finding links to the way he creates in theatre. The film is significant not for its critical or audience reception, but for its importance as a transition point from one medium into another, for displaying Lepage's ability to express his theatrical creativity through film. Critics in Québec observed that 'If *Le Polygraphe* signals a new stage in the work of Robert Lepage, it is because, more than *Le Confessionnal*, this film constitutes a flowering lesson in the use of the cinematographic medium' (Anon. 1996: 47).

The enormous social and political upheaval after the failed 1995 referendum on Québec's separation from Canada provided the context for the film's reception. Lepage communicates Québec's slow process of realisation that separatism should be about who Québecers are at the present moment and what their personal truth is, rather than about their interpretation of the past. The closing decades of the twentieth century constitute the period in Québec where localism and cultural protectionism began to decline, in favour of a new awareness of an outside world of global cultural references and shifting and migrating identities.

Lepage is aware that if his films are to be popularly accepted, which implies reaching international audiences, he must adapt the narrative to the film industry's requirements of form, genre and audience reception. His authorial independence in the making of *Le Polygraphe* therefore intentionally allowed some concessions to commercial pragmatism. During the process of selecting material, François' homosexuality, which featured in the theatre play, was omitted from the film narrative. Marie-Claire's relationship to François has also changed: just a good friend in the theatre play, she is François' girlfriend in the film. These are concessions made to the global narrative, since an unhappy ending and a homosexual character could potentially alienate an audience. Moreover, in working with the conventions of a murder mystery, François' character appears to be more vulnerable if Marie-Claire is his girlfriend.

It is clear that the starting resource for the film *Le Polygraphe* was the theatre play of the same name, but it is interesting to consider how Lepage achieved this transformation? Moreover, why did he choose *Le Polygraphe* to be his second film and how is it relevant to his preoccupation with memory? This chapter will address the central theme in *Le Polygraphe*: the questioning of our ability or inability to find out personal truth about the self – 'who am I?' It also seeks to draw out the full parallels between the selection of narratives from theatre and their transposition to film.

'Le Polygraphe' – the project

The 'project' of *Le Polygraphe* spanned eight years and a number of narrative cycles, including changes in artistic medium: from theatre improvisations and performance to a published text and finally a film. Lepage first experimented with transforming one medium into another when he collaborated with Peter Mettler who directed a television film in 1991 based on Lepage's theatre production of *Tectonic Plates*. The film version of *Tectonic Plates* collaged actual theatre performance with filmed events, departing from the theatre space into interior and exterior locations relevant to the story. From the outset, the film *Le Polygraphe* used narratives from the theatre play as a starting point in order to create cinema and not a film version of the theatre performance.

The stage narrative of *Le Polygraphe* developed as a work in progress, starting as a set of improvisations by the actors and authors; Lepage, Marie Brassard and Pierre Phillipe in the winter of 1987–88. These improvisations were then shown to a limited audience in open rehearsals in Québec City. The response was evaluated, and influenced the development of the first phase of the narrative that opened in May 1988. A second version was built on the experiences from the first phase, and opened in November of that year in Montréal. Subsequently, *Le Polygraphe* was translated into English and premiered in London in February 1989.

The narrative continued its cyclical development and a third version opened as a bilingual performance in Toronto the following year. Throughout the narrative transformation there was a perpetual process of feedback: an analysis of what had worked with the previous narrative and what had to be discarded. Each phase included the responses of the group, the critics and the audience as stimuli for starting a new set of explorations. The final version of the narrative was published at the end of the performance development in 1990, making *Le Polygraphe* the first published play by Lepage, collaboratively written through continuous performances. As a stage play it was often produced by other theatre companies and continued to be performed around the world. In 1996 the narrative cycle achieved yet another transformation, evolving from a theatre play into a film script. In this transformative process Lepage looked for 'Valuaction' – valuable action in resources (in this case the theatre 'text') – and selected the actions that would transform it into the film narrative.

The shift from theatrical to cinematic narrative in *Le Polygraphe* occurs through this process of selection, Valuaction, which is a montage of different threads of the narrative that will be kept and developed further, and which will eventually find their way from theatre into the film narrative. The process of changing the narrative and deciding what to develop is the Valuaction part of the RSVP Cycles. The process of Valuaction, much favoured by Lepage, involves selecting and redeveloping the personal scores of the initial characters and adding other characters. Valuaction literally means looking for value in action, meaning performed action.

In theatre, collective creativity implies that group decisions are essential for making the narrative. Brainstorming, feedback and selection are important in order to understand what makes the dramaturgical material. However, Valuaction can also have a more general application as the process of selection, incorporating changes based on the feedback and outcome of the previous narrative-creative cycle. As Lawrence Halprin has explained:

> The ideal relationship in complex situations exists when Valuaction (V) becomes part of the entire procedural pattern and is used as a feedback mechanism to encourage growth and change during Performance (P). Valuaction (V) is here

meant as an observation of process as well as a judgement oriented selectivity. (1969: 28)

A common obstacle in adapting from one medium to another, for example from a novel or theatre play to film, is the need to overcome the requirements of expression inbuilt within one medium. The narrative of one medium has to be translated or transposed into the language of another one. One of the advantages of working with the RSVP Cycles is that the narrative is not perceived as a product or fixed entity, but rather as a flexible combination of various 'scores' (characters' repertoire of behaviour), which are independent, but can form a unity with any other score. Breaking down the narrative into scores allows an easier selection process in order to determine which of them could be kept and developed further.

The group collectively looks for value in what they already have, and changes the narrative based on responses and feedback received, both from the audience and critics. An example of Valuaction in progress is provided by Lepage's response to early audience feedback. The general comment in the reviews of the first phases of the theatre play *Le Polygraphe* was that the boundaries between dream, fantasy and reality were not clear. Solange Lévesque, the French-Canadian film critic, observes:

> In this first version of *Polygraphe*, nothing is told, but everything is evoked by means of precise details, or shown literally (the dead is a real skeleton, present on stage), in such a way that the spectator is constantly kept alert and forced to, following the example of a detective, reconstruct what has happened. Using the clues he has been furnished with as a starting point, he has to organise the story and decide which of the fragments belong to the world of dreams, the world of fantasies, or to reality. Because it is quite evident that we will only have fragmentary access to Truth or Lies (if they are at all distinguishable). (1988: 153)

The narrative in the final version, published as a text, took these difficulties into account. Continuing with the process of Valuaction, the narrative was placed in the realm of personal memory and guilt, structured according to the new production goal, creating a film narrative. Although the narrative transformed, the starting resources – truth, reality, fantasy, representation in cinema, science that dissects life – remained the same in the first phase and in the film narrative. Therefore, through Valuaction, narrative is evaluated and reformed so that the driving creative intentions are presented in the most appropriate form.

The price of artistic freedom meant that Lepage never made much money on films; any surplus funds tended to be reinvested in other theatre and film projects, created at his home base in La Caserne. His decision to work on a small intimate theatre play, originally involving only three actors, and then develop it into a film, tells us much about his views on film production. The success of *Le Confessionnal* could have placed

Lepage in a league of bigger-budget film-making with increased access to technology, funds, actors and marketing. However, his need to have artistic control over his work and his interest in the cinematic medium as a means for personal expression prevented him from taking a commercial approach to film-making. From his experience in *Le Confessionnal*, Lepage learned that the more people involved as a 'collective auteur' which decides what goes into a film – according to the interests shaped by society, culture, economy and industry – the lesser the creative space for an individual auteur and his own impulses. To diminish these tensions and negotiations between industry and personal creativity, Lepage chose a production model suitable for him as a film artist: total authorship over film.

The existence of the published text and the fact that it had been co-authored by Lepage and Brassard allowed them easier access to production rights. The subject matter of *Le Polygraphe* warranted funding from Canadian and Québecois programmes. By making the film, Lepage achieved two important production objectives required by government funding bodies: first, a culturally specific narrative about Canadian life and, second, a film that contains global references, understandable worldwide. The story itself had international appeal. The whole film can be placed within the realms of the 'whodunit' genre, which not only has commercial appeal, but also involves the examination of the truth, imperative to every culture.

As a text, the stage play of *Le Polygraphe* is intrinsically no more cinematic than any of Lepage's other plays. In fact, his previous plays *Needles and Opium* and *Elsinore* successfully combined cinematic vocabulary within a theatrical environment. One of the reasons that contributed to the adaptation of *Le Polygraphe* from theatre to film is that the exploration of cinematic representation of life was a starting resource; one of the themes of the theatre play was the making of a film. In addition, the theatre text itself borrowed from the detective murder mysteries that have long adorned global screens.

Another important factor in choosing the text of *Le Polygraphe* was the quality and quantity of personal references in the material. As with other aspects of Lepage's work, the starting resource for *Le Polygraphe* had personal resonance, coming from a real-life event in which Lepage was involved as a student. One of his friends at the Conservatoire in Québec City died in suspicious circumstances and the entire group of friends were individually considered to be suspects and investigated until it was established that the death had actually been a suicide. The group members also started to suspect each other and eventually their friendships suffered.

Lepage was not interested in creating a psychologically detailed murder mystery with clear objectives; this is rather the background to an introspective journey into personal memory and interpretation of reality. François, the main character, can be seen as Lepage's alter ego, which places him within the context of the story. Individual memory is an important creative instrument that gives Lepage freedom of approach to creativity that is a direct result of Cocteau's influence on Lepage.[1] This implies that the basis for his art is introspective. When Lepage works with material that is not based on his memory, he uses characters he can identify with as a presence in the narrative through which he can communicate with the audience. He explains: 'It's one thing to do a play about great people but if you want to move the audience you have to give them something to identify with, so I created this character who is an alter-ego of myself' (Anon. 1993: D5).

Narrative structure

Le Polygraphe is an introspective story that details the search for personal truth. The film focuses predominantly on François, although his story is only one of multiple narratives that exist within the theatre text. The action of the film takes place simultaneously in Québec City and Montréal at the end of the 1980s, and the main narrative revolves around a group of friends, François, Judith, Claude and Marie-Claire, now disbanded after the murder of Marie-Claire and the investigation into her murder, involving everybody as suspects.

François (Patrick Goyette), a political history student and part-time waiter, is going through a difficult time. For two years François has been haunted by the murder of Marie-Claire, his former lover. He is also a prime suspect in the police investigation. To clear any suspicions against him and to reassure himself of his innocence, François agrees to undergo a polygraph test. The results of the test, however, prove to be inconclusive. Things do not improve when François learns that a screenplay based on Marie-Claire's murder and written by his friend Judith (Josée Deschênes) will be filmed. Adding to his already emotional and tormented life, Lucie (Marie Brassard), François' friend and neighbour, takes the role of the victim (Marie-Claire) in Judith's film. François becomes entrapped within an emotional state of instability and guilt, to the point where he no longer sees the difference between the actual events and the murder he is accused of. Doubting his memory and innocence, François asks his close friend Claude (Maria De Madeiros) to be his alibi. Eventually, it is revealed that Claude was so intensely jealous of François' relationship with Marie-Claire that she planned and carried out the murder. On the night of the killing, François was angry with Marie-Claire; Claude took on his anger and killed Marie-Claire. At the end of the film, Claude returns to François' vacant flat and sets herself on fire in another act of immolation, re-enacting the actual murder of Marie-Claire.

Lepage's use of camera and editing to create transitions of time and space, making the *mise-en-scène* relevant to the characters' search for answers, resembles Alain Resnais' cinematic language of time/space puzzle. The film narrative of *Le Polygraphe* consists of fragments that are slowly put together into one unity. This approach resembles Alain Resnais 'in the sense of the splitting of primary unit – the world is broken-up, fragmented into a series of tiny pieces, and it has to be put back together again like a jigsaw' (Dormachi & Doniol-Valcroze 1985: 60).

The narrative of *Le Polygraphe* puts back together the pieces of a jigsaw in an attempt to reconstruct a whole from the fragments. The truth is intended to be found

Figure 7 *Le Polygraphe*: Françoise taking a polygraph test to establish the truth

by examining a variety of points of view, not only one dominant vision. Like Resnais' work, Lepage's film structure resembles cubist painting because reality consists of fragments that are edited together. The emphasis on montage follows Eisenstein's idea of film montage as a primary tool to create the film's reality. On the level of form, Lepage is trying to unify opposites. Each shot has its own autonomy and simultaneously seeks to establish a relationship with another or several other shots. This is also reflected on the level of content: through a dialectical approach, Lepage contrasts seemingly opposite ideas and cinematically looks for a connection between dissimilar objects, fragments such as the polygraph and *matrushka* dolls. Scene after scene, the polygraph asks the audience to acknowledge the uncertainty of reality where private personal truth could never be part of tangible scientific reality. In this sense, the film narrative could be seen as Lepage's meditation on the limitations of personal truth, which is always hidden behind appearances and answering the question 'who am I?' As in a hall of mirrors, one reality is revealed only in order to present the existence of another one.

The main conflict is embodied in the character of François and his own view of himself, his innocence or guilt. Intertwined with this is the external conflict. For two years, Marie-Claire's murder has affected François, isolating him from his closest friends and reinforcing self-doubt. Every person François comes into contact with is somehow linked with the murder. However, the principle that brings the characters together in the subplot is coincidence and chance. These characters are strangers who meet one another and whose meetings underscore similarities both in their personal stories and their relationship to the core intrigue of the film. This pattern will be fully explored in Lepage's following film, *Nô*, where the dramatic mechanism involves misunderstandings as a result of coincidences.

In the theatre play, mirrors were used to create theatrical effects representing the deconstruction of human anatomy. Mirrors had the function of symbolising the duplicity of life, its possible reflections and changes. Throughout the film, Lepage often used mirrors and reflections to show the characters appearing in multiple images and in different perceptions. For example, when Lucie sits to audition for Judith's film, Judith's face is seen through the glass where Lucie's face is reflected. The Russian dolls have a different function in the film narrative than in the theatre play. In the play, the dolls are bought as a present for Lucie; they are not the significant personal objects they become in the film narrative. In the play, Christof's remembrance of Anna comes as a result of Lucie showing him how to cry so that it looks real. This triggers the memory of his escape. When Christof finds out that Anna has committed suicide, he voluntarily begins the process of remembrance. It is thus the outcome of a message rather than a subjective memory that comes to the surface having been suppressed.

Mirrors in which we see one or multiple reflections and the *matrushka* dolls (where opening one doll serves only to reveal another) appear as dominant motifs of the film narrative and are important visual images for the search for truth about one's identity. The complexity of the development of the narrative is closely linked to the accumulated layers of opposite meanings. Lepage explains that in the film 'death is also an important theme that is constantly linked to sexuality' (in Charest 1997: 90).

A similar principle of contrasting meanings in order to create a new one is evident in *Le Confessionnal*, where juxtaposed narratives create another narrative that is more revealing of personal truth. Lepage communicates the story through the process of compiling a mosaic of meanings which are multiple and metaphoric. The film narrative in *Le Polygraphe* is not so much a combination of different multiple narratives as one narrative created through associations of meaning.

Multiple narratives meet at the intersection of individual and collective histories, betrayals, passions, escapes and the inability to hide from the past. The multiple narratives in the film following François' and Christof's stories reveal the personal and political truth hidden behind layers of appearances. The physical space in the film is real – it depicts recognisable sites of urban Québecois and East German living. However, the characters' personal interpretation of their own environment points to a space existing somewhere between reality and fantasy. Both Christof and François constantly question the possibility of forgetting and reconciliation in their attempts to deal with a past that unrelentingly grips them.

Looming over both of them is the question, 'what is my reality?' The answer to this question is hidden in a set of identical appearances. The paradox of hidden truth is exemplified in the image of a *matrushka* doll that opens up to reveal identical dolls that become smaller and smaller. The truth remains elusive, distant from human capability to fathom its full complexity. On the level of plot, the search for truth is initially impossible since the murderer is unknown and even François is uncertain about his innocence. The missing connection prevents François from reassembling his life: is he guilty of a murder, and if not him then who? His relationships with other characters influence him from within, creating an external pressure of guilt, which then becomes internalised, triggering his quest for personal truth, much like the quest of Marc to find his real father in *Le Confessionnal*.

As in *Le Confessionnal*, the person who can solve the mystery is someone with power. In *Le Confessionnal*, Massicotte, a former priest and current politician, holds the keys to the family mystery surrounding Marc's birth. In *Le Polygraphe*, Hans, a criminologist, knows that François is innocent, yet both these characters keep this information hidden, not only from the main characters but also from the audience. However, this is not for personal reasons, but because the characters are trapped within the protocol, the way the system functions, which prevents them from revealing these secrets. In *Le Confessionnal*, Massicotte is constrained under the Rule of Silence and in *Le Polygraphe* Hans cannot divulge François' innocence because the case is not closed. Hans explains that when the guilty party has not been identified in a police enquiry, everyone is kept in ignorance. Therefore, the audience is also kept in ignorance and deprived of the information necessary to answer the main character's quest which, through the process of identification, becomes the audience's own quest. It is interesting that the audience are made to associate themselves with the characters on the margins who are victims of the circumstances. This disempowers the audience, which is relevant to Québec's position of 'otherness' or the insecurity that stems from a marginalised social and cultural condition in relation to the empowered centre.

Multi-perspectivism of Sub-narratives

Cinematically, Lepage plays all sorts of tricks on the audience to lead them to believe that François could be the murderer, directing the audience's attention to all that is inconclusive. The film opens with François producing inconclusive results at the polygraph test, which means that he is still a possible suspect. François' relationship with Lucie is full of ambiguous innuendos. The slow-motion sequence in the restaurant where he spills red wine over her, supported by a menacing musical score, might imply that he is a murderer. Furthermore, Christof suspects François and questions Hans about his guilt. François' own insecurity and self-doubt until Claude's suicide adds to the audience's uncertainty. In fact, from the opening sequence of the film with the polygraph test through to the end of the film with Claude's suicide, it is the notion of

François as a possible murderer that underpins the entire film narrative. Similarly in *Le Confessionnal*, the audience does not know who Marc's real father is, which implicates Massicotte as a possible suspect. The audience's unease is maintained until the very end of the film when the mystery is resolved.

For example, in *Le Polygraphe*, Lucie and Christof go out for a meal at the restaurant where François works to celebrate her getting the part in Judith's film. François sees them and goes over to say hello. When he finds about the occasion, he congratulates Lucie, but his discomfort is evident. At this point the film turns to slow-motion although the soundtrack remains running in natural time. Here, Lepage brings in music to emphasise dramatic tension. François walks to the serving screens and turns to look in Lucie and Christof's direction. He picks up a coffee jug and as soon as his hand touches the jug, the music stops abruptly and Lucie and Christof's laughter is heard. François turns to leave, this time using the other side of the screen. All the time the action still runs in slow-motion. François' footsteps are heard and he moves towards Lucie and Christof's table. The rest of the restaurant is now empty and all the tables have been restored to their usual settings. This suggests the passage of time, clearly making time relevant to François' introspective vision. Above the silence and the footsteps, Lucie and Christof's laughter is heard. François reaches the table and pours coffee into Christof's cup. François then moves his arm swiftly across the table knocking almost a full bottle of wine over Lucie. Seemingly he does not notice and continues clumsily pouring the coffee. There is a mid-shot of Lucie falling backwards off her chair, her body covered with red wine. She lies on the floor, almost motionless. There follows an up-shot of François' face and Christof comes into view. There is still no music, but the sound of coffee swilling in the jug can be heard. Stringed music begins reinstating real time and the picture cuts to black, suggesting a death. However, the next image shows François, Lucie and Christof walking home. Lepage manipulates the audience into viewing François as he is coming to view himself.

In summing up the main theme of *Le Polygraphe*, one could point to the notion of reality as personalised, dependent on character's point of view and never separated from other external and internal influences. Levi-Strauss' idea that in this world nothing comes 'raw' – meaning that everything is 'cooked', processed through, and working within, a series of relationships – implies that reality does not exist on its own, but as part of a system of relationships and values. Here, the characters' reality exists within the frame of reference made of the interaction between personal and collective points of view. Although the main storyline centres on François, *Le Polygraphe* has multiple narratives consisting of a number of different characters' points of view. This is less evident in the film narrative than in the theatre play which essentially consists of three equally important characters and interwoven narratives: François, Lucie and David (Christof in the film).

In the theatre play, the victim is a young student who has been raped and murdered. Against this news item, Lepage and Brassard juxtapose fragments of stories that result in a polyphony of meanings and various intermingling symbols of fantasy and reality. The multiple narratives, as in Lepage's other projects, are the outcome of the actors'/authors' improvised scores and associated ideas around similar themes.

The decision of what to select for the film narrative was centred in the murder investigation. The play starts with David, a pathologist who carries out an autopsy on the victim, Marie-Claude (Marie-Claire in the film), revealing the extent of the victim's injuries. The problem of a divided Berlin in François' political science lecture is superimposed onto the victim's autopsy and heart, which is split into two parts. The film opens with the shots of François' polygraph test taken by Hans, the criminologist, who is a friend of Christof. In the play, the murder occurred six years before and lives in memory, whereas from the beginning of the film, the polygraph test proves inconclusive and François is still a suspect of an ongoing investigation for a murder that happened two years ago. This event, which serves as a connecting device between characters in different stories, is shifted from the background into the main focus.

However, in the film there is a need for each character to tell his story, breaking through the murder mystery plot structure and bringing a personal truth. Still, this personal truth is inevitably influenced by society. Although the police know that François is innocent, he is still a suspect and therefore perceived by society as a potential criminal. There is a conflict in the characters' environment between their own personal truth and the one known by society. François has his own self-doubts and this is reflected within his group of friends in his own social environment. There are two groups of characters: the first group consists of the three characters from the theatre play: Lucie, François and David (renamed Christof); the second category of characters mainly belong to François' narrative and are the original friends – Judith and Claude – directly affected by the murder of Marie-Claire, and Hans, who conducts François' polygraph test and controls the investigation.

The point of view of each one of these characters creates a reality that corresponds to one aspect of the story. Multiple narrative realities exist in layers, as a set of appearances of truth, or as one reality hidden within another, as symbolised by the Russian doll. It is therefore important to consider each these characters' strands of the narrative. To highlight the essential nature of *Le Polygraphe* – the existence and interaction of multiple complex perspectives – we will now examine each main character's perspective in turn: François, Claude, Christof, Lucie and Judith.

François finds himself to be the main suspect and feels his identity disintegrating under increasing pressure and self-doubt. His point of view is defined by this event, which is evident in his relationships with Lucie, Judith and Claude. His social reality is simple and easily recognisable to almost any audience; a struggling PhD student who lives in a small rented apartment and has to work as a part-time waiter in an elegant restaurant to support himself. Throughout the film, we see François with Lucie more than with any other woman. They are neighbours, but it is unclear whether their relationship involves anything more, although the audience is led to believe that François is jealous of Christof, who is having a relationship with Lucie. François and Judith appear to be long-term friends. Judith is a writer who has used

François' private story of grief and turmoil as inspiration for her film script, causing François great distress. Claude is in love with François. They haven't seen each other since the murder. In the scene between François and Claude there is a suggestion of unfaithfulness on Marie-Claire's part. François admits that after the murder there was 'une partie de moi qui s'est senti soulagé'. Claude guesses that he was relieved because now Marie-Claire will not belong to anyone else. The character of Marie-Claire is represented briefly and is generally absent from the film narrative; we do not see them together. We are shown a scene where François remembers the night when he wanted to see Marie-Claire, but she was in Judith's apartment and did not want to respond to his calls. That night Marie-Claire was killed.

Claude is the daughter of an ambassador and belongs to a higher social class. She is in love with François and wants to be his best friend and confidant. Of all the characters, Claude is the most ambiguous. She commits a murder and kills herself out of love for François or out of guilt. The film does not give a definite answer regarding her motives for murder although it is suggested through Claude's memories that she was obsessed with François and jealousy is implied. We see the outcome of her action, but not what motivates it.

When François goes to see Claude for the first time since the murder, he tells her about the polygraph test. Claude's point of view is best revealed in the dialogue of this scene:

François:	Listen, I'm going to tell you something, but you have to promise not to tell anyone.
	Claude nods.
François:	When Marie-Claire died, there was a part of me that felt relieved.
Claude:	Relieved of what? That she wouldn't belong to anyone else?
François:	It scares me. Because my sentiments aren't clear.
Claude:	She is dead. Forget her.
François:	I can't. I am not capable of it.
Claude:	François, how do you think I felt? You drop me just like that from one day to the next saying I would always be your best friend, your confidant, but that Marie-Claire is like...
François:	She was just a girl!
Claude:	She was an embarrassment!
François:	I want you to reassure me.
Claude:	Reassure you of what?
François:	I want you to tell me that I was here on the third, that I was here on that night with you.
Claude:	You were here that night. Like on any other night that she showed you the door. You were with me. Oh, François, I love you. You are the person I love the most in the world. And do you know what I am for you? An alibi. Leave now. Leave.

It is left open to interpretation whether François and Claude's relationship has ever been consummated. It is also unclear whether François reciprocates her feelings or not. The revelation that Claude is Marie-Claire's murderer comes in the climax of the film when she visits François' vacant flat. Posing as a prospective tenant, Claude sets the apartment on fire and commits suicide.

Christof's (Peter Stormare) story runs parallel to the mystery of Marie-Claire's murder. He is a political refugee. As an outstanding pathologist, he is headhunted and lured to the west from East Berlin by Hans (James Hyndman) who works for the Canadian police. Christof has vanished from his old life leaving his wife Anna (Rebecca Blankenship), an opera singer, behind.

Cristof's life is a practical illustration of François' PhD thesis on 'cultural alienation and loss of identity in the context of political exile in the era of the Cold War'. François' interest in identity and the political history of divided Berlin is juxtaposed with Christof's story. François' idealistic engagement with politics is contrasted with the actuality of exile. The implied hostility between François and Christof evokes the potential insularism of Québec from the harsh real politics of the wider world.

Personal and political histories meet in these two mirroring characters. In order to understand themselves, Christof and François have to resolve events from their immediate past and without that piece of the puzzle they are incomplete as human beings. Like the priest/politician Massicotte in *Le Confessionnal*, Hans has the same function as keeper of the truth; he knows the answer to François' puzzle. Although he knows François is innocent, he will not reveal the truth. When confronted by Cristof who is worried that Lucie might be in danger from François, Hans tells him: 'He's not a threat. They know who did it.'

Even as Christof's relationship with Lucie develops, he does not tell her about his wife and his past. The *matrushka* dolls that he took with him before leaving are the only remaining link to his previous life. Christof's relationship towards the dolls represents the process of *depaysment* – the disorientation that he is experiencing. When he finds out that Anna has committed suicide, we see him locked in his room listening to an aria from Ariadne auf Naxos (*Ein Schönes War*) by Richard Strauss. In a flashback we see that Christof is remembering: the day of his defection when Anna was rehearsing the same aria. He took the *matrushka* dolls and, pretending to go out to buy wine, crossed the border into West Berlin, where he met Hans in a cafe.

Lucie (Marie Brassard) is an actress. She lives in the apartment opposite François, whom she perceives as very gentle and supportive, a good person to talk to. She has given François the keys to her flat so he can feed her cat when she is away. The first time we see Lucie she is auditioning for the role of the victim in Judith's (Josée Deschênes) film about Marie-Claire's murder.

Lucie is the character that connects François' and Christof's line of perception. Her character is defined through her relationship with these two men. They essentially exist through their connection with the past whilst Lucie embodies the present. Coming back from an audition, Lucie witnesses a suicide in the Montréal metro and is helped to recover from the shock by Christof who takes her back to her flat in Québec City. They have sex, which François interrupts by bringing back the cat. Christof and Lucie start seeing each other casually and the relationship is shown to develop throughout the film. She gets the part in the film and while filming she moves in with Christof in Montréal. Once she finds out from Judith that François was a suspect in the murder, she still believes and trusts that he is innocent. Accidentally, she finds out from Hans about Christof's wife. She is the one that takes Christof to the airport and we see her reflection through the glass in the departure lounge as Christof is crossing the security gate.

Judith's point of view is represented through the making of a film about Marie-Claire's murder. Judith belonged to the original group of friends that included Marie-Claire and François. It is through this experience that she comes to write a screenplay, which she sends to François, based on the murder of her friend. When she contacts him, he refuses to meet her to discuss the script and accuses her of opportunism. Like François, Judith was deeply affected by the murder of her friend and by the police investigation. Although initially she believed François to be the murderer, she is convinced of his innocence after being asked to identify suspects at a police line-up, where all the suspects are women. She reveals this to François at the climax of the film when they finally reunite. Like François, she has her own memories of the event. The screenplay serves to exorcise the negative feelings and emotions that were oppressing her. In her film she makes a policeman responsible for the murder:

Lucie: Judith, the police are guilty of what exactly?
Judith: Of suspecting me of the death of my best friend, of making me doubt myself, my friends, of making me point to those I love.

Parallels with 'Le Confessionnal'

Like *Le Confessionnal*, on the surface, *Le Polygraphe* is a 'whodunit' film narrative that uses a murder mystery as a connecting device between different sub-narratives. However, the suspense is intended to show the main characters' own dilemmas and inability to separate reality from fantasy. The murder plot serves as a dramaturgical device to open up deeper levels that are relevant to the discovery of the character's own truth. This task is not easily achieved, because truth is nebulous and depends on each character's perception.

Le Polygraphe takes place in the present and, as in *Le Confessionnal*, the events from the past do not allow the characters to move on or find a way to live with themselves. However, unlike *Le Confessionnal*, the present in *Le Polygraphe* is not dependent on finding an answer to a question from the past, but on the ability of characters to reconcile their own present with the past. The need to move forward is embodied in the images at the end of the two films. If the ending in *Le Confessionnal* suggests a new beginning for Québec, embodied in Marc's son who is taken across the bridge to the other side of the St. Lawrence River, then the ending of *Le Polygraphe* is the voyage outside Québec into a world where Christof returns to Berlin for the first time after his escape and François lectures on a divided Berlin to his students.

In *Le Confessionnal*, Lepage brings two sub-narratives together through parallel editing, evoking personal memories and memories that are involuntarily recalled. *Le Polygraphe* continues this principle, but only focuses on specific important moments where memory is used to enlighten the characters' hidden truth. For instance, the audience see and hear Christof giving an autopsy report regarding the human heart, which is then crosscut with François delivering his thesis about the dividing of Berlin at the end of World War Two. The interrelating dialogue heightens their emotional importance. Berlin is instantly recognised as a heart under dissection and, vice versa, the blockage in the heart leads to its failure, just as the Berlin Wall caused the death of a once-healthy political organism. François' lecture is accompanied visually by Christof's escape from East to West Berlin. Lepage's parallel editing introduces this third element, which gives the audience an insight into Christof's memory. Lepage thus brings together associated ideas containing the linking themes.

The connection between fragmented scenes is achieved through extensive use of tracking shots. This is best exemplified in the scenes connecting Lucie's audition with the suicide in the Montréal metro. We see Lucie in the audition. She is asked to improvise a state of panic. She remains fixed in the foreground while the background revolves around her and changes to show people on the metro waiting for a train. The use of the tracking shot and continuous editing is utilised in the climax of the film where, through a combination of these two conventions, Lepage achieves a culminating effect. We see Claude on the floor of François' vacant flat ready to set herself on fire. The camera moves in a single, steady motion from her recumbent body to a bar where she is playing pool with François on the night of the murder. Lepage's skilful use of editing combines imaginary space with real space, extending the present moment with memories through flashbacks. Memories and the present moment are put together through continuous editing, which generates the sense of a flow without the traditional distinction between past and present, characteristic of flashbacks.

The use of flashback pertains to *Le Confessionnal* and *Le Polygraphe*. The flashbacks underscore the transitions between past and present in which the past becomes the present. This equality between past and present is relevant to the impact of memory on the present moment and is also a cinematic technique and convention used to narrate past events. For example, Christof's background is represented through personal remembrance inspired by objects and news from his old life: television reports of the fall of the Berlin Wall in 1989 and the process of German unification, and through association with the thesis that François is working on. Christof's story is revealed through a set of flashbacks.

The idea elaborated in *Le Confessionnal* of the 'past carrying the present like a child on its shoulders' is reflected in *Le Polygraphe* through Christof's and François' relationship to their past. Christof's political exile influences his assumed identity in

Canada; and François' self-imposed exile from his friends mirrors Christof's attitude. Both characters have personal resources that objectify their intentions. Christof's material resource is the *matrushka* doll he carries, whilst François' physical resource is his PhD thesis, which is embodied in the notes he has written on the wall of his apartment and the graffiti on the roof of his building. It is interesting that in both films the past is directly linked with walls. In *Le Confessionnal* Pierre is unable to disguise the past, which comes back at him embodied in the stains made by old photographs. In *Le Polygraphe* François uses walls to reconstruct the past. This is amplified in his yearly breakdown of historic facts regarding post-war Germany and his use of the 1917 Soviet Revolution slogan 'The history is being written with blood'.

In a similar manner to *Le Confessionnal, Le Polygraphe* incorporates the making of a movie within one of its narratives. The reality is mirrored by fiction, so the filming of the murder in *Le Polygraphe* brings the past into the present moment. Using a film within a film – and more precisely the process of filming – is another way in which Lepage undermines the notion of authored and factual history. The story is manufactured by the narrator; the 'hi-story' is imagined and told through personal and social conventions. It is performed. It is as if the material did not exist in its own right, but constructed by the discourse, by the conditions and circumstance of storytelling. The idea of using film within a film, or in fact one medium within another (as in Lepage's *Nô* where theatre is used within the film) is an outcome of Lepage's multi-disciplinary and multi-perspective approach to creating. It is only natural that in his films Lepage shifts between different media as this represents his professional engagement with the arts. He works in theatre, opera and film; he acts, designs, directs and writes.

The real digesis in the film narrative of *Le Polygraphe* is reflected in the mirror showing cinematic reality, where the murder of Marie-Claire is fictionalised and placed onto film. Once again, Lepage uses cinematic conventions within his film narrative to expose the differences between reality and the representation of it. The presentation of a murder in Judith's film, although faithfully staged, does not correspond to the truth because it blames the police rather than the actual killer. The film within a film represents one version of reality (Judith's) and thus corresponds to the metaphor of the polygraph as another possible personal truth.

Using accelerated and decelerated motion is another technique that Lepage fully explores in *Le Polygraphe*. In *Le Confessionnal* acceleration occurs only once, suggesting a passage of time. The scene where the frozen salmon that has been given to Marc is being defrosted is presented through accelerated time. However, in *Le Polygraphe*, the passage of time has a subjective function, deliberately juxtaposing 'real' and 'personal' time, emphasising the mental state of the character during specific moments. Consequently, Lepage makes increased use of acceleration and deceleration motion techniques. In order to create suspense, Lepage manipulates time by deliberately fast-forwarding or slowing down action. The audience is not made to feel certain of François' innocence or intentions until Hans divulges the truth to Christof. François' relationship with Lucie is deliberately left open to interpretation, maintaining the suspense and the belief that she could possibly be his next victim. In representing François' subjective position and emotional state, Lepage technically manipulates time. Accelerated time is always connected to Lucie's presence or to the murder scene, which is filmed in the exact location of Marie-Claire's death. The example of the restaurant scene, explained in the section on audience perspective, points to the use of acceleration and deceleration as a cinematic technique to create suspense.

No exit

If the film narrative is seen as a journey characters embark on, a passage between two points, then François' character appears to be unable to move beyond the entrapment of his initial situation: the murder of Marie-Claire and the investigation that followed. François is desperately searching for an exit. Everything that happens to him throughout the film is not a result of his own action, but rather of action that happens to him. His life is full of unauthored, involuntary memories that are confusing his search for the truth about himself. For example, by comparing François' behaviour to that of other characters in the film narrative, we can see the degree of his passive 'engagement' with his environment. Unlike François, other characters demonstrate varying degrees of progress or the ability to move on. Lucie auditions for the film and is given a part. She meets Christof and they enter into a relationship. Judith writes a screenplay that is converted into a film. Claude has killed Marie-Claire and at the end of the film she sets alight François' old flat, committing suicide in the process. Christof's progress is materialised not only through space but also through time. The audience is shown his life story from the point at which he emigrates from East Berlin to Canada, leaving his wife Anna, beginning and developing his relationship with Lucie, to his final destination, returning to East Berlin, to reconnect with his past.

The end of the film takes place five years after the main narrative occurs. François has become a lecturer and is explaining to his students the notion of dichotomy within a unified Germany: nostalgia for the old life and the capacity to embody the present. In his lecture François states:

> In the eyes of the rest of Europe, she has been devastated, divided, reconstructed and, more recently, re-unified. The question at the moment is to know whether Germany will have the capacity to reconcile itself.

Faced with the empty stares of his students, François uses an example to clarify what he is saying. This explanation turns into a voice-over that provides a running commentary to Christof's return to Berlin in an attempt to reconcile with his past after his wife's suicide. We see Christof going through airport security at the airport. A guard examines the *matrushka* dolls, suspicious of the shape and content. This search is accompanied by François' voice:

Thus, in our increasingly mixed society, trust is the only way towards reconciliation. What is difficult even today ... to claim it through the body, conscience and the feelings of human beings, the soul remains a mystery that hides another that hides another, and ... it kills itself ... until the infinite.

Through François' character, Lepage expresses Québec's inability to move on, or rather, the forces that keep Québec submerged in a constant redefinition of national identity and past. François' passivity is caused by memories that press him and keep him locked within a world he cannot escape.

In selecting actions from the multiple narratives of the play to develop further in the film, collaborators were caught between the multiplicity of a layered symbolism and conventional psychology and morality of a 'whodunit' murder mystery. In *Le Polygraphe* the multiple readings of the text worked less successfully than in *Le Confessionnal*. It misses clarity of narrative and perspective. The characters' stories are neither clearly demarcated enough to present entirely oppositional readings nor did they constitute one unified viewing presented from different perceptions. Continuing to explore cinematic expression as a tool of narration with the extensive use of fast-forward and slow-motion to suggest internal time and space, visual experimentation ultimately dominated relevant and meaningful aspects of the story and characters.

CHAPTER FIVE

Nô: Where am I going?

Nô in Context: Personal Stories

The film *Nô* (1998) opened Montréal's World Film Festival in 1998, only the second time in the last decade that a Canadian film had done so. *Nô* was released as a small-budget film, without big marketing promotion, perceived as an in-house La Caserne production made by a group of theatre friends. It went on, however, to receive an award for Best Canadian Film in the 1998 Toronto International Film Festival. It is a truly independent film where Lepage, as author, had control over its development and could advocate his own views regardless of producers' objections or predictions; there are no Hollywood stars, special effects, or intriguing cinema technology on display.

At its premiere, Lepage explained that he made his first film, *Le Confessionnal*, for the producers; the second one, *Le Polygraphe*, for the critics; but that *Nô* was made for the people. Apart from providing welcome publicity, this statement reveals Lepage's intention to make a film that in an ironic way looks again at the local mythology of 'October Crisis', humorously questioning national indecisiveness about the future. He chose to focus on a local theme that had particular historical and political sensitivity to Québec, the interpretation of the events of crisis of October 1970. This political situation garnered the FLQ international attention and contextualised Québec's separatism within the world scene. Separatists considered the October events to be an example of their political struggle and evidence of their oppression; any other reading but the 'official' separatist one could be considered heresy, a breaking away from the canon and a betrayal of the nationalist cause.

Nô was Lepage's third film and the second one based on a collectively devised theatre play, in this case, *The Seven Streams of the River Ota*. This chapter will examine further the way in which Lepage uses scores (the RSVP Cycles) as multiple stories to transpose the narratives from one medium to another. The creative process began in 1994, originally as the Hiroshima Project, a devised theatre piece, which developed over a period of four years into the stage play *The Seven Streams of the River Ota* and finally into *Nô*. The film was produced with a budget of fewer than $1 million (Canadian) and shot within 17 days, primarily in La Caserne, Québec City and Montréal.

Nô, as with *Le Polygraphe* before it, interweaves personal and political references. However, these references relate specifically to Québec in their examination of the mythology of the October Crisis. Sophie and Michel, the film's protagonists, are in a relationship and faced with a range of political and personal decisions. The narrative develops by attempting to answer the question, 'Where am I going?' Significantly, *Nô* deals with circumstances in the present moment, with characters' actions referring to their future much more than their past. This can be seen as an important break from Lepage's previous two films, where the characters' engage with discovering a secret in the past in order to make the future better. *Nô* is about what happens now.

The story thus evolves around the relationship between a man and a woman. Sophie (Anne Marie Cadeau) is an actress from Montréal engaged with her theatre company in performing George Feydeau's farce, *La Dame de Chez Maxim*, in the Canadian pavilion at the 1970 World Expo in Osaka, Japan. During the tour she discovers that she is pregnant. Although not entirely sure of the father's identity, she telephones her boyfriend, Michel (Alexis Martin), a playwright and FLQ sympathiser. Before Sophie can tell him the news, the conversation is interrupted by a loud knock on Michel's door. It is four o'clock in the morning in Montréal on the day Canadian Prime Minister Pierrre Trudeau invoked the War Measures Act. Michel's friends, members of the FLQ who are planning a bomb attack, come to stay with him in order to avoid being arrested.

Back in Osaka, Sophie is unsure about what to do regarding her pregnancy and seeks advice about a possible abortion from her Japanese friend, Hanako (played by Marie Brassard) who works as an interpreter in the Canadian pavilion. Meanwhile, Michel and the other members of FLQ are involved in preparing a communiqué to the media, but seem to be more concerned with the grammar and syntax of the language than with the actual bomb device. In Osaka, Sophie attempts to get rid of an unwanted admirer, a fellow actor, François-Xavier (Eric Berner). She meets an inept Canadian diplomat and his bourgeois wife for a sushi dinner. This couple, despite being Québecois, are conservative in their tastes and act French, preferring mainstream French culture to indigenous Québecois culture. Over dinner Sophie becomes entangled in Québecois issues which point to the divisions existing between Québecers. The opportunist and self-centred diplomat Walter (Richard Fréchette) is interested in taking Sophie to bed while his obnoxious wife, Patricia (Marie Gignac) is full of scorn and disrespect for Sophie as an actress. Since Patricia has to leave for Kyoto, Walter uses the opportunity to spend the night with Sophie. However, Patricia misses the last train and comes back to the hotel to discover Walter and Sophie together. Sophie goes back to Québec.

Running parallel to this, Michel's group is preparing to plant the bomb while unknowingly being observed by two policemen. As a result of bungled timing, the bomb explodes prematurely and destroys Michel's apartment, though Michel and his friends escape. Upon her return to Québec, Sophie arrives at the destroyed flat. While being apprehended by the police for questioning, she has a miscarriage. At the end of the film, ten years later, Michel and Sophie follow a new referendum on Québecois independence on television. They are now middle-aged and middle-class, witnessing the loss of their dream of sovereignty over a glass of red wine. Their earlier passionate idealism has faded, and they greet the news with a degree of detachment. The film ends with their decision to proceed with a common project, an allegory to the national political project: having a baby.

Despite uncertainty about Lepage's political credibility to discuss the subject of the October Crisis, and the general claim that the film's narrative and characterisation were shallow, *Nô* found considerable success with audiences, reviewed a crowd pleaser. The critical reading of the film points to its location within the realm of Francophone and Anglophone binary opposition, a projection of personal, political or artistic positions. Anglophone commentators used the term 'terrorists' to describe the Québecois characters involved in the FLQ crisis, whilst Francophone commentators referred to them as FLQ members. In Canada, the general view on the film's political dimension was summed up in *Maclean's* as 'an anti-colonial farce steeped in Québec references, [that] gave the local audience reason to cheer' (Johnson 1998: 52). Internationally, this opinion was echoed in the *Time Out Film Guide*, which summarises *Nô* as 'Lepage's offbeat blend of farce and socio-political satire … which doesn't quite succeed as a comment on various kinds of commitment, but passes the time quite agreeably' (Andrew 1999: 740). On the other hand, a lack of psychological and realistic credibility was noted in *The Nation*: 'To sum up Sophie's unsettled situation in the world, Lepage reduces her to the cliché of obstetric symbols, the woman who is pregnant and can't decide what to do' (Klawans 1999: 26).

Most of the general interpretations of Lepage's *Nô* arguably miss the point of the film's intention. Trivialising the film's narrative by making it literal, or contextualising it only within a political framework, undermines the world that Lepage seeks to represent in this film. If it were really only about the personal struggles regarding the FLQ crisis or a pregnant actress's indecisiveness regarding the potential termination of her pregnancy, it would amount to a cliché, influenced by American films; a Hollywood-cultivated understanding of one truth. The truth lies in the characters' depths, partially hidden under visible expressions. Only through struggle and by overcoming obstacles are they becoming better people, gaining further insights.

This take on psychological realism is not confined in the situations Lepage imagines. Unlike his two previous films, the characters in *Nô* are not involved in soul-searching or inward-looking journeys; event-led, the characters have more of a function within a set of farcical misunderstandings that are without psychological depth. This device – the depiction of people who are trapped in their own circumstances – is similar to the way that director Mike Leigh shapes characters in his film narratives. In *Nô*, the situation is more important than the characters; they observe circumstances that are larger than their own abilities to deal with them.

The political references in *Nô* deal with very sensitive issues in Québec's recent past surrounding the October Crisis in 1970, which internationalised the question of Québec's sovereignty. *Nô* takes an ironic view of Québecers' inability to make a decision regarding their separate identity. The two main characters are making decisions about their own lives at the present moment; their inability to effectively do so leads to farcical consequences. Their personal lack of a 'common project' is equated with personal and political failure, both in their relationship and in Québec's separatist politics and the FLQ crisis. Sophie's unsuccessful pregnancy is equated with Michel's frustrated and disorganised political action. Turmoil in their personal relationship has political relevancy as it is used to represent Québec's troubled and ambiguous national project.

The October Crisis began with the kidnapping of British diplomat James Cross by the FLQ on 5 October 1970, and escalated five days later with another kidnapping, that of the Québec Government's employment minister, Pierre Laporte. This resulted in the proclamation of the War Measures Act on 16 October by Prime Minister Trudeau. The Canadian army took control of the major cities, and more than five hundred people were apprehended without trial on the basis of being 'FLQ sympathisers'. Laporte's body was found a week after his kidnapping and the heavy military presence on the streets of Québec's cities led to a departure from FLQ's radical separatism to political nationalism and non-violent resistance, focusing on the emerging Parti Québécois and culminating in the Parti's election in 1976.

The end of the Crisis set the context for Québec's approach to winning its sovereignty through referendums. The October Crisis also gave voice to the concerns of independence; as part of FLQ demands their manifesto was read on CBC/Radio Canada. The political arena shifted from the streets to the media, where ownership and information of the media proved to be more effective for the Canadian government in shaping public opinion and generating a crisis that influenced opinion polls and public consciousness. The Canadian government successfully made the association in the public consciousness between Québec's sovereignty and economic crisis, intolerance towards natives and immigrants, and feelings of isolationism. Nevertheless, the October Crisis was not entirely abortive, as it succeeded in making visible the struggle of Québec for independence, and ultimately became a staged drama theatrically played out in the mass media.

These events are re-worked in the plot of *Nô*, Lepage's interpretation of the October Crisis. He chose to show the subject matter through a comic lens, and his satirical approach received a lot of criticism; in separatist circles the memory of the Crisis is sacred. In a press conference he explained:

A lot of people have their doubts about whether we can make fun of the October Crisis. But we're not making fun of it, we're just presenting the comical aspects, and we're an amateur enough society to do that. There was something maladroit in this crisis, and that's what I tried to express, without mocking the political ideals of the time – ideals that I still share today. (In Johnson 1998: 52–3)

Although he did not want to create a political film, its references situate it within the realm of Québec's wider cinematic treatment of the FLQ crisis. A number of reviews evaluated *Nô* in comparison to similar films that also dealt with the FLQ crisis; to a certain extent, *Nô* should be situated in this tradition, because it shows how a national event of major political significance can become farcical, particularly through the process of remembrance.

According to Bill Marshall (2001) there are two fiction films that substantially deal with the October Crisis: Michel Brault's *Les Ordres* (1974) and Pierre Falardeau's *October* (1994). *Les Ordres* won Brault the Director's Prize at the Cannes Film Festival in 1975 and is generally considered to be an important part of Québec's national cinematic canon. Its influence on *Nô* can be seen in Lepage's mix of black and white and colour footage, which in Brault's case was the result of a lack of funding. To a certain extent, limited funds were also a factor in the filming of *Nô*. Nevertheless, Lepage's mode of creating allows him to use resources and adapt them into his own scores/narrative. Thus, the obstacle of having to use black and white film was overcome; as a solution, it was used to represent the scenes in Montréal. Furthermore, *Les Ordres* was situated in the tradition of *cinéma direct*, through its attempts to create the feel of a documentary, or a testimony to the political event through fictional material. Lepage employs the style of *cinéma direct* in his filming of the Montréal scenes, deliberately quoting from this style and subverting it to create a farcical situation that humorously presents inexperienced and clumsy terrorists.

The plot of the other film, Falardeau's *October*, revolves around four members of the FLQ who are engaged in the kidnapping and killing of Laporte, and the police's pursuit of one of the members after the accidental discovery of a communiqué in the metro. The action is located in the place where Laporte was held captive. The film had very strong political, psychological and philosophical undertones, and centred on the lack of memory that informs the group's current and future actions. It examines the relationship between kidnappers and kidnapped and the consequences that arise. Similarly, there is an absence of memory, and only the present moment exists; the circumstances that outline present and future action are by no means rooted in an understanding of the past. Lepage's film also uses four characters, here preparing to set a bomb, locating the action in Michel's apartment. The main concern is to create a communiqué; unaware, they are under observation by the police in the apartment opposite.

Lepage opts for parody; deliberately, through the characters' flaws, he creates comic situations, focusing on the grotesque aspects of their situations. His take on the FLQ crisis is one of the sub-narratives in the film *Nô*; in fact it represents a background setting for the personal misunderstandings between Sophie and Michel. The other sub-narrative revolves around Osaka, a direct extension of the theatre play *The Seven Streams of the River Ota*. The film uses references to the play within a play by constantly shifting between the representation of Feydeau's farce and Sophie's farcical experiences. The theatrical references of Feydeau's farce in the Osaka sub-narrative are mirrored in the theatricality of the October Crisis. Lepage uses the public and media-related theatricality of the crisis to fashion his farcical representation.

It is this farcical aspect that really separates Lepage from other Québecois directors who have dealt with the October Crisis. A tragic farce, his 'revolutionaries' are sympathetic idealistic well-wishers, seeing not only from the Québecois perspective as people suffering for the cause, but also from the Canadian position that is traditionally cynical towards Québec's separatism. His position on the October Crisis is simultaneously a witness for defence and prosecution.

In *Nô*, Lepage did not want to recount political events or embody the historical essence of Québec's uprising in the 1970s. The story was filtered through the lens of his memory and personal mythology. The question 'Where am I going?', against which the film narrative develops, is presented largely through broad humour, and thus may constructively be viewed from the perspective of a bewildered but amused child. Lepage explains that, as a twelve-year-old boy he was entertained by the sight of a soldier in camouflage, with branches sticking out of his helmet, in an otherwise completely urban environment. This twelve-year-old's view of the October Crisis largely defines Lepage's interpretation of the events in *Nô*. The bungling, pompous conspirators resemble comic-book buffoons in their absurd pedantry and dangerous confusion of time. This childlike view combines with the Feydeauesque, creating a burlesque cinematic representation of political and personal life.

Unlike the film's farcical treatment of events where important decisions have to be made regarding personal responsibility and political action, the quotation of television reports within the film implies the seriousness of the official version of reality, and the solemnity of televised documentary excerpts contrasts sharply with the stylised burlesque of the film. It is not a coincidence that the film begins and ends with a television report. The FLQ crisis is presented on the television and the characters watching this are arguing over its representation. The film ends around the time of the first lost referendum on sovereignty, with Michel and Sophie's debate over having a baby as a common project mirrored by the counting of votes on television. Their personal story is played against television and the political reality constructed through the medium of television, a reality that they now accept as their own.

The Quiet Revolution in Québec permeated the public domain through television, 'served' directly into people's homes as a game of appearances. Access to personal and cultural identity is controlled by those who, either through economical forces or ideology, have the right to decide the way reality will be constructed and represented, and more importantly, the context in which one can pose the question 'where am I going?' Ideas have become regulated by market laws; therefore, only those ideas that are presented and packaged in such a way that they are acceptable can continue to exist. This approach is relevant to Québecois art, particularly cinema. Throughout the 1990s, Québecois film narrative was not dominated by local separatist political consciousness, but rather by economic and international factors regarding spectatorship, co-production and distribution. In the light of this, *Nô* can be seen as a farewell to the politics of national protectionism of the past and distinctly Québecois (French) culture in favour of a more mature society where the past is open to different interpretations, where a new awareness of national identity distanced itself from controlling the past as one unified narrative.

Each time Lepage reverts to the Montréal sub-narrative, documentary footage is always present, be it in the foreground or background. When the curtain call ends in the theatre play we return to Québec, where documentary footage is shown, telling of the mass arrests on the streets. Once more, Lepage plays a conflict against the backdrop of a farce, also creating a farce out of the Québecois media system when Trudeau appears speaking English with no French dubbing or subtitles for the Québecois audience.

Narrative scores and cycles

Although *Nô* was developed from a theatre play, the narrative scores impacting on its development as a performance, came from another film, Alain Resnais and Marguerite Duras' *Hiroshima Mon Amour* (1959). The creative process of *The Seven Streams of the River Ota* began in 1992, when Lepage went to Japan on a fellowship programme. During this first visit he wanted to see Hiroshima, and his hosts gave him a good account of the city's history and their own experience with the atomic bomb. One of Lepage's hosts during this visit, Takahagi Hiroshi, explains that 'we couldn't have imagined at that time that his visit would become the germ of his "Hiroshima Project", begun in 1994' (1995: 84). Lepage explains in the official programme for *The Seven Streams of the River Ota* that his own impressions of Hiroshima as 'a place where you are confronted with sensuality and eroticism, despite the name being an international symbol for death and destruction ... We wanted to explore this theme of devastation and destruction coupled with rebuilding and survival.'

Lepage was fascinated by the way life regenerates itself after massive destruction and the unknown consequences of radiation, but even more fascinated by the coital symbolism of the primary landmark Yin and Yang bridge over the River Ota, which he interpreted as an image of rebirth after death. Lepage's long time collaborator, actor and writer Marie Brassard points out in an interview that the starting resources for the group to devise a performance were found in *Hiroshima Mon Amour*:

> It became clear to us quite quickly after we started talking, that we didn't want to do a historical show where we would fill in facts on the stage. I think that

the movie *Hiroshima Mon Amour* is very important. There is such a profound and strong eroticism in that movie. We talked about what happens after a war, when there's devastation, when everything has been so horrible. What's left is for everything to grow again a contact, relationship, and love. (*The Seven Streams of the River Ota* theatre programme, 1996)

This film provided a unified point of reference that the whole group could use to start their improvisations. Brassard's interpretation of *Hiroshima Mon Amour* fits Lepage's description, which was also included in the programme for *The Seven Streams of the River Ota*: 'sexuality can be a metaphor for survival, not just in our private lives but even, in an urban context, for society and how we run our lives'. The film *Hiroshima Mon Amour* explores memory and uses collage and images to present the love story between an Eastern and a Western person, the A-bomb experience and the German occupation of France during World War Two. Indirectly, the themes from *Hiroshima Mon Amour* are reflected in *The Seven Streams of the River Ota* through the characters' relationships and more directly associated in the film *Nô* through Michel and Sophie's relationship. Resnais' film investigates a new narrative technique, which was adopted in the *mise-en-scène* of the performance narratives of *The Seven Streams of the River Ota*. It consists of balancing image and text, and flashbacks of memory. In this way, *Hiroshima Mon Amour* offered the group a number of possible resources for scores.[1]

The Movement Through Forms and Media

As outlined in chapter one, scores are the repertoires of actions used in the characterisation of a persona. They are used creatively in collective improvisations, forming a resource in the creation of new narrative, the material from which a film's *mise-en-scène* is composed. The use of scores in the creation of a performance, as an essential part of the RSVP Cycles, is similar to the traditional understanding of dramatic scenes; except that scenes are bound to the narrative structure, to the cause and effect of plot development, while scores are relatively independent. Scores, then, can be viewed separately from the narrative, thus forming different events or multiple sub-narratives that can be interwoven into the master narrative of a film.

It has been generally accepted that *Nô* is an adaptation of the theatre play *The Seven Streams of the River Ota*. However, the film is not strictly speaking an adaptation of the theatre play, but rather a new narrative cycle that facilitates the scores of the theatre performance in order to create a different artistic expression. Lepage's perpetual metamorphosis of medium extended the narratives of *The Seven Streams of the River Ota* from a theatre performance, to a written and published text, a website (there were also plans for an on-line CD-ROM), and finally a film. This transformation results from the cyclical nature of work where scores can be used to initiate a number of different narratives. Therefore, in this cycle each different medium services as a storytelling device that can use previous cycles as a resource to create its own narrative.

The version of the narrative of the play performed in Vienna in June 1996 served as the basis for the published script (see Lepage and Ex Machina 1996). However, up until the end of the touring schedule the performance narrative continued to change, and differed, although not drastically, from the version recorded in the published text. Part five of the theatre play was chosen as a resource to develop the scores for the 'Nô' screenplay, developed by Lepage and André Morency – brought in to help shape the filmic material from the devised theatre performance – in 1997. The whole Montréal sub-narrative in the film was developed from an incident in part five of the play, in which Sophie unsuccessfully attempts to call her Montréal-based boyfriend from Osaka. Lepage emphasises that the group felt this part of the play had not been fully explored and offered the potential for extension into another medium. The specifics of production played a significant role in the development of this narrative into a film. The film's subject matter – the Québecois issue of separatism – found Lepage local support, thus decreasing the necessity for international producers. This in turn gave him more artistic freedom.

After making the film, Lepage posted the work on the Internet. He intended to create an interactive web site, attempting to extend theatre into virtual reality. Information technology employs aspects of theatre and film as starting points to create its own artistic expression; it is therefore possible to see how the narrative develops in different media. The metamorphosis of medium can be seen in Lepage's other projects: *Le Polygraphe* (theatre performance, published drama text and film), *Tectonic Plates* (theatre performance, printed photo album and television film), *The Seven Streams of the River Ota* (different phases of the touring theatre production, published play, pre-text for a film and website development), *Geometry of Miracles* (theatre production and extensive video documentation of the rehearsal development). Each phase of the performance in itself constitutes a narrative that transgresses its present state and becomes a different narration in another performance cycle.

As a theatre director, Lepage borrows from film directing, a way of making narrative by 'editing' and putting together already existing material. In theatre, he uses the actors' improvisations; in film he uses a montage of shot material. Thus, Lepage as a creator of narrative, either performed or filmed, is in the position of a 'montager' of various individual or group scores. He uses the performances in front of an audience in theatre as a sort of editing room, where he tests the material and then re-works it based on the response. It is important to note that 'public rehearsals' can only occur if there is something to be shown to the audience, a need from the group to present their work in progress and seek confirmation on their progress in the creative development. In this way, the audience's response becomes a test for the effectiveness of the narrative, thus serving as a 'master editor'.

As outlined in chapter three, the use of a collective method of writing and development of the film narrative over a long period of time is the result of work in theatre. In this, Lepage mirrors Mike Leigh's directorial methods. Both directors start by improvising a narrative with a group of actors who work intensively for months in theatre-like conditions. Once the characters are generally defined, the actors are sent away to research the social environment, and explore their emotional and psychological depth. The actor thus becomes the author of his/her own text.

There are also important differences in the two directors' working methods, however, which result in dissimilar film narratives. Leigh works closely and individually with his actors through improvisations and their personal observations. Once the actors have laid out their characters, they are introduced to each other and improvise together in the situation devised by Leigh. He is positioned at the centre of the creative process and has complete control over each character's behaviour and inner self, which the actors can only discuss with him. Before shooting a film, Leigh fully rehearses the narrative, giving the improvisations their final shape. The idea behind this is to create a finished script. Once filming starts everything is defined and fixed. This way of working uses devising as a way to develop a script, as a playwright workshop. Leigh as director is in the position of master editor/writer who puts together all the pieces.

Lepage's film narrative does not engage with social themes in such a detailed fashion, or the creation of multi-layered characters. Lepage deals chiefly with events, locations and situations, and his characters are often stylised. This is particularly true in *Nô*: the characters serve an emblematic function and do not allow us to fully know them. In his narrative, scores are not limited to the behavioural repertoires of character, but may also be inspired by locations, the visual image of the space in which action takes place. The two main characters in *Nô* are in different locations and their respective narrative scores are emphasised as such – Sophie in Osaka and Michel in Montréal.

The film did not recognisably point to the city-space of Montréal, as Lepage's two previous films did; both *Le Confessionnal* and *Le Polygraphe* made abundant use of referential Montréal landmarks. Nonetheless, and somewhat ironically, the decision to open the Montréal Film Festival with *Nô* was more in line with providing a site-specific film that would renew the relevancy of local events. In fact, throughout the 1990s there was a strong emphasis in Québec's films on inaugurating Montréal as a recognisable city space, rather than a generic city in American and European films, or individually imagined and interpreted through colonisation or immigration.

Lepage's film works consist of a multitude of sub-narratives that are associated and linked through themes rather than through a structured storyline. Through the selection process, Valuaction, outlined in chapter four, the scores can be selected to create any given number of narratives. The film narrative *Nô* came out of the Osaka score in the theatre play *The Seven Streams of the River Ota*, where a pregnant actress is attempting to speak by telephone to her boyfriend in Montréal. In the theatre play we never see her partner but his existence is present in the score, and the film narrative takes this information to develop its new story. Thus, in the film *Nô* the action shifts between two locations and two main scores: the Montréal scores and the Osaka scores.

The main action thus occurs simultaneously in Osaka, Japan at the 1970 World Expo and in Montréal, during the October Crisis.

The narrative mix between Montréal and Osaka, political and personal, is also represented in the style of the film. Japanese references to traditional Noh theatre are intertwined with Feydeau's traditional French farce, mixing and subverting tragic and farcical situations. Apart from playing with the sounds of the words, the political 'NO' in the 1980 referendum on Québec's independence is presented in the title of the film in a way that resembles the spelling of Japanese traditional Noh performance. The juxtaposition of Osaka and Montréal creates the main intrigue of the film. *Nô* sets out to show what happens when two people in two distant locations are simultaneously placed in situations that resemble a comedy of errors. The scenes are based on a set of misunderstandings – cultural, linguistic, political and sexual – that generate the main conflict. As in *Le Confessionnal*, Lepage uses colour to distinguish between locations in his parallel editing. Montréal scenes are shot in black and white, whilst scenes in Osaka are placed in a full colour setting, emphasising shades that are bright and strong.

The plot structure of *Nô* is built on simultaneous scores: the characters' actions that are happening at the same time in different locations. Lepage's theatre performances often use simultaneous scores showing both at the same time on the stage. In cinema, the idea of presenting a story through events that are happening at the same time in different locations could have been technically achieved using split screens. The audience would be invited to follow the main action via the means of louder audio. Lepage considered experimenting with the simultaneous presentation of multiple narratives in *Possible Worlds* by showing action simultaneously on screen. However, he abandoned this idea for fear that it would alienate the audience. Instead, he makes judicious use of creative cinematic techniques to represent and highlight his juxtaposed narrative score.

The opening of *Nô* underscores the cinematic quality of Lepage's mixed dual narratives through continuous editing. The Osaka sub-narrative begins with Sophie's score and her discovery that she is pregnant. This is crosscut with the Montréal sub-narrative and Michel's involvement in the October Crisis in Québec. From the beginning of the film narrative, Lepage sets up a conflict in the film by giving the audience the time and location of two different realities, that of Montréal and Osaka. The film begins with the words 'Montréal 15 Octobre 1970' being typed and a voice-over from a television broadcast announcing:

Prime Minister Trudeau rejected outright the demands of the FLQ, the Québec Liberation Front. He delivered an ultimatum giving the kidnappers a six-hour deadline to free the British diplomat and the Minister of Labour. The kidnapping took place in quick succession. Shortly after, the FLQ issued communiqués demanding the release of political prisoners being held in Canadian jails. The government has stated Canada has no political prisoners.

The next shot is in black and white. We see two 12-hour clocks indicating 11.32 and 1.32, which we can hear ticking at the same time as the broadcast.

During the voice-over, the camera tracks down a pile of books. We then see a hand rip out a page from a typewriter, suggesting the frustration of the character we later know as Michel. The camera continues to track, revealing newspapers on the floor with titles depicting the FLQ crisis. We now see the picture of the actual television broadcast, which shortly changes topic to the Osaka World Fair. We are shown an Asian Canadian Mounty, emblematic of Canada; a stylised symbol whose substance is used as an attraction in the Fair, but challenged in the context set up by the FLQ crisis. The next shot presents an external view from the street of Michel's flat, which we will later discover is being observed by police. After this brief moment, we are back to Michel watching a report on traditional Japanese culture and Noh theatre, 'a theatrical form dating back to the samurai'. The shot now jumps forward and into colour, taking us directly to the Noh performance in the Japanese pavilion in Osaka. The credits of the film are shown on the background of the Noh performance.

We see Sophie and Hanako watching the Noh performance. Sophie leaves the play and the camera cuts to her in the bathroom, where she washes her face, not feeling well. When the camera cuts back to the Noh performance, the Noh actor is also washing his/her face. Although distinctly different, these two images reflect one another. In the foyer, after the performance, Sophie and Hanako discuss Sophie's ill health. The camera cuts to a doctor's surgery. Hanako translates for Sophie and tells her that she is pregnant. Sophie is in shock and says she cannot continue her pregnancy. This event introduces a problem for Sophie, and initiates the subsequent actions on her part; we may see it as a device to develop the plot. Sophie wants an abortion, but it is difficult in Canada. Her inability to have an abortion in the country is played out against a social background where abortion was made legal only a year earlier, in 1969. Hanako could get Sophie into a clinic if she were to stay in Japan for another week. These two scores introduce the main conflict present in the two sub-narratives, the FLQ crisis and an unwanted pregnancy. Throughout the film, these two conflicts will be intertwined, creating the narrative of the film.

Towards the end of the film, Lepage collages different scores simultaneously, creating a story out of their juxtaposition. The simultaneous events occurring in the photo booth are a good example of this. The two acts – the FLQ group leaving the flat and François-Xavier beating himself in the photo booth – happen within the same time frame, signified both by the inter-cutting of images and through the continued use of black and white cinematography. This crosscutting demonstrates duplicity, comic and tragic, political and emotional, personal and collective. Very quickly the camera cuts to the police and the landlady rushing to the window to see what has happened. François-Xavier leaves the photo booth, still weeping. The glass in front of the camera is smashed. The shot reveals the view through the window, down into the basement flat. There is nothing but blown up furniture, and on the top of the pile, a mangled typewriter – symbols of the struggle between language, politics and violence.

The visual image serves as a metaphor for the Montréal sub-narrative. Focusing on an object to tell a story is a device that Lepage uses in his theatre directing, turning physical resources into material that can stimulate the performer to produce the narrative. In a film, the physical resources are independent because they can directly communicate with the audience through the eye of the camera.

Throughout the film, Lepage predominantly uses the camera from a fixed point, very rarely moving it within a shot, unless to demonstrate a space, as with the newspapers on the floor of Michel's flat. Due to the multiple and simultaneous scores, editing between various locations of the film narrative becomes essential for the audience to understand. To a certain extent, Lepage was unable to clearly present the story to the audience. Occasionally the use of crosscuts is confusing in creating the narrative: some of the suggestions they create can infer different meanings, particularly if the background information is previously unknown to the audience.

The decision to make the film *Nô* is part of the 'coming back to Québec' phase in Lepage's work. This phase started with the Hiroshima Project, and coincides with the launching of Lepage's new company, Ex Machina, and multi-disciplinary performance space La Caserne in Québec City. Christi Carson observes that Lepage is moving away from generalisation in the production *The Seven Streams of the River Ota*, dealing with stories closer to his home:

> While the comments this show makes about the Holocaust or AIDS might be somewhat vague, specific points about issues close to the director's heart, such as ideas about translation and representation through language and the media, are made clearly and poignantly. (2000: 74)

It is not a coincidence that the protagonist of the film is a woman and that the story of pregnancy has actual strength and weight, in contrast to the antics of amateur terrorists and incapable police. The Montréal sub-narrative has more to do with the boys playing roles than anything serious and life-determining; whereas the Osaka sub-narrative carries a life importance; decisions that ordinary people make, which are significant in their lives. This dichotomy between feminine and masculine principles is well represented in Québecois cinema culture. Lepage often paraphrases what Michel Tremblay said, that women in Québec have to make real decisions because there are no men, referring to its matriarchal society.

We may see two major strengths in Québec cinema: in the first the national position is constructed through masculine principles and Oedipal terms; the second challenges this national position. The latter's more heterogeneous 'narratives of failed masculinity or of alternative gender and sexual identities may point to the historical specificity of Québec's position as "minor" rather than "major" culture, and to the desirability of exploring the positive implications of that status rather than rejecting it as deficiency' (Marshall 2001: 109). Sophie could be seen, allegorically, as representative of the Québec nation, a signifier for Québec as a physical entity. The different characters that emotionally relate to Sophie represent one of the following positions relevant to Québec: Michel, the clumsy political games of the FLQ; François-Xavier, naive romanticism; Walter, the irresponsibility and manipulation of the federal government; Patricia, the pettiness of the local bourgeoisie with French European aspirations; and Hanako, the multi-cultural and international community. Lepage finds that matriarchal roots inherited from Native cultures are essential in defining Québec's collective self, pointing out that the main characters in Québec's theatre or cinema are women and gays, 'the man are quiet or absent'.

Although the relationship between Sophie and Michel is at the centre of *Nô* they are never represented together, except at the conclusion, but are portrayed in their separate locations. Sophie is on tour in Osaka and Michel is at home in Montréal, until the very end of the film, ten years after the primary narratives, when they are presented together, residing in cosy domesticity. It is interesting to observe that until *Possible Worlds*, Lepage never showed a protagonist in his film in a relationship with a woman. In *Le Confessionnal* Pierre is not in a relationship and in *Le Polygraphe* there is not a single scene that shows François and his ex-girlfriend, Marie-Claire, together. Woman, as an object of love, is hidden, absent, idolised or pregnant.

Theatre Within the Film

The choice to set the film in 1970 was not only politically relevant, but also aesthetically important. The fashion and lifestyle of the time were very theatrical, very exaggerated, and in a way farcical. This theatricality is complimented by the use of theatre within the film. Stylistically, theatricality offers an alternative reality to the one of personal and political crisis represented in the form of pregnancy and revolution. Many of the comic devices that Lepage uses come from boulevard or farcical theatre. The physical presence of Feydeau's farce and Noh theatre performance are scores that influence the development of a number of visual images, interweaving politics, romance and absurdities in the characters' reality. In fact, the characters' reality merges with that of the theatre play. The shifts between references in the theatre and everyday life are continuous throughout the film. At the beginning of the film, when Sophie is in her dressing room half made-up for her role in the Feydeau play she is telling her colleagues about the telephone call she had with Michel and his abrupt termination of the call as unexpected visitors arrived. The only explanation is that it must be a mistress. This corresponds directly with the play that Sophie is in, which is predominantly about adulterers. This is how Sophie introduces her own plot into the frame of the farce.

The narrative uses the 'comedy of errors' mechanism of developing a plot through a sequence of misunderstandings and flaws. Sophie and Michel, as well as the film's other characters, will encounter a series of misunderstandings in their communication. The absurdity of characters' actions in the Feydeau play is echoed by the action in the plot of the film; misunderstandings are the outcome of differences in what one characters wants to do and what another is actually doing. This creates a set of different coincidences that profoundly affect the characters' lives. To this end, the characters' actions are mechanical and respond to external sources that are out of their control.

An important factor that perpetuates misunderstandings in the narrative is the element of time. Sophie rings Michel at four o'clock in the morning, believing it to be four o'clock in the afternoon, to tell him about her situation. After an argument she tells him only that she is staying in Osaka for another week. Their conversation spirals into one of a troubled relationship: their hours of work or lack of it and their personal irritations. As the argument heats up, someone knocks on Michel's door and he hangs up. Sophie suspects that Michel is having an affair. Michel's flat becomes a refuge for a small FLQ faction trying to plant a bomb. The telephone brings these two conflicts and sub-narratives together into the narrative of the film.

Another example of farcically confused timing concerns the handling of the bomb. We see the FLQ group typing out a new communiqué, after an argument in which Michel objected to the previous one. This is crosscut with a news report on the crisis on Michel's television. Michel accidentally discovers an error – a misunderstanding involving the clock used to set the time for the bomb. Since the clocks were identical and twelve-digit, they mistakenly used the one showing Osaka time, meaning that the clock on the bomb is set to go off within minutes. The panic of Michel's explanation is crosscut with Patricia missing her train in Osaka. The audience sees her running up a corridor and then walking back towards the camera having missed it. The voice-over is Michel explaining what has happened to his two FLQ friends and the delivery courier.

The misunderstandings in the relationship between Sophie and Michel are complemented by those of another couple, Walter and Patricia. Each actor, as a character, has his own score to develop in opposition to his partner, but also serves as a dramaturgical device to propel further the misunderstandings in the plot. This is achieved by having a counterpart in characters with entirely opposing points of view. This way of working also resembles Mike Leigh's: in his films he 'pairs figures who are, in effect, each other's antitypes' (Carney & Quart 2000: 15). Opposing Sophie and Michel's characters, who are politically and socially marginalised (struggling artists and FLQ sympathisers), are Walter and Patricia, characters who represent the mainstream, the Canadian Cultural Attaché and his 'cultured' wife.

A particularly comical misunderstanding occurs when Michel orders the food for the conspirators in his flat. The camera tracks through the group, past Michel, out of the window and into the window opposite, with a focusing shot on the reel-to-reel tape recorder that is recording Michel's call. The camera cuts to the two policemen at the window. Unusual pairing is represented through two mismatched policemen. They are trying hard to be perceptive and outwit each other but appear to be very unintelligent. Not only are they mismatched in this way, but physically they are entire opposites: one is small and stylish, the other is tall and unsophisticated. The absurdity of their situation and 'police thinking' is emphasised by their argument revolving around the group number in relation to their food order. The one decides that there must be four group members based on their order of three Cokes and a coffee while the other suggests that maybe one of them would drink a coffee and a Coke or maybe two Cokes.

There is then a knock on the door. At first they ignore it, but when the landlady, who is trying to show a homosexual couple the premises, tries to enter, the larger of the policemen barricades the door whilst the other hides all of their equipment, which would demonstrate their work as under-cover officers. This also adds duplicity to their roles. When they allow the door to be opened, the smaller of the two is lying on the fold-out bed. There is a knowing nod between the two potential tenants, which is both comic and telling of Lepage's interpretation of a police stake out as a possible homosexual affair.

Language, or rather languages, have an additional important role in generating farcical confusion in communication between characters in *Nô*. In addition to French and English, there is Japanese. Communication and the inability to communicate are used as a backdrop to a politicised language – Québec's French. The attempts of communication between Sophie and Michel are intensified due to different time zones. The issue of language is central to the debate concerning Québec's national identity and yet Lepage locates the exposition of the linguistic debate against the background of a farce, and explicitly uses farce to explore the issue.

The film shows us scenes from Feydeau's play, and then we are shown the audience watching the performance, some wearing headsets. We are then shown the translators' boxes. Lepage allows us to hear French, Japanese and English simultaneously. We are shown the very end of the play, where all the characters shout 'Vive la France'. This episode can be seen to embody a key political theme central to Lepage's illumination of Québecois culture and politics, and is taken up by Sophie as she dines in the Japanese restaurant with Walter and Patricia. She becomes exasperated by the irony of the situation: Québec sending a French play to the World Fair. Ultimately, this paradoxical cultural relationship underpins the problematic nature of Québec's independence. Their first language is Québecois-French, not Continental French, hence when Michel and his FLQ counterparts are sending a communiqué to the press, Michel wants it to be linguistically perfect; sending a message to Québecers, not just the French. He wants it to be grammatically and comprehensively correct, not slapdash or untidy. Sending the bomb and the communiqué produces an argument, mainly with regard to the language of the communiqué. As the time bomb ticks towards premature detonation, the conspirators argue over semantics. Michel states: 'We must transcend an impoverished language, make it sovereign.'

The scenes in the Japanese restaurant with Patricia, Walter and Sophie are taken directly from Lepage's the theatre play *The Seven Streams of the River Ota*. Initially, the stage actors who had written their own lines improvised the scenes in the play. The characters represent contrasting points of view, which they slowly work into a conflict

Figure 8 *Nô*: Sophie having dinner with the Canadian cultural attaché and his wife in a restaurant in Osaka during EXPO

throughout the dinner. Patricia has not enjoyed the play and makes several sarcastic remarks. The tension builds, climaxing with Sophie's outburst:

> On top of that you're diplomats ... Why did we bring a French director to Montréal so we'd use a French accent in a lousy French play to represent Canada at the World's Fair? I'll tell you why. We're colonised ... Colonised, fuck! Yes, fuck! I said 'fuck'.

This outburst is met surprisingly well and, for the first time, Patricia seems almost compassionate, seeing Sophie not just as a down-and-out actress playing a whore in a play she hates, but an artist with emotion and pent-up aggression. Patricia leaves to catch her train, and Walter must apologise for his wife's behaviour, suggesting that she is merely jealous because she always wanted to be an actress and Sophie is so talented. He lavishes Sophie with crass attention until she falls into a fit of drunken laughter.

The ensuing nightclub scene is a mix of kitsch nationalism, sleaze and exaggerated 1970s fashion. The whole scene is very theatrical. We see François-Xavier standing in front of a screen projecting images of Canada. There is a brightly coloured statue, with its hand raised to its forehead. François-Xavier does the same, creating duplicity of imagery, while he looks into the crowd. Sophie has actually gone to use the telephone, trying to contact Michel. She is unable to get through. We hear all her money drop but, drunk, she walks away, leaving it in the telephone. She goes back to find Walter. Catching sight of François-Xavier she tells Walter that she wants to leave. The two of them struggle through the crowds to get out. In the background, the audience can see

François-Xavier clambering his way through the same crowds trying to get to Sophie, frantically attempting – and failing – to communicate.

Another interesting example of the direct use of farcical communication is to represent the political interpretation of the October Crisis in the lavatory of a karaoke bar in the hotel where they are all staying. In the bathroom, Sophie finds out from twin hostesses of the Canadian pavilion about the FLQ crisis while the 1970s disco party is going on. The twins are dressed in the same hotel-like uniform, smoking marijuana and laughing about the small size of Japanese condoms. They bring Sophie in on the joke. Offered a joint, Sophie takes it and listens while the twins talk about the events occurring in Québec. Sophie panics and splutters making the twins laugh even more. The way Lepage contextualises this event tells of his position towards the remembrance of significant events, such as the October Crisis. Once outside of Canada, these events are seen in a different light, as part of a global narrative, presented alongside small condoms and someone's coughing fit, making the point that all people do not have the same relationship towards 'important' historical events.

The subsequent scene of bedroom confusion, miscommunication and discovery is pure farce. Sophie runs to her room where she tells Walter to leave as she wants to go back home immediately and will not be seeing him again. He begins to get dressed and Sophie continues to tell him to leave, whilst hurriedly trying to pack her belongings. Someone knocks on the door. Walter goes to answer believing it to be room service, but when Patricia calls his name he panics and hides himself in Sophie's closet. At this point, Lepage draws together the film narrative and the theatrical farce. Sophie opens the door and Patricia completely ignores her, shouting for Walter to come out. Eventually, Patricia takes note of Sophie's presence and apologises, not for interrupting, but for being late because she missed her train. At this point, Walter leaps out of the cupboard, closing the door quickly explaining that Sophie was not feeling well and so he escorted her home. Patricia asks, 'So why were you hiding in there?' He answers, 'I thought you were room service.' Patricia is not convinced by Walter's story, but is interrupted by another knock at the door. It is François-Xavier, who arrives to declare his love for Sophie.

This section is a direct reference to the Feydeau play, even using some of the same lines. Indeed, when Sophie has had enough and is desperately trying to make everyone leave her room, she goes to open the doors for them, only to find the stage-set doors used in the performance behind them. As the porter from the play enters the entire space is transformed. Sophie opens all doors to find the exit and by doing so reveals the set of the theatre play behind each door. The other stage characters from the farce enter to take their place in the curtain call; left to right we see the vicar, Patricia, Walter, Sophie, François-Xavier, Mme Pepynon and the lady with the dog. They all exit and come back on leaving Sophie, who in the new line-up exits through the audience. We hear the music of the Noh performance and the same red curtains close the piece. This represents the dichotomy between the reality of the farce of the play and Sophie's reality, seen by us as a set of images that Sophie is experiencing – her inner world.

The problematic communication is also exemplified by the FLQ group, based in Michel's flat, planning to plant a bomb, and who are trying to negotiate a way around the one-way street system of Montréal. The central comedy arises from the misunderstandings involving the road works, of which some of them are aware, and arguments over which streets are one-way and which are closed due to the police. Having already planned how to get the bomb out of the apartment, they call for a take-away delivery. This is a cover for them using the telephone, which they know to be tapped. Michel is made to make the call to 'Acropolis BBQ', which is run by a French-speaking immigrant, another of Lepage's jokes.

Sex and frivolity, adultery and promiscuity, are an important part of bedroom farce intrigue. As a genre, it relates to the audience by subverting the norms of accepted social behaviour and bringing marginalised behaviours into the main focus. Farce is essentially ritualistic; it releases needs to follow an established order and gives us a taste of the disorderly. Fertility and sexual activity were important starting resources for the theatre play, and were linked to the cycle of death, rebirth and regeneration, inspired by the bombing of Hiroshima. The audience are situated within Michel's bombed out apartment. Inside the flat and looking out, we see Sophie's legs emerging from a taxi. She walks towards the camera as two policemen come towards her, one from either side. They accost her, and a struggle ensues. We do not see anything but their legs and we hear their voices. We are still watching in black and white. The camera moves and we see Sophie's wrists handcuffed behind her back. The camera tracks down, just after she has stated that she needs to go to the hospital, to reveal her inner thighs, which are bloodstained. When the camera is just set to expose her bloodstained white tights the shot snaps into colour. Once more, Lepage not only uses pregnancy in the character narrative – as with Rachel and Françoise in *Le Confessionnal* – but also miscarriage.

Figure 9 *Nô*: The view from the bombed apartment on Sophie's arrest after arriving in Montréal from Osaka

The overlapping score that utilises pregnancy and miscarriage in *Nô* and *Le Confessionnal* is the fact that the father of the baby is unknown – Rachel from *Le Confessionnal* knows who the father is but no-one else does and Sophie is unsure of the paternity of hers. Both Sophie and Rachel have a miscarriage. However, in *Nô*, Lepage uses pregnancy and miscarriage as a metaphor for the political conditions in Québec. By equating fertility with Québec's identity, he suggests that Sophie's pregnancy serves as a metaphor for the FLQ crisis; when she suffered a miscarriage this corresponds directly with the failure of the FLQ's mission. Also, the reproductive score highlights the failure of the Parti Québécois in the 1980 Referendum on Sovereignty, in contrast to Michel's proposition to have a baby to share in a 'common project', using political terminology being played on the television in the background. Thus the characters' new maturity and acceptance of themselves and each other is symbolised by the implied fruition of their relationship and the continuity of life.

The score in which François-Xavier is in the photo-booth remembering Sophie and slapping himself is simultaneously happening with the score of the FLQ and the bomb. The camera cuts to the four of them (Michel, the two FLQ men and the courier) getting into the delivery car, an old Volkswagen beetle, as quickly as they can. The car does not start until the third time, adding both to the suspense and the comedy of it all. Once they are just out of shot, the shot flits back to François-Xavier in the photo booth. He worked himself into anger that culminates with punching the screen in front of the camera in the photo-booth. This is followed by the external shot of the flat exploding.

Perspectives of memory

Lepage invites the audience to partake of a privileged perspective, enabling them to see behind the external reflection: we view the play from backstage, and see inner fantasies in the photo-booth. From behind the stage, we see the curtain call as well as the stage mechanics – props are removed to make way for all of the characters. Throughout the film narrative, Lepage plays with the audience's view. This underpins his use of voyeurism, the looking out and looking in that is used continually throughout *Nô* and *Le Confessionnal*. In this instance we see out from the stage to the audience; in *Le Confessionnal* we see out from the screen to the cinema audience.

In *Nô* particularly, the audience are very aware of looking and the gaze of the camera: we are shown into rooms, shown other screens, allowed into the privacy of the photo-booth and the characters' memory, shown backstage mechanics, close up detail of fabrics, into dressing rooms, bathrooms, clubs and pavilions. The use of the camera also places the audience in the role of a voyeur, never caught, but always watching from a hidden location.

As an example of the way in which Lepage asks us to witness his characters, we see the curtain call from behind the scenes. The 'characters' (actors playing actors) line up across the front of the stage in typical boulevard theatre costumes. From the left to the right we can see a bourgeois lady of the house, priest, M. Pepynon, the protagonist and main adulterer (played by François-Xavier); Mme. Pepynon, his stage wife and a porter. Sophie runs in to join the line between the priest and François-Xavier. They all wave to the audience and red stage curtains drop, as we saw at the close of the Noh play. Throughout this curtain call, we are shown both sides – from the audience's point of view and from behind the stage. Using multiple scores and editing into the film narrative, Lepage makes the audience omnipresent, all-seeing, all-hearing and ever-witnessing.

For Lepage, the photo-booth is a magical device that reveals the fantasies of the characters, their inner world, while they are photographed. All of the photo-booth scenes end by exposing personal memories. The audience is introduced to Walter and Patricia as they enter the Osaka World Fair, where a mundane incident is used to set up their characters. We see Patricia and Walter trying to get through the ticket stalls. Patricia has entered and is waiting for Walter who has lost his pass and wants to buy another one at the entrance. He is busy explaining who he is, wishing to purchase a full ticket rather than a day pass to see the performance that he officially came to see. She accuses him of wanting the full ticket only as an excuse to get drunk on free drinks in the Québec pavilion. Walter has to have his photograph taken to put on the pass. As Walter steps into the booth, we see him from the photo booth camera's point of view, and in black and white. Patricia never stops talking and insisting on a response. The first three photographs taken are of him either answering her aggressive questions or of his sheer disbelief at her behaviour. However, the audience then see his memory when two hands come from behind the curtain and he fondles a beautiful young woman.

Walter's memory could be seen as indicative of politicians and their place in the filthy underbelly of society, interested in illicit sexual exploits, excessive drinking, and so on. François-Xavier is seen entering the photo-booth after a failed attempt, yet again, to convince Sophie to accept his affection. He is crying. He looks into the camera, where the audience are situated, and begins slapping his face, first on one side and then the other. The audience are then taken into his memory, which is also depicted in black and white. There, François-Xavier is rehearsing a scene of the Feydeau play where Sophie has to slap him. The rest of the cast are watching and laughing, but Sophie just can't quite get it right and hurts him. She keeps apologising and he keeps laughing it off, making them go through it again. This memory and his action within the photo-booth are inter-spliced so that the audience feel as if they are seeing the two simultaneously.

The third time the photo-booth is used as a score is when Hanako and her boyfriend have their photographs taken. Hanako was blinded in the Hiroshima bombing, rendering her an *ibakusha*, an injured survivor of the bomb. In Japan, she explains, *ibakushas* are not found attractive as they carry the signs of the bomb, which may then be passed on to their children. Hanako's American boyfriend does not feel this way, because he is not part of the Japanese cultural mind-set. The audience are looking from the point of view of the photo-booth's camera. For the fourth photograph, Hanako takes off her sunglasses (which she has worn permanently throughout the film), revealing her eyes. The flash goes, and turns into the image of the Hiroshima mushroom cloud, which explodes behind Hanako's eyes. This clip ends just as a different flash ends, that of a police officer photographing the debris of Michel's flat after the bombing.

Due to the cross-cultural reading in Lepage's films, the position of the spectator is aligned to Lepage's own as a film auteur, simultaneously aware of the signification of the material within and outside of its cultural context. The characters in Lepage's films bring into Québec's milieu a different cultural position, a cultural baggage acquired whilst being outside. This creates a difference between local Québecois reading and the international perspective, the inside view is now challenged by elements from the outside that often expose Québec's inbuilt cultural attitude as ridiculous or petty, relevant only to its own momentum. *Nô*'s film narrative follows Lepage's elaborate and consistent interest in the contact between cultures and experiences of travelling, a journey of narratives that occurs in transition between locations separated in time and space. Himself in a position 'in-between' the worlds, he brings to *Nô* his interest in Asian cultures and his own experiences of theatre on international tour.

In this context, the main accomplishment of Lepage's film narrative can be seen as the ability to translate 'national idiom' into an internationally understood and relevant narrative. He is not alone in presenting Québec from the perspective of the outsider looking in, and in many ways he bears a resemblance to the film directors of non-Québecois origin, but who are part of multi-cultural Québec – Léa Pool, Paul Tana and Michka Saäl – and bring with them questions about roots, memory, remembrance, belonging, otherness and exile. Exile in Lepage's film is a quest to redefine and reconstruct personal identity, and by doing that, he presents an alternative vision of Québec, a Québec that does not have to be perpetually centred in on itself, but can engage with the world.

Lepage's version of the 'intercultural' has been the subject of numerous critical observations and more often than not a reason for accusations and disputes. The main line of negative criticism centres on Western appropriation of Eastern cultures as a free source to build its own material regardless of the cultural and historical significance of the 'resource' culture. This view aligns itself with a critique of cultural imperialism within a neo-colonial setting. Lepage's appropriation of Eastern cultures does tend to be aestheticised or romanticised, and Western representation of Eastern culture is not without prejudice. In other words, making an artwork out of any material requires a sense of free interpretation and subjectivity, which is necessary in order to create. Yet the audience's ability to interpret images from other cultures largely depends on their own experience and ability to read their own self into the 'intercultural text'. Lepage has never claimed to be making a production about the East, but is rather offering his personalised view. In that regard, he always depicts his alter ego as a French-Canadian character on a journey into an 'other' culture. His approach to the intercultural material is rather an outcome of the way he works, a cultural resource for the creation of narrative and *mise-en-scène*.

Furthermore, Lepagee accepts cliché as the key to open doors that can lead to discoveries about human life, revealing the cultural content hidden behind accepted perceptions and understandings. In a creative process one first encounters the stereotypes, which are often discarded in order to discover more original ways of interpretation through continuous artistic 'research'. Thus we gain more intimate knowledge about our existence. Lepage likes to begin with a cliché, and look for hidden material behind social and cultural stereotypes, as a contemporary mythology. He compares this approach to an archaeological discovery where the actual material is buried, hidden behind the surface that often reveals little. He uses the clichés of other cultures, particularly Eastern artistic traditions, as objects that create his *mise-en-scène*. Similarly, he is appropriating inter-culturalism by turning the 'other' cultures into material for his *mise-en-scène*, transforming objects into aesthetic material. This could be explained as giving primary importance to the aesthetic concept of other cultures rather than exploring the real meaning behind them. His intercultural gaze is a view from the outside, a tourist visit, an observation of the different cultural processes occurring within other cultural codes in order to construct its own sense of identity, but not necessarily to comment about the East itself. This suggests that the 'polycultural' was implemented as an artistic device to create the 'language' of a *mise-en-scène*. The term 'Oriental' represents something that is romantic, exotic and mysterious, different from the Western approach to life. It is an invented, constructed terrain made of fantasies and collective projections, a necessary balance to rigidity. The materialisation of the Orient depends on the context in which it is situated by the (Western) observer, who appropriates it according to his/her own understanding.

Nô's *mise-en-scène* may be seen as a 'collage' of cultures, using different cultures to create a counter reading of history (that is, the interpretation of the October Crisis). Nevertheless, because of the centrality of the dominance of one culture over another, this interaction becomes one-sided and can result in subversion and domination of other cultures, or their inclusion within a frame of 'Americanising' and perversion of their original essence. It could also be said this cultural process is reversed in Lepage's films. His main characters are generally from a marginalised social and cultural circle; they are artists trying to find their place in the world and make some sense of their lives. A look towards the East provides escape from the dominant centre of Western capitalism and depersonalising consumerism. Instead, it provides an alternative model, an idealised, romanticised construction of the East in contrast to empty, hypocritical, Americanised Western ideologies.

CHAPTER SIX

Possible Worlds: What is my real world?

Performance of Memory

For several reasons, *Possible Worlds* (2000) provides a startling contrast to Lepage's previous film work. Choosing to direct from the text of another author rather than his own, the film is based on the stage play of the same name written by Toronto playwright and mathematician John Mighton. Significantly, it uses English rather than French, and more than any Lepage's previous films, the external environment plays a key visual role in the cinematic language.

Originally, the play *Possible Worlds* was mounted on the Canadian Stage in 1990, directed by Peter Hinton. It received the Governor General's Award and was produced across Canada. According to John Mighton, Daniel Brooks directed the most accomplished performance of the text in 1998 at Théâtre Pas Murail in Toronto, using a minimalist set with visual and sound cues to create different worlds. Lepage had seen the videotape of the Brooks production becasue the play had been chosen to participate in the Carrefour Festival in Montréal. He thought that the production would make a good film, so when Mighton approached him with the idea to direct the play for the screen, he accepted. The actual performance of the play *Possible Worlds* was thus the starting point for the development of a new narrative cycle, a film script. Using the theatre play as the 'Performance' part of the RSVP Cycles, Lepage proceeded to develop the film narrative. In this way, Mighton's writing becomes performance, enabling Lepage to look at the text as a resource for his cinematic creativity. Rather than using a fixed text, therfore, Lepage is approaching text as performance which gives him freedom to bring in various visual influences and cinematic references, specifically in the treatment of the relationship between memory and identity.

The film *Possible Worlds* consists of multiple narratives organised around the question 'What is my identity?' The narrative of the film progresses as an attempt to answer the complex question about the main character's existence in parallel lives and his relationship with the woman he loves in each life; although she appears to be the same physically, she has different characteristics.

As an artist, Mighton is interested in what determines identity – is it a continuation of memory or character's behaviour or something entirely different from conventional psychological reality? In *Possible Worlds*, Mighton recognizes that our identity does not consist of one unified source or influence but of different fragments, often contradictory multiple sources or influences; Lepage was attracted to this mixing of worlds within one identity. For Lepage, Mighton's play reinforces the Renaissance idea of blending the artistic and scientific. The same ideas have attracted and inspired Lepage's work in theatre from the beginning, notably with his first solo show, *Vinci*, where he sought to make a connection between the human brain and Renaissance architecture. Lepage's interest in Mighton's work also comes from this combination of arts and science. It is not surprising that Lepage was attracted to questioning memory and identity at the crossroads of arts and science; this is Lepage's personal theme and the exploration of technology and media is a central and ongoing trait of his work.

The theatrical qualities of Mighton's play have a strong impact on the film's narrative. Despite the fact that Lepage wanted to move away from a sense of the theatrical by exploring exterior visual images, the shifting between various narratives and worlds is achieved through the transformation of objects and space, which does evoke his theatricality. He himself considers that the film *Possible Worlds* was framed and scripted in a very theatrical manner (see Bilodeau 2000). Mighton provided the dialogue for the film's script and Lepage came up with the location and the visual references; the connection between film and theatre is very present in the cinematic language.

The story in the film script of *Possible Worlds* is relatively simple. At the beginning, George Barber (Tom McCamus), a successful financial consultant capable of exceptional mathematical thinking, is found dead in his apartment. Nothing has been stolen; however, the victim has been robbed of his brain. Soon, we discover from the police investigation that there has been another murder, where the brain of an influential consultant, who had knowledge of important information in the corporate world, is missing.

Interwoven into the police narrative are the lives that George lives in parallel worlds. The audience see on the screen the different worlds that George's consciousness constructs. In one world he is married to Joyce (Tilda Swinton); in other worlds, they are perfect strangers. In the scene following the murder scene, George enters the cafeteria of a hospital and meets a woman, Joyce. He knows her, or at least seems to know her. She does not know him. A few scenes later they meet again in a trendy bar. This time she is the one who introduces herself to him, as if they were meeting for

Figure 10 *Possible Worlds:*. The view from the outside in as the window cleaner discovers the body of George in the opening shot of the film

the first time. It is revealed that George's brain is still alive; it has been stolen by Dr. Kleber (Gabriel Gascon) for scientific research and his multiple lives are the dreams and manipulation of memories that result from Dr. Kleber's experiments.

George has no control over the shift between possible worlds; he involuntarily moves from one existence to another. The multiple narratives not only point to problematic reality, but also have a number of levels of interpretation. On one level, the consciousness within George's brain journeys through a labyrinth made of different realities of intertwined worlds. On another level, the main intrigue of the film is fundamentally a detective story concerned with finding out who stole George's brain. However, the police officers in charge of the case and the doctor who stole the brain are engaged with the philosophical question of what human imagination is and why we have it. On another level, the film is also a poem about the immortal love between George and Joyce.

Possible Worlds focuses on the parallel realities created in the brain; it is the life of a brain separated from the body that is dead. The film subsequently questions the foundations of our perception, knowledge and information about what constitutes identity. In *Possible Worlds*, Lepage returns to the pattern of a conventional detective murder-mystery, a 'whodunit', in order to convey his story. As in *Le Confessionnal* and *Le Polygraphe,* he uses this genre to achieve the marriage between his own interest in personal and collective memories and Québec's reality, whilst ensuring international audience involvement in the intrigue of the story.

The murder-mystery serves as a unifying device for the overlapping sub-narratives, providing a context for the relationship between George and the various Joyces. As in Lepage's other films, the sub-narratives have their own independent structure but, put together, create a new superstructure. In this way the meaning is composed through juxtaposition of various events from different narratives. When put together, the multiple narratives compose one master narrative that communicates to the audience via its segments or sub-narratives. For example, in *Le Confessionnal*, the narrative of two time periods, 1950s Québec and 1989 Québec, collages into a master narrative; likewise in *Nô*, two events happening simultaneously in different locations, Japan and Québec, inform the master narrative of the film. The multiple narratives in *Possible Worlds* bring together a number of visual images that take the viewer on a journey through the narrative labyrinth in-between the worlds inhabited by George. The cinematic labyrinth through which the main character journeys is more evident in *Possible Worlds* than in any other of Lepage's films because the narrative consists of a plurality of events that have the same quality – a similar scene is played over and over again. There is no 'centre' to the film; each sub-narrative has its own gravitas and equal importance for the viewer.

Visually, the labyrinth is represented through continuous shots connecting different generic and unspecified locations. Using *Reservoir Dogs* (1992) and *Pulp Fiction* (1994) as examples of the same technique, Lepage points out that 'instead of cursing this vocabulary, we have to ask ourselves how to utilise it to make it into a form

Figure 11 *Possible Worlds*: Detective looking at George with missing brain

of art' (in Dossier 1995a: 27). Like Tarantino, Lepage wants to create a film narrative that can be 'read' regardless of the point of entry into the narrative, one that can be moved in various directions, which 'possesses a framework in the form of a labyrinth' (ibid.).

The structure of *Possible Worlds* is closer to that of a poem than a chronological narrative because multidirectional editing allows the flexibility of different readings – the viewer has the flexibility to enter the film narrative from a number of different angles. In the press release accompanying the film's publicity material, Lepage calls it 'a cubist love story' or a 'mathematical poem' (*La Caserne* 2000). This difference is underlined by the interpretation of time in the poem and in fiction (chronological narrative).

The multiple narratives in *Possible Worlds* invite multiple points of reference from which we can observe George's reality. By moving through different aspects of consciousness we are allowed into the possible lives of the main character. However, Lepage's view of life remains fundamentally individualistic. The character is confined to his own self, with experiences that are private and solitary regardless of the fact that they have been observed and interpreted by multiple points of reference. George is convinced of the continuity of his world and attempts to escape from the labyrinth in which he is trapped. His attempts are complicated by alternative life scenarios, which are outside of his control (echoing the characters in Alejandro Amenábar's *Abre Los Ojos* (1997) or its Hollywood remake *Vanilla Sky* (2001)). George's movement between the possible worlds is an involuntary action, in the same way that in *Le Confessionnal*, involuntary memory transports the existence of the past into the present. George is bound to a perpetual present from which he cannot escape. He exists in a moment in time in which fantasy, dream, and reality have equal validity. In the cinematic labyrinth of *Possible Worlds*, the absence of a central point of reference – a central world – makes anything possible. As Normand Provencher has explained:

> *Possible Worlds* weaves a strange canvas, which will transport the viewer between dream and reality, to the limits of the unconscious, with everything this elliptically constructed surrealist exercise supposes about desertion and loss of one's points of reference. (2000: B12)

Possible Worlds consists of three main sub-narratives. The first is characterised by George's absence, except as a lifeless body at the beginning. This narrative involves the police investigation into George's murder and the theft of his brain. George is only referred to as an object, the brain. It begins with the discovery of George's body and focuses on the search for the criminal. Two policemen, a younger one and an older one, forming an odd couple, are the main characters in this sub-narrative, and the comic undertones in the representation of the two police officers are similar to those in *Nô*. The police officers are incapable of understanding and dealing with the circumstances of the crime as the application of their conventional State-sanctioned wisdom proves inadequate to the task.

The second sub-narrative revolves around George's relationship with Joyce, a scientist in this world. This relationship is a romance, which is developing into love. George attempts to date Joyce who refuses him at first, being passionately dedicated to her work, unsociable, and strongly suspicious of men from the business and financial world. She is clearly not interested in casual relationships. To win her over, George relies on the information he has gained about her in other worlds and lives. After a number of failed attempts, George convinces her to go out with him. They develop a relationship.

In the third sub-narrative Joyce is a stockbroker. The nature of George and Joyce's relationship in this sub-narrative is primarily sexual. The character of Joyce is in binary opposition to the one from the previous world. Joyce relates differently to George, whose feelings for her remain the same. Initially, she approaches George, who has been drinking, and takes him to her home where they have sex. George wants to know whether she is interested in a relationship. She says she is unreliable and likes challenge rather than stability. In a very general way, the roles are reversed, with George now seduced by Joyce.

The multiple realities are created for the viewers by taking them through narratives, moving from one location to another, giving the impression of switching television channels. On a number of occasions, Lepage has emphasised that television, of all media, has had the most impact on him. The contemporary habits of channel-hopping while watching television, seeing fast-paced music videos and commercial spots with strong visual messages, having the opportunity to fast-forward and rewind video films, has had a substantial and acknowledged impact on the construction of the narrative in Lepage's films. In the world of the televisual medium, cause and effect progression and psychologically justified action have to an extent been replaced by fragmentation, temporal and spatial dislocation, automated response and superficiality in characterisation.

Lepage's cinematic labyrinth helpfully includes a guiding figure, as it were, assisting the audience to negotiate the many complex aspects of the narrative. As in *Le Confessional*, where Father Massicotte connects the two narratives, *Possible Worlds* features a character that appears in all the sub-narratives and serves as a connecting device – Dr. Kleber, the brain surgeon. Dr. Kleber is physically present in the film, directly and indirectly serving as an opposing force that fundamentally dominates George's life. The presence of a character that has all-embracing power over the destiny of the central character, or has the answers that character is seeking, can be seen to symbolise the basic disempowerment of Québecois society and culture in relation to the outside world. Someone from the outside holds the strings and has the ability to determine the character's life, reinforcing the colonial position of Québec in regard to France or America. In highlighting Dr. Kleber's omnipotence, Lepage invites the audience to share Dr. Kleber's elevated and unifying perspective on the multiple narratives.

Time and space of memory

The main character in *Possible Worlds*, George, exists in a space in-between worlds, a non-location consisting of possible realities. Each of these realities has a different scenario, one which is transitional and temporary and it is difficult to contextualise the story within a cause-effect plot development. The complexity and inaccessibility of the film was inadvertently captured by one reviewer – the film synopsis in London's Institute of Contemporary Art's July 2001 programme attempts to encapsulate the film's story by inventing a location and narrative sequences that do not exist in the film: 'As two detectives set out to investigate his death, we're allowed back into various scenes from George's life, and his relationship with Joyce in a small northern town.' This description substitutes the absence of coherent time and space in *Possible Worlds* by creating the location of a northern town and contextualising the story into a chronological set of flashbacks. Memory is central to *Possible Worlds*, not as a device to recount the past, but rather the plurality of memories is seen as the perpetual re-living of a present moment and accumulation of possible multiple present existences. Lepage explains: 'We make plans for the future, we invent scenarios for the past, we are living in possible worlds whilst passing very little time and spending very little energy in living in the present?' (in Bilodeau 2000: 19).

Mighton's idea for the play came from a view of the world as an illusion where 'we are just imagining everything' (2002). He was attracted to the narrative where different versions of the same event are repeated. The story in *Possible Worlds* was inspired by experiments with epileptic patients in the 1950s, where, as Mighton explains, scientists separated the two halves of the brain, finding that they were able to function independently from each other and appeared to have a separate consciousness. This opened a series of philosophical questions on personal identity which, combined with Mighton's interest in the Cartesian problem of duality between mind and body, created a ground from which the play started to grow. Interestingly, Mighton, like Lepage, is not an author who starts from a story or synopsis, but rather from a set of random events which are slowly revealed into a story. Reading about this experiment, Mighton had images of the physical brain being stolen, which provided the starting material. His text focused on the dialogue, leaving directions and location of the events to the director. This implies that Lepage had to create a visual world in which cinematic images could produce locations that exist in-between realities, as well as transforming one reality into another.

The images chosen by Lepage to represent George's worlds have a non-specific location: the space is deliberately ambiguous and has an unreal atmosphere. There is a deliberate disjunction between interior and exterior shots. Exterior shots are in a rural picturesque costal landscape of high windy yellow hills and rocks overlooking the sea, while all the interior shots suggest an urban location. For example, the interiors of the police station hint at a conventional representation of a busy urban police station similar to those portrayed in 'cop' series such as *NYPD Blue*. George's job interview

Figure 12 *Possible Worlds*: First of many encounters between George and Joyce, here in front of a huge glass wall with water (rain) falling down

similarly takes place in a high-powered corporate environment. Scientific laboratories and a cafeteria with endless numbers of researchers in white, and a fashionable designer apartment, suggest more of a 'yuppie', urban lifestyle. These images could be anywhere; they could be places in our imagination.

The non-location in *Possible Worlds* has a distinctive absence of given circumstances, of specific identifications of where and when. The film's *mise-en-scène* exists in a perpetual present and cannot be contextualised in a cause-effect storyline development. In *Possible Worlds* non-locations are subjective and continue Lepage's established treatment of personalised events in films such as *Le Confessionnal* and *Le Polygraphe*. The boundaries of what is real and what is fantasised are blurred in a non-location, where all forms of reality are possible, because they are the outcome of our personal invention, constructs of our own memory. Each of these could be seen as a virtual archetype from the landscape of the modern psyche.

The life that goes on inside the mind is represented on the screen through surrealist images. As in Cocteau's cinematic aestheticism, Lepage presents alternative worlds by dislocating the space, transforming it into dreamlike reality and images. Unlike Lepage's previous films, where the past is brought to the present through remembrance, *Possible Worlds* resists the past by having multiple existences in the present moment. The replacing of a single reference by a multi-referentiated system, which transforms one reality into another, functions through a vivid visual imagery with strong surrealist expression. Lepage deliberately removes the single references to time and space in order to create a general ambience, where 'timelessness' and 'spacelessness' are replaced by invented or found space and time.

The film's visual images are similar to a poem through their interpretation of time. Time is measurable through the collision of two events or narratives, but Lepage's use of time in film is less measurable, and suggestive of a poetic sensibility. The images digest experience and meaning, amalgamating them through symbols and visual metaphors. His approach reinforces the ideas of one of Canada's best known writers and acclaimed poets, Anne Michaels:

> A poem is like putting a needle through material and looking at a pleat, where the fabric is joined together with a single piercing. What you have is a gathering together of a cluster of pleated gestures. In some ways, this ability of a poem to pleat times is closer to our actual experience of memory, of the passage of time. We notice time most when one event suddenly collides with another, providing us with a perspective. As Einstein might say, as far as time is concerned, a moment must be witnessed: 'all our judgements in which time plays a part are always judgements of simultaneous events'. The time of the train's arrival is relative to the person on the platform, the co-ordination of time and place. (2002: 10)

The film narrative of *Possible Worlds* internalises time, as well as place, erasing boundaries between past, present and future, in a dreamlike explosion of limitless possibilities. Lepage creates a perpetual present where the fragmentation of George's narration uses transformation in the same scene from one event or world into another, whilst attempting to reinstate this into a cause-effect narrative. In this, Lepage reflects Gilles Deleuze's notion of time. For Deleuze, the present is split 'in two heterogeneous directions, one of which is launched towards the future while the other falls into the past' (1989: 81). The characters in *Possible Worlds* exist within the present time frame. Time is not objectively measurable in the film; for the most part we see projected events that happen within George's brain. There is a feeling that the narrative is locked within a constant present moment. This approach is similar to the way internal time is condensed in our memory. To an external observer, the process of remembrance could take a few seconds, while internally the person could have been on a whole journey involving months or years.

This poetic treatment of time and space is similar to Alain Resnais' cinema, where the *mise-en-scène* is created through the manipulation of time and space as a way of escaping the constraints of linear plots and presenting continuous sequences of realistic events. Guy Phelps and Ralph Stephensen explain the manipulation of time as essential to the film structure in Alain Resnais' work:

> In opposition to conventional films Resnais aims to construct a purely mental time and space and to follow the mind which goes faster, or slower, than

reality – dodges, skips, doubles back, lingers, repeats, and creates imaginary scenes, parallels and possibilities ... *Last Year in Marienbad* [1961] goes further and succeeds better in enabling the spectator 'to come to terms directly with subjectivities', than anybody might have thought possible before it was made. One might also say this film constructs poetic as well as a mental time and space, and is virtually the first film conceived as a poem, that is, in which the traditional dramatic construction is replaced by non-narrative construction. (1989: 114)

The interweaving of different times and spaces is cinematographically achieved through parallel cuts and tracking shots. To achieve this, technically, as in Lepage's previous films, parallel cuts and tracking shots are used. The temporal transitions, the displacement of space, surreal treatment of events, and plurality of narrative threads are reminiscent of Resnais' *Last Year in Marienbad*. In Resnais' films, psychology is replaced by supra-personal memories, feelings, and personal and political histories, which is the same approach Lepage takes in *Possible Worlds*. Resnais' cinematography appears to influence Lepage's work although he has never openly accepted links with the French auteur. As pointed out in the previous chapter, the use of Resnais' film *Hiroshima Mon Amour* was a starting resource for the theatre play *The Seven Streams of the River Ota* and subsequently the film narrative of *Nô*. The extensive use of tracking shots in *Le Confessionnal*, also present in other films by Lepage, were inspired by Resnais. *Le Confessionnal*, like Resnais' *Marienbad*, resonates in narratives composed through flashback techniques in order to create a recollection of the past. Resnais explains that when he discussed *Hiroshima Mon Amour* with Marguerite Duras, his scriptwriter, they decided 'to have no flashbacks and to work on the principle that what goes on inside our brain is as real as what we see. In other words, that our actions are determined by our memories' (in Duynslaegher 1997: 16). Lepage's *Possible Worlds* reflects Resnais' belief that 'we use our memories to decide what to do next' and that 'everything we do is coloured by our memories' (ibid.).

In *Possible Worlds* memory creates material that can be 'performed' as real life. The parallel montage replaces what could be considered a traditional flashback with continuous action in order to construct the present. Action determined by memory is an overall narrative principle in *Possible Worlds*; the treatment of George and Joyce's relationship reflects the multilayered narrative of remembrance in Resnais' *Marienbad* where the imaginary 'place' itself becomes the subject of the film. Similarly, the brain-on-a-life-support-system not only serves as the central image of *Possible Worlds*, but is also the place where the majority of the action happens and other worlds are inhabited. As Resnais explained:

When we read a novel we use fragments of cities in our imagination. Even if the novelist states that we are in a house in London our imagination may well locate this house in New York or Ghent. I try to find counterparts for this in cinema. That's why I like to build the cities in my films from a patchwork of locations and to cut from one space to another in a reverse-angle editing technique. (in Duynslaegher 1997: 16)

Resnais' explanation is relevant to Lepage's *Possible Worlds* in more than one way: we see each world that George lives in only as a fragment of a whole made of a patchwork of different settings, ambiences and locations. This is similar to the process of remembering, where only key moments and events are kept, and once put together by our imagination, they are played as one continuous master narrative.

Language as performance

Making films in English has a mixed legacy in Québec culture, since nationalists see English as a persistent threat, one that undermines the French language. However, figures such as Francis Mankiewicz, Claude Jutra and Denys Arcand have made films in English. Lepage's approach to the English language is pragmatic, not out of commercial interest or a need to adopt the language of the dominant culture as a sign of becoming anglicised or to equate Québecois identity with the immigrant other. He deliberately employs English in *Possible Worlds*; as discussed in chapter two, Québecois identity does not only have to be expressed through French. The globalisation of the national narrative and the world has shifted the relationships between inside and outside, particularly in the context of hybrid cultures and identity seen as a mixture of a plurality of cultural references. The use of English can make the story more accessible to the international audience, thus creating a wider reach of communication. It can also be an attempt to bypass the limitations of the distribution of non-English films and avoid labels of 'art house' and 'ethnic' cinema.

To put it simply, Lepage uses English to gain greater access to the international audiences, but as he explains, the use of English also gives him greater control at the time of release:

> One thing about filming in English that makes me happy is that the film has a greater chance of being shown almost everywhere, in Germany for example. In another language, it would have been dubbed. For me, this is a way of conserving a certain artistic authenticity. But we are not talking about [filming in English as] a career decision. (In Provencher 2000: B12)

However, using language as a reference is a common practice explored in Lepage's theatre work. Usually, his theatre productions are performed in French first and then an English version is developed for national and international touring. In his films, the language and the subject matter are distinctly Québecois; however, he always references English as an outside influence, either through foreign characters, media reports, or live translations. In *Possible Worlds*, English, as the main language, loses this idiosyncratic marginal position, and subsequently loses its power as a device for contrast and as a symbol of mainstream politics and culture.

In choosing to work in English, Lepage is availing himself of an existing international resource: there is nothing more global than the use of international English, which is indirectly or directly present in most cultures, mainly through cinema and television. Pragmatically, regional film-makers are accustomed to utilising international points of reference accommodating to the demands and requirements of the mainstream film industry. It is in this context that Lepage opts to work in English. Certainly, he is not the first Québecois director to use English as a film language and to work from an English theatre text. In 1993 Denys Arcand directed *Love and Human Remains*, his first film in the English language and the first not based on his own screenplay, but rather on a theatre play by Brad Fraser. Lepage's decision to use English is not an ideological one; rather it responds to an audience that has been overwhelmingly exposed to Hollywood films and shaped by Anglophone culture.

With *Possible Worlds*, Lepage wanted to capture international attention and step outside the small art-house frame where his films are usually shown, in his own words, as 'good Québecois films'. He also wanted to move away from Québecois themes that he had previously worked through; not to be compartmentalised by the film industry into a particular cultural background associated with otherness or alternative films. Lepage points out that directors such as Lars von Trier are not questioned about why they film in English when that is not their first language. However, contemporary Québecois cinema has been criticised for its talkativeness and intensive use of dialogue, which is mainly a feature of theatre, but is not imperative for the cinematic means of communication. Yves Rousseau (2001: 17) points out that Québec's cinema, with its funding limited, is involving itself in a cinema of words, calling it a film of 'chattering' (*bavardages*). Instead, he argues, Québecois film is not showing visual images but talking about them. In this context, it is liberating when language is stripped of localism and from accent in order to target the international audience.

In order to convey the narrative of *Possible Worlds*, Lepage made very clear directing choices in terms of style: the actors' mode of representation, the use of language combined with expressionless faces shot in a close up, with all background sounds dimmed to emphasise dialogue. Language represents the characters' thoughts as most of the film's narrative is concerned with what George's mind constructs. Lepage chooses to use an emotionless and automated style of language, almost devoid of any traceable human characteristics.

In one of the more striking images of the film, he ambitiously deconstructs language in general, reducing the repertoire of an entire (hypothetical) linguistic community to three words. The image consists of a lighthouse, rocks and sea where we see two people moving stones and mechanically repeating the words block and slab. Dr. Kleber explains to George that these people belong to an ancient civilisation that has three words in its language: block, slab and hilarious. The words block and slab relate to construction, to building, as we see two characters shifting blocks of stone, echoing the myth of Sisyphus. Dr. Kleber elaborates, explaining that millions of dictionaries would be needed to explain all the meanings of these two words. The scene reinforces Lepage's insistence that language is ultimately personalised.[1]

Emotional detachment in the relationship between George and Joyce is observable throughout the film. George generally wears an emotionless expression, and is absent and detached from his surroundings. This is justified by the fact that his character lives different lives and has accumulated knowledge of his different existences. This emotional detachment can also be explained by the fact that George is physically dead and thus represents an image of himself constructed by his mind. In terms of character traits, he has a lot of information about people (having met them in different lives), is capable of great mathematical thinking and is exhausted from shifting between lives. Joyce (or rather different 'Joyces') accuses George of appearing to be a million miles away and made of smoke, with no physical substance.

Using a central character that does not reveal emotions is something Lepage developed with his first film, *Le Confessionnal*. Critics observed that Lothaire Bluteau's interpretation of Pierre in *Le Confessionnal* lacked passion. This has been interpreted as an added value of the film aligning it to postmodernism; others criticise the absence of emotional expression on screen. Lepage outlined this position shortly after the release of *Le Confessionnal*, and suggests an equivalent audience response in film and theatre:

> It is not up to Lothaire to arouse emotion. Emotion belongs to the public and to no one else, not even to the character that you see on screen, on the stage or in a novel. Everyone works towards emotion taking place in the auditorium, the only place where real emotion is needed. I have always believed this. Why do I often find theatre and film flat and boring? It is because the people on stage look moved all right, but you are not. The people on screen look like they are going through incredible emotions, but you go: 'OK, I have understood, but where is our emotion in all this?' (in Dossier 1995a: 25–6)

Lepage is more interested in having emotions alive in the auditorium rather than on screen between characters. This approach – taking response into the audience – is a direct outcome of his theatre work, where he positions the audience as a partner in the creation of narrative. Lepage wants to translate the liveness of theatre into cinema so that the emotional response occurs in the auditorium rather than on the screen. However, language in theatre is alive, which does not always translate to cinema. This could explain the lack of humour in the film, and its inability to play on the initial meaning that existed in the theatre text of *Possible Worlds*. For example, the absurdity of George's situation is not fully realised. The end of the film results in the reworking of a typical problem of confused and unfixed identity rather than offering a new exploration for Québec's 'in-between' position, where Québec's collective, and Lepage's individual, position of being captured between worlds translates into George's situation.

Thematically, *Possible Worlds* makes links with the narrative of memory and its loss, which is characteristic of a number of contemporary films such as *Memento* (2000), *Nurse Betty* (2000), *Mulholland Drive* (2001) or *Vanilla Sky*. Using the loss of memory and thus identity is an essential driving power behind the plot structure of these films.[2] However, in *Possible Worlds*, over-remembrance and plurality of narratives, each relevant to George's memories, become the film's main problems. It is not surprising that the incorrect synopsis of the film in the ICA's pamphlet attempts to give precise time and space coordinates for the film narrative. George's questioning of reality is resolved at the end of the film when he realises that his identity consists of a collage of different memories (lives) put together into one. He would be happy forgetting, or at the best escaping, his alternative lives and memories rather than attempting to remember his multiple histories. The emphasis in North America on questioning memory and identity comes from a postmodern sensibility of artificial stimuli from the environment where sameness, branding and consumerism, induced through media and cinematic reality, force the audience to question who they are (a question which they are encouraged to answer through consumer choices). The plurality of George's memories can also be seen as a matrix of media-generated realities.

Thematically and linguistically, Lepage was hoping to widen access to his film. Traditionally, as with his theatre work, he uses international festivals for the promotion and commercial distribution of his work. Interestingly, *Possible Worlds*, unlike *Le Confessionnal* and *Nô*, did not make any significant achievements at the festivals. The film was refused by the Cannes Film Festival and absent from the Montréal International Film Festival. Instead, it premiered in Venice in 2000 shortly before appearing at the Toronto International Film Festival in September of the same year. *Possible Worlds* was shown together with Denys Arcand's film *Stardom* (2000), which opened the Toronto festival. Arcand's film is also in English. In Québec, Lepage's film was presented for the first time in Montréal in October 2000 at the Festival du Nouveau Cinéma et des Nouveaux Médias.

Lepage was not altogether disappointed with this state of affairs, arguing that the film was an attempt to experiment further with the cinematic medium:

When Piers Handling proposed different positions in the programme of the festival of Toronto, I told him from the start that I would much prefer to be lost in the programme so that people watch the film without expectations. (In Bilodeau 2000: 19)

Although Lepage wanted to play down the expectations of the audience regarding high art and implied élitism, the fact that the film was presented at art-cinema venues already defines the audience, to an extent, and the audience's interpretation of the film. This in practice limits the film's accessibility to larger audiences. Even though there was more funding available for *Possible Worlds* than for *Nô*, it was still considered to be a low-budget film, largely funded by Canadian and Québecois government bodies – confirming its status as art cinema.

Depending on the cultural background that defines the point of entry into the aestheticism of the film narrative, critics gave different readings of this cinematic reality. Québecois critics generally agreed that Lepage's vision did not successfully translate to the cinematic form, which resulted in an air of detachment, one-dimensional characters, and a cerebral and hermetic narrative. The main criticism was practical, based on the fact that the film narrative did not hold the attention of the film audience. Reviewing the Toronto Film Festival, Luc Perreault observes:

> During half of the film Lepage intrigues with the combinations he uses to tie his characters. But little by little, these combinations exhaust themselves and one loses interest in this heightened existence. It's as if once his message has been formulated, the director himself has forgotten to have faith in his imagination. Moreover, the film carries an impression of coldness. It is too cerebral. (2000: 12)

The view of the Québecois critics – that the film is a theoretical exercise and an unsuccessful screen translation – could be explained by Lepage's apparent 'desertion' of the French language and his creation of an Anglophone film. This is the first film narrative in which he does not focus on Québecois characters or explores themes directly linked with national Québecois cinema. A far cry then, from the generally accepted obligation of Québecois film auteurs to 'celebrate' Québec's social and cultural reality and engage with Québec's political conscience, detailed in the use of French language. The English reviewers, on the other hand, generally considered Lepage's aestheticism to be the main value of the film. For example, the review in London's *Time Out* magazine describes the film as:

> Simultaneously an intellectual murder mystery, a philosophical poem about identity and the nature of consciousness, and a luminous romance that embraces different versions of desire as it searches for the unpredictable kernel of affection … Offering a telling thesis on cinema's own ability to generate realities, he's crafted not simply a possible world, but a truly dazzling one. (Andrew 2001: 91)

Interestingly, Québec's critics focused more on the value and clarity of the narrative, while elsewhere focus was on the film's form, style of representation and aesthetics.

Poetics of art and science

In *Possible Worlds*, the existence of the brain remains contextualised within the controlled environment of a scientific lab. Mighton points out that as an artist in

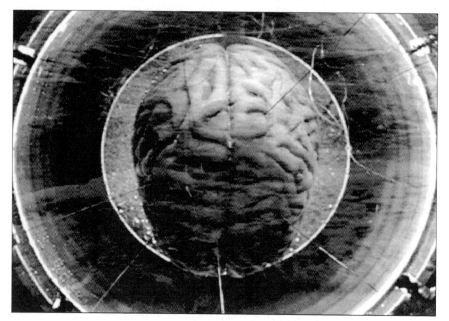

Figure 13 *Possible Worlds*: George's brain on a support sytem superimposed on the waves

his work he was provoked by 'the way science consistently is redefining boundaries of imagination much more than the arts' (2002). Lepage wanted to respond to this provocation and explore the relationship between art and science. The question for him is how to use technology to narrate, to tell the stories. At the same time that he was editing *Possible Worlds*, Lepage was working on a new solo show under the title *Moon Project* that would, eventually, become *The Far Side of the Moon*. This same period is also characterised by his work on a collective production developing a new theatre performance, *Zulu Time*. All three projects utilised new technologies as a vehicle for artistic expression, interweaving scientific discoveries and philosophical questions of human existence.

The relationship between art and science is an interest that Lepage fully explored in all his solo shows. In fact, from the beginning of his theatre work, he showed an interest in exploring new technologies and their interaction with narrative. In the film narrative of *Le Polygraphe*, for instance, there is a strong presence of science and scientific understanding of the world, which often collides with the everyday mythology of the characters. In *Possible Worlds*, scientific discoveries radically influence the way we construct our existence. Mirroring and exploring this effect, Lepage interweaves various influences from mathematics, science and poetry in creating the narrative.

In *Possible Worlds*, as with Lepage's other work, the existence of new technologies allows him to explore different meanings of expression and, accordingly, a new variety of themes. With the arrival of new media, such as the Internet, Lepage believes that we are encouraged to develop multiple personalities; that we do not really live in the 'real' world. The ability to construct a cinematic reality, as opposed to mirroring the world's reality, is an important aspect of the aestheticism in *Possible Worlds*.

The visuals in the film are dominated by the central image of a brain in a glass with a watery liquid. This provides an aesthetic tone, which informs the style – clinical and cold. In keeping, the verbal and visual languages are clinical, emotionless, deliberately pronounced and removed from any indication of location. The brain survives on an artificial life support system that allows it to stay alive and to 'think', functioning as a live organism whose scenarios or lives we see. This image of the brain surrounded by water in a glass container becomes the central reference point; hence the opening shot of the film is of water on a huge glass widow. Water symbolism recurs throughout the film, as Lepage points out, it 'developed this whole aesthetic' (in *Take One* 2000: 16).

Throughout the film, the image of a rat's brain on a life-support system is juxtaposed with the image of George's brain on the same system. The early image of a dead body whose brain has been removed, continuous images of a live brain in liquid inside a glass container, and the revelation at the end of the film that the possible worlds George inhabits are narratives created by his brain, echo Descartes' celebrated dictum 'I think, therefore I am'. These images are a visual representation of the mind-body dualism. The film poses the question initially brought up by Descartes' dualistic division of reality: what exactly is the nature of consciousness, and what is the relationship of consciousness with the physical world? Not only does

Figure 14 *Possible Worlds*: Reality constructed as an alternative world by George's brain

the mind in question have no body and functions independently, the film narrative refers to new scientific evidence regarding brain activity that challenges the traditional notion of indivisibility of the mind. These scientific findings present the possibility that the unity of human consciousness is an illusion, with mental functioning 'an uneasy amalgam of a host of semi-autonomous and often quite loosely co-operating subsistence' (Collingham 2000: 119).

Spontaneous discovery and accidental creativity play an important part in Lepage's way of working on theatre performances. He perceives creativity as a scientific experiment where all elements of the environment have an important part to play. Lepage uses La Caserne, his home base and studio in Québec City and a creative laboratory that brings together different arts and media of expression, for his ongoing search for new theatrical and cinematic language. La Caserne is also the home for other artists and companies working in the field of computer design, creation of visual images, special effects, scene and costume design. However, the nature of the film medium and the costs involved in the filming process do not allow the possibility to play with the resources until the narrative is found through improvisation; rather, Lepage works very thoroughly on the film script before shooting starts. In *Possible Worlds*, he and Mighton went through a number of versions of the film script – Mighton's drafts were followed by discussions with Lepage, which in turn prompted a new draft. The decision of how to end the film could be linked with the presumed emotional response of the audience. Leaving it ambiguous, the audience is given the responsibility to 'write' a conclusion. In *Possible Worlds*, the film narrative and the ending suggest a number of possibilities. Towards the end, in what is by now just one of the possible worlds, Joyce has to decide whether or not to keep George's brain alive on a life-support system; in another world (or scenario that his brain plays for him) he is a criminal in prison. The film ends with the world where George and Joyce are at the beach, lying in each other's arms, when suddenly Joyce points towards the sea to a red light coming from the distance. We are shown what she sees but there is nothing. The same lines are repeated a few times finishing with:

Joyce: Someone is trying to signal us. What shall we do?
George: I do not know.
Joyce: It stopped.
George: Thank God.

However, the ending of the film was the result of an accident that Lepage used to his advantage. The filming of *Possible Worlds* closely followed the screenplay; however, he allowed accidental discovery to influence the shooting, as he would do in theatre with improvisations, finding resources by chance and adapting to them. Mighton explains:

There is one scene when they went across some sort of grass hill and they look down at the ocean and they can see some kids playing and stuff, and I thought

Figure 15 *Possible Worlds*: George and Joyce on the beach realising that someone is trying to communicate with them in the distance

that was absolutely brilliant and I guess he just found it. He'd already thought there'd be kids involved but I think they actually found that pan across going down to the water. I think the cinematographer was very good and had that, and between the two of them they came up with the shot which is spectacular for that scene. So I was surprised at things like that but he would convey to me pretty clearly how it looked beforehand. (2002)

Artificial reality

In *Possible Worlds*, the popular genre of the detective thriller is used in an ironic interpretation. Police are there to establish the truth; however what is the truth in the multiple realities where George has different versions of such reality? Overlapping with the detective search are elements of the science fiction genre. Science fiction films are rare in Québecois cinema because generally, films in Québec engage with the realities of Québec's existence – Yves Simoneau was criticised for the Americanisation of his science fiction film *Dans le Ventre du Dragon* (1989) (Marshall 2001: 296). However, Lepage was careful to point out that *Possible Worlds* deals with scientific reality. In the film, the borders between science fiction and science reality are blurred, establishing artificial reality with endless possibilities. These realities could be the outcome of memories or dreams generated by the brain itself or they could be the work of external forces stimulating from the outside through chemical or electronic impulses.

Visually, the film uses images that, in a surreal way, connect space and time between the various worlds: the brain in a container and the character of scientist, Dr. Kleber. The images deliberately lack specific references to place, language or landmarks that could give a sense of location. The decision to have interior shots in a typical urban setting as represented in television series on detectives, hospitals, bankers and lawyers, and exterior shots, in a postcard rural setting surrounded by the sea, points to deliberate use of artificial reality. Dealing with the general ambience of a city, beach or countryside without recognisable names or places allows the viewer to project their own memory into the story.

Narrating from memory is indicative of a loss of place and central focus, of a process of personal and global deterritorialisation. This raises the possibility that our world, or the way we perceive, is conceptualised by someone else outside us, perhaps those who, like Dr. Kleber, have the power to create and own the information, to contextualise 'mind' within a controlled environment suitable for their own 'experiments'. In late-capitalism, human interactions are becoming increasingly complicated, with imposed ways of behaving, social rules of engagement, information overload, promotions and advertising that disperse any meaning, drowning it in a sea of multiple meanings. Conversely, the information we receive is also controlled, owned and edited. In the contemporary age, thinking is contextualised by the social and cultural matrix created by the multiple realities of media culture: television, radio, Internet, films, press. Dr. Kleber explains to the inspector investigating George's murder that in the future there will be drugs that can erase unpleasant memories and even stimulate new, pleasant ones. In the age of human cloning, we might already be on the doorstep of artificial memory.

We live with the misleading presumption that the world we live in is a unified global village. The notion of a global village suggests a community of communities with an underlying common interest, where the rules of engagement are known, unified, simple and equally accessible to all. However, the access to, and control of, resources, and the distribution of information and knowledge are in the hands of a few. And, where exactly is the centre of the village located in contemporary multi-referentiated urban living? We do not live in the same village but in a cluster of small villages in perpetual conflict for dominance. The image of a 'village' is better replaced by a megalopolis, an urban jungle of multiple groups and sub-groups in a constant chaotic movement and collision, seemingly unified by economic interests, circling around the social centre in the conflict over control.

Our connection to reality becomes determined by television and cinema. Philippe Gajan (2001) observes that in a strange turn of events, Québecois film that started with *cinema direct*, evoking strong connections with reality, is now beginning to resemble the artificial reality constructed by television. *Cinéma direct* has come full circle in Lepage's artificial reality cinema; after all, the images in *Possible Worlds* do not have to be part of the audience's direct experience because we know them from films and pictures in designer magazines and tabloid journals. What we see in *Possible Worlds* is a mediated experience of cinematic reality already shown in other works of media culture. Lepage reinforces the idea that the understanding of the world increasingly comes from a visual culture where viewing experience is part of every day life, where reality is manufactured in media, fabricated and fictionalised.

If we take the image of the scientific experiment with the human brain in a glass container full of liquid as a metaphor to represent human existence in the contemporary world, then the mind becomes an entity contextualised by those who control the experiment. Knowledge of the world is not necessarily the result of our own existence but of an artificial experience made of an infinite number of possible realities. The film narrative develops in response to George's question, 'What is my reality and my existence; in what world do I actually live?' The question is, then, how much of our experience is actually implanted as our own by the dominant centre? Who controls and owns information?

In *Possible Worlds*, Lepage suggests the possibility that science and technology will make the hitherto accepted duality of mind and body obsolete, separating the fact of the body from the reality of the mind. In this complex cinematic mosaic of multiple realities, Lepage moves towards a new aesthetic for a new art form, matching the complexity and plurality of his art with the unimaginable complexity and plurality of human existence.

CONCLUSION

Possible Endings

It is difficult to draw conclusions about the work of a film-maker such as Robert Lepage; hard enough to critically engage with his perpetually transforming and multi-referential way of creating, let alone be definitive in comment. To date, Lepage is the author of four films; he is in his mid-40s and intends to continue producing work for some time to come. His career could still take unpredictable paths as he continues to experiment with theatre and film. Consequently, this 'conclusion' will in itself be a work in progress, an unfinished chapter, a reconsideration of some of the key philosophical points that Lepage raises in his film narratives, and open to change.

At the time of writing, Lepage is at work on a new project, a potential film with the working title *Tourism*. It is a story about the illegal trafficking of human body parts. Although there is no script as such, but a set of ideas improvised with actors, he intends to create narrative material that can then be used as a resource for mainstream cinema technology. This new project demonstrates Lepage's inclination towards hybrid forms of media, mixing the ways of working in theatre and cinema. As part of this work, for the last two years, Lepage has been filming with a DV camera the rehearsals in his La Caserne studio, using the way he devises theatre to create material or a 'recorded text' as a starting point for a future film.

At this point it is not possible to know exactly what form the project *Tourism* will take, or whether it will materialise as a film, theatre production or something else. However, the general outlines that emerge from conversation with Lepage himself make it obvious that the project is a continuation of the earlier feature: exploring human nature, body and memory, technology and communication through performance and cinema. Regardless of whether this project becomes a motion picture or not (which depends largely on funding processes and the outcomes of production games), Lepage intends to combine artistic disciplines, creating and recording rehearsed events with a DV camera, and then using these recordings as an ongoing creative workshop to make a film as a work in progress. This combination of theatre and film clearly points to a new synergy of arts, styles and technologies that in the future could perhaps form a new and different artistic expression.

The context reviewed

Lepage's film directing has the ability to take the regional, local context of Québec's reality and expose it to the international audience by using a wide range of references. This achievement should not be underestimated given the proximity and overwhelming influence of Anglophone culture and the Hollywood industry. In Québec, 'until the 1940s, "the cinema" meant Hollywood films in English (the vast majority) or films from France' (Marshall 2001: 299). The shift in the Québecois public's perception of cinema coincides with the rise of political consciousness towards the definition of national identity and independence.

Since the 1960s, the development of Québecois cinema became closely linked to the representation of Québec's social reality. Québecois cinema was both an element, and crucial reflection, of the complexity of national identity as defined by ideological criteria. In 1977, the Québec National Assembly passed the Charter of the French language, making French the official language of the state, in education and the work-place, thus ending linguistic freedom of choice. The Charter was more then a language act: placing emphasis on the protection and development of Québecois distinctive-ness, cultural politics equated territory with national identity. Funded by government bodies, media and film played a crucial role in supporting the ideological position of Québec's separatist tendency.

However, in the 1980s, with the growing popularisation of multi-cultural concepts, minorities and hybridity, the primacy of the linguistic issue gave way to the need to express and reflect the newly recognised cultural plurality (gay issues, interest in Oriental cultures, recent immigrants, the finding of new identities rather then the preservation of old ones). These themes are much reflected in Lepage's work. His cinema enters into the context of the immigrant other as 'becoming' a new mixed identity of Canadian or North American rather then 'being' a fixed identity in relation to France. His characters, socially marginalised or culturally or physically displaced, tell us about their own Québec from human perspectives that relate to different cultural backgrounds. If the role of film is viewed primarily as ideological and didactic, criti-cism of Lepage's work has suggested that he reduces art and life: ironic and detached, he plays a superficial game of narratives with a set of 'clever' ideas. However, by using familiar content and exploring aesthetic qualities, which place emphasis on form, Lepage communicates through a cinema language in which form *becomes* content. He relates recognisable stories and one does not have to know about 'Québec' to be able to engage with his films.

Theorising communities

Lepage's world is one of perpetual movement between different cultures and locations. His attitude towards community is based on the understanding that contemporary communities – particularly urban communities – are not defined by national contexts and politics of the state as by their own historical and contemporaneous circum-stances. Each community has its own identity and should not relate to one prescribed by the political national discourse.

Canada itself is a country in the making, a mosaic of communities and cultures that has been attempting to see itself as a multi-cultural community since the 1980s. Québec, as a strong cultural centre, plays an essential role in this process. In postmodern criticism, the process of explaining Canadian reality has focused on the existing polarities between unstable shifting identities without an evident coherent centre (Hutcheon 1988), and on the concept of finding and building a nation. However, this process is not confined to questions of resolving identities; it is also preoccupied with social interaction between various groups. Lepage often points to an implicit difference that he perceives between Montréal and Québec City: the cultural and financial dominance of Montréal and the political significance of Québec.

Lepage's unwillingness to bend to the established 'ways' of social and cultural hierarchies has often placed him in conflict with Montréal's cultural 'gate- keepers'. This is understandable: in every nation there is not just one centre, but multiple centres that at any given point in time can succeed one another (for example democratic election or revolution) and which are in perpetual conflict over dominance and control of the cultural, historical, biological and geographical 'territory'. Communities, regardless of citizenship, have more in common with each other then nations, sharing, as they do, the content of human experience, which is becoming increasingly homogenised. On the other hand, however, communities within a national context can have completely different historical, social and cultural experiences. In large cities, such as London or New York, urban identities can vary greatly from the presumed homogeneous national identity; for example, compare the cosmopolitanism of London with any regional centre in the North of England and you may be talking about two very different 'countries'.

Future direction

Since art is a medium for communication, the individual experience as artistically expressed transcends the boundaries between communities, and the nature of that experience shared through stories brings people together. For Lepage, film is a form of communication, a way of telling stories of people at the point of change, willing to make a break from the forces that constrain them. His cinema simultaneously conveys and translates the paradoxical feeling of wanting to escape from a location, whilst at the same time wanting to stay.

The cinema of Robert Lepage is thus a personal and poetic interpretation of reality, not a mimesis of life, and in this he shares the approaches of other authors such as Jean Cocteau, Federico Fellini and Emir Kusturica. Each uses film as a vehicle for personal poetics, and regards the medium as an inappropriate and inadequate way to record and reflect on the 'real' world. The notion that Lepage can be considered only in the terms of Québecois film tradition, as a social commentator with strong ironic undertones, limits understanding of his work. To exclude Lepage from the global and international cultural and social context is to do injustice to his films; his narratives are about living in a world where it is has become more important to discover one's own history, to understanding one's own actions and what one want from life. His narratives are also about being free from imposed collective thoughts. It is in the creation of this poetics of personal and collective memories that Lepage excels and it distinguishes his work.

Within the canon of Western culture, these preoccupations are not only relevant to North America or countries with colonial inheritance and consciousness, but also to Europe. The global movement of people through integration, displacement and migration results in hybridity, which is inevitable. In turn, this hybridity necessitates the need for a sense of the personal past.

Lepage's characters, Pierre and Marc Lamontagne, Francoise, Sophie and Michel, and George, all demonstrate an inability to accept and understand the meaning of the life that occurs in their own surroundings. Their need for the discovery of an authentic life, hidden behind the surface of the mass market, media and information, beneath the artificial reality, is a natural response to the desire to comprehend existential, moral and intellectual consequences of life. In a world where the growing control of global information systems imposes one version of the truth, and the use of science works to increase the predictability and manageability of human action for greater economic and political profitability, the need for fantasy, personal truth and freedom from the official story – the CNN version of the world – strengthens.

The characteristic features of Lepage's theatre and film work have been illuminated here in an attempt to explain the social and cultural context and process of his work from the perspective of new auteurism cinema with a global message and international reading. Lepage's understanding of art reinforces what is essentially a traditional view expressed in Eisenstein's famous credo, 'there is no art outside conflict' (1968: 42). Conflict for Lepage is not fabricated and illustrated in simplistic plots, characters and elaborate pyrotechnics and visual effects. Like Mike Leigh, conflict in Lepage's film narratives derives from the characters themselves, from their own insecurity with regard to their identity and environment. However, they are all engaged with the worlds that exist outside of social realty, where personal and collective mythologies and memories exist alongside fantasies, dreams and alternative existences, where past and present merge.

Simultaneously, Lepage approaches cinema as a medium for poetic expression. Like Jean Cocteau, for whom cinema is a 'medium for poetry as an art' (1994: 32), Lepage's cinematic style uses visual language, transformation of meanings and symbols in a poetic way. The fates of his characters are conveyed for the viewers in a multi-perspective and multi-layered fashion, giving a variety of points of view to what is fundamentally a narrow, limited and superficially defined existence. Moreover, he explores cinematic language by finding new ways of engaging with the struggles and demands of our age when cinema is re-defining itself, through film's stylistic potentials.

For Lepage, creativity is not about finding answers, but for posing questions and provocations. Creativity is ultimately concerned with the nature and representation of memory. He is interested, as an artist, in showing how time and historical events shape characters and the individual interpretation of history. Such themes are relevant to events that are experienced indirectly on a level of collective memory. As a director, he does not look for solutions to the conflicts and dramas of human existence in sociology or psychology but rather within the individual. His films are intensely Québecois in their relevance to social and cultural milieux whilst representing personal stories and allowing a subjective vision. It is the unity of his work that makes it consistently relevant: the manner in which he expands his multi-disciplinary theatre performances into film, his mixture of realistic and poetic representation, memories, fantasy and reality, past and unpredictable future, human nature and choice.

APPENDIX:
INTERVIEW WITH ROBERT LEPAGE

Aleksandar Dundjerovic: There is a sense of marginality and displacement in your films. Is that relevant to the time you spent growing up in Québec, developing against the position of the mainstream, Francophone dominant centre?

Robert Lepage: The theme of the family is very important in Québec, as it is, I guess, in Irish culture or Scottish culture. I think it has a lot to do with the fact that the cultural community here has survived because of family and their blood relations. It explains some of the nationalism, Québec nationalism. My family in particular was a bit strange though because it was a mix of all kinds of things: children who had been adopted and children who were biological. So, that created a certain kind of tension in the family; also the fact that the two adopted children were adopted in English Canada, so they were brought up in English and we were brought up in French. This is a bit of a metaphor for Canada, a cultural metaphor.

Your cultural environment was of working-class Québecois, a strong French background where multi-lingualism was not common.

No, not common, certainly somewhere like Québec City. Montreal was more bi-lingual but Québec City and the rest of the provinces were uni-lingual French. I always saw it as an advantage to have this kind of bi-cultural upbringing; but it has also been the root of conflict. We were very ordinary, a working class family, normal children, but the situation was very abnormal compared to that of many other families. I think that today you appreciate that and see it as an interesting point of view, an interesting place from which to look at society. But in those days it caused an obstacle, it was problematic. At one point I was very unhappy about that. So, as a result, when the whole social context of separatism and bi-culturalism became a preoccupation, I had a different experience of it because in my family I'd been living the reality of it. My older brother, whose name is Dave Lepage, had an English first name and a French surname. When he went to school, he went to an Irish Catholic school. Of course, everybody would beat him up because he was considered by the French Canadians to be an English Canadian. Then, when he went to New Brunswick to continue studying English, he had a French name and a French girlfriend and he was considered to be French Canadian. Now he lives in Ottawa, the only official bi-lingual city in the country because it's the capital and their civil servants have to speak both languages. It's the only place where his life is really possible.

Looking back to the 1960s and 70s, how would you describe Québec, and the tension between localism and internationalism?

The 1960s were very important in Québec; before that it was really driven by a moralist Catholic church, under its control. At that time, Montreal was the biggest city in Canada, well before Toronto because of its bi-culturalism; it had the potential to invite international events and with Expo '67, it put Canada on the map. Suddenly people went, 'Oh there's a country called Canada, there's a city called Montreal'. Expo '67 was very, very modern. So, suddenly Montreal back-flipped and became this completely international, cosmopolitan, modern society obsessed with technology and the avant-garde. Though, of course, it did not have the structure to support that, but it remained quite an illusion for a while in the 1960s and 70s. There were two forces. Part of population was trying to become this big international city, opening on the world, and then there was the inner politics of Québec – like in the early 70s with the October crisis. So it was a very difficult time, in which Québec really woke up. It's interesting that earlier on we were talking about the poetics of memory, how that's a recurring theme in my work. There's something about film, certainly for someone who comes from the theatre, film is about recording. It's about leaving traces and remembering how things were and what they meant. One of the big revolutions of the 1970s in Québec, in the early 70s, was that they changed the license plate. Québec used to be called Québec La Belle Provence and now it's Je me Souviens. I remember.

Aside from memory, themes of politics and sexuality, within the larger question of identity and nationalism, appear to be relevant to your work. In all of your films there is 'man' and 'woman' and there are essential clashes, which demonstrate their inability to have a relationship. This seems to relate to your own 'coming out', in political and sexual determination, in the mid-1990s.

I have always been very interested in sexual politics but not in the way people usually are. Gay directors usually want to discuss their sexuality as a theme. I'm not interested in that. In a sense, it's not an interesting theme for me to explore. I don't have anything different or new to say about it. What I find interesting about sexual politics – and it's something that Michelle Trembley, who's our most important playwright, developed in the 1960s – is this realisation that we are not a patriarchal society but a matriarchal society. The culture survives because of the mothers, the women. In this society the women are the fighters, they are the ones who are the leaders, the people who speak on the TV the politicians. It's a matriarchal system that has been inherited – not by the French and not by the English, because they're both very patriarchal. In Québec I think we have inherited it from the North American Indians because the aboriginal culture here is matriarchal. The men go and hunt and the women take care of the politics; they are the ones who decide. Québec society, its heritage of the Native population, is the matriarchal thing, and because of that we don't have a lot of men who speak; it's the women or the gays. So, if you look at Québec culture whether it's theatre or cinema, it's that difficulty that's expressed a lot. The characters, the main characters, are usually women; the men are quiet or absent; and the gays are there, talking, showing their problems.

In the mid-1990s you started to talk openly about the whole question of political position in Québec. Why was that?

In 1995, when there was the second referendum, it was an interesting time, not just for Québec. What is separatism? Separatism is a part of a country that says 'we want to have our own…' and it necessarily has to be a selfish thing, it has to be, 'this is what I need and I want it now, and it means separating with the rest of this country'.

Like with Yugoslavia?

With the case of Yugoslavia you try to create a federation of different cultures and it only holds for a certain time and there's a moment where people make love or they fight. You can't have two communities that live together without meeting; you have to meet one way or the other. The thing about 1995 that was interesting for the referendum was that it wasn't just about Québec, it was about Canada. It was saying to English Canadian people, 'you have to redefine yourself'. If the referendum said 'yes' or 'no', it's not important. What's important was what that this debate was about redefining the whole federation. It was about saying 'Québec wants out'. I became more comfortable speaking out about my political positions because I was more involved with working in English Canada than Québec. I had a real relationship with the English Canadians. I had a real respect for them, because I knew them. When you don't know the other culture, you say 'no'. When you know them you can say, 'Well then, this is why we should not be part of the same country'. I think that I had the better knowledge of what English Canada had to offer. It's interesting, English Canada believes that the only culture in this country that is strong is in Québec. So they don't want to lose us, because if they lose us they lose their shop window of culture. But it's not true. Yes, we have a vibrant culture, but English Canada has another kind of culture that is as interesting and strong. The problem is that English Canada is being de-possessed of its excellence because the United States just takes talent. If you are an excellent writer, director or actor, you're taken, and the country is being emptied. In Québec we keep our excellence a bit more.

You are one of the few directors whose films have gained artistic success outside Canada. Are you drawn to Hollywood?

They've asked but I would be very uncomfortable. I don't want to go through the burden of having any kind of Hollywood career. It's the worst place you'd want to live and work. You want to have artistic control and that's the reason why, when I want to do a film, I ask for little money. You don't want to have more than one producer above you; I understood that early. If I want to do the things I want to, work with the people I want to, I have to keep it small. The moment you do something with ten million dollars it's over. They completely destroy the artistic project. It's impossible. I'm not ambitious, for cinema I mean. I think it's an interesting medium and I'm interested in exploring it. I love the influence it has on my theatre work, but I've never taken it seriously.

Before you made Le Confessional you appeared in Jesus of Montreal. Had you appeared on screen before?

I did a bit of television before that and I ended up in a couple of student films with friends but the first real part I got in a film was in *Jesus of Montreal*.

What impact did working on this film have on you?

I got to see a professional team working hard. It felt like a very free improvised thing and that had an impact. I was misled, though, because it was probably the Québec film with the biggest budget. Also, Denys Arcand has a vision of what cinema should be; because it is so prepared, so scripted, he does not feel that he is looking for his film as he shoots it. For him, it's done. So I was misled in that sense. I was there doing this film and I thought, 'Oh there's so much space, there's no tension, there's a place to try'. When I came to do my own film, first of all there was not the money that there had been on *Jesus of Montreal*, far from it. Also, I don't really write things, and you have to really have something written so then you can improvise.

What was your experience with the TV film of Tectonic Plates? Did you have a hand in that project?

I didn't know a thing about film so I collaborated. I think it's problematic to film my plays. Because my shows use a cinematic language people think 'Oh, it's going to be so easy to take this play and make a film of it', but to the contrary, it's very difficult to translate.

How did you find that with Le Polygraphe?

That was probably the time it was the most difficult, because you are doing something with another kind of poetic system, which is based on reality. Film is interesting when it's hyper-realistic – when you have to go beyond that realism. It's all about close-ups, about showing details, showing you something that you haven't seen. Theatre is about pushing away, about showing an ensemble. The people are far from the object, they're far from the situation. So it's about looking at things. Cinema is about looking with a close up.

You work as actor, performance artist, film and theatre director. In each, you are evaluated separately. When you're doing a solo show you are evaluated as a performer and the critical opinion is that you're a very good performer, and when you do your theatre directing you're evaluated as a theatre director and when you do a film, you're evaluated as a film director. Yet you bring in your work all these media together.

I have never played in one of my films and I think I should do that. Then I would be preoccupied by something other than directing. When you are on the stage you write a play, you direct it, you do the stage design, and you perform it. Because you perform it, you are not always looking at it. You are looking at it from a place that's in the centre so you imagine what people see, you control from the middle. Not in film. That's one thing about Woody Allen that's so extraordinary. He's not as obsessed by what the film looks like as much as what it feels like. And I think I would be a better actor, director and writer if I was in the middle of my film and I haven't had the courage to do that yet.

It sounds like you're in the middle of the solo shows.

When I did *Far Side of the Moon* I understood that relationship between media, because it's a theatre, so people don't even see my face if it's badly lit. But there's a little microphone so, like in cinema, they get my voice, a close up of my voice. That means I can be very cinematic with my acting, using theatrical, visual physicality.

Your solo shows have that cinematic quality. Which medium affects which – theatre the cinema or vice versa?

I think that it depends on the narrative, on the story that you want to tell. I don't have a theatre upbringing, I went to theatre conservatory, where they tried to show me how you do theatre, but it's very boring. If I had been brought up in Europe, I would probably have been more in contact with theatre but here theatre is for the bourgeois. You don't go and see theatre. But you see a lot of TV, a lot of film.

So these are the references in your work?

Yes. That's how you tell a story. Naively, the amateur actors and companies, think that they can do cinema on stage. They think they don't have any education of theatre. They see something on TV and they try to do that. That's where it becomes art.

In your theatre work you are constantly re-writing and transforming narrative, but as a film director how do you work? Do you have a fully written script? Is everything worked out in advance?

It's written, but sometimes it's more of a canvas to which I just add some lines.

What about with Le Confessionnal?

It was the first time in my life that I sat down and I wrote alone. That was a nightmare.

And you decided to confess to cinema? You wrote the script then what happened?

It's more complex than that, because it starts where film starts today, which means there's no story, there's no script or anything, there's a name. This producer comes to me and says, 'You have to do cinema' and I say, 'Well, no, because I'm doing a lot of theatre and if I do cinema you have to have time, you have to have money, it's very expensive'. He said, 'With your name, no problem'. So I didn't start at film school and then make a first film with two thousand dollars. They said they'd find four million and they gave it to me and they said, 'You do your first film'. It's the way it happened then and it's the way it happens now. People that really are good film-makers and have things to say are not making films because they don't have names.

What is the most important thing for you as a film director once you are on the set? How do you work on your 'mise-en-scène'?

I think it's the exploration moment. I was very prepared during pre-production for *Possible Worlds*. So, I knew what I wanted at every level, except when the actors came in the morning and we did the first blocking there was no time to explore. I was reading Stanley Kubrick who said that even if you prepare for five years for a scene, the moment is really when the actors come out, just before they go to make up. You have this blocking moment where you say 'Okay, the camera will be here and you come in, or maybe put the camera there'. This is half an hour that they give you to try to find out how you're going to shoot it. That's where it happens, you know, and for me that's really exciting and that's where the thing comes to life, but it's half an hour. It's terrible. We should shoot for half an hour and spend the rest of the time doing this. Blocking is where it's all happening. But cinema's production system is not made that way. That's why we have so many people breaking away from the system, either abandoning it or creating Dogme or saying we have to get away from all this and bring back the storytelling and do it with more money. People are trying to unplug, they want to do it unplugged, because it's become a complete PR thing cinema and it's not an art form.

How do you work with your actors?

I don't direct like other directors. I don't spend a lot of time discussing the psychology of the character and trying to make the actor act. I believe actors are intelligent, if you work with good actors. They're actors, yes, but they are storytellers, the ones that people will listen to. I try to help them tell the story and make it interesting then they decide how to do that. If they're intelligent they'll find how to make it. There is not enough time to do that in the cinema, unless the actors are also writing the story with you. Then you don't even have to say anything to them, the actor already knows what to do. With our new project, that's how we're working. You don't need to direct the actor because there is this inner understanding of what the story is and what everybody should be doing. Because I knew *Possible Worlds* was something I didn't write, I asked for the actors to be there earlier. I wanted more rehearsal time because I felt we had to understand what this thing was about.

How long was your rehearsal process for Possible Worlds?

One week. Usually you have one day here.

The cinematography in Possible Worlds I haven't seen you use before. There are many exterior shots, paintings, connections with surrealist imagery.

I have to admit that up until now, it's been difficult for me to really point out the advantages of doing cinema, because theatre always satisfies me. Except when I did *Possible Worlds* I kind of went, 'Oh wait a minute, we're stranded on an island and we're shooting exteriors, surrealist exteriors and all that, and I've never done this before'. I mean I've done some establishing shots, out in the snow for *Polygraphe,* and I did the bridge, but in *Possible Worlds* the film only made sense if was shot outside. When you do cinema you don't say 'Oh, that's interesting dialogue'. When you do cinema, you say, 'This is in the North Pole and we'll have a helicopter'. You do something that you can't do with theatre: you try to grasp nature, you try to grasp cities, the logic of urban sprawl, the logic of continents moving and the logic of how lights move in a huge environment. I thought, 'If I continue doing films it has to allow me to do that'. Like in the cafeteria in *Possible Worlds* there's all this glass and there's rain. In the earlier films when it rains it's in a little window.

In Possible Worlds you have all these transformations of objects, complex transformations of scenes, when one event transforms into another one.

It's always about going from one place to another and how you get there, and it's the way you get there that gives the language to the film. For me, that is important: how it plays with its space and how it plays with time like in *Le Confessional*. Film is about 24 frames giving the illusion of reality and movement. It's about set sequences, it's about crossing through what you cannot do in real life. Like going from light to dark, from today to yesterday, from the future to the back, from one place to another in one magical moment. But it is not just cut and edit; it could also be a way of informing the audience. I think that *Possible Worlds* is a complex film but for me it was where I felt I had a better hand at the craft.

The use of space is very interesting in your work. The characters in your films are generally located in terms of a global reference, for example Québec or Osaka. It seems that Possible Worlds does not even specify itself globally.

My strongest subject in school when I was a kid was geography. All my work is about geography so it could be that geography includes cultural differences between two countries, it includes travelling but it also includes the geography of space. It's not just going to Europe in a plane, it's also the geography of the human environment and what that means and how does it have an influence? I worked in Japan a lot and I know that in Japan there is no space. People live in small houses, so when they go to the theatre, the curtain opens and there's nothing on the stage and there's a little tree and then the actor comes in, but they all go 'Ohhh'. They go 'Ohhh' to the space. I think that's the thing, that's what I'm saying. When we did *Possible Worlds* we wanted to shoot something that with the opening image people would go 'Ohhh', but they don't go 'Ohhh, it's beautiful, it's big' they go 'Ohhh, it's space'. The story takes place in this space or this space has something to say in this story, and that's important, where you shoot it, the places, the locations you choose, what do they have to say? Not just locations in a conscious way, sometimes it could be unconscious. The whole story of *I Confess,* by Alfred Hitchcock, was supposed to take place in Boston. Then they wanted to do it in Chicago, and at one point he said, 'No we have to set it in a place where people will believe that this Catholic priest and this Catholic church has power'. So the only place was Québec, and it happens that the location was interesting, cinematically interesting for him to explore. *Possible Worlds* was a very, very challenging thing, because the place is the brain. There's no real place. So we would go somewhere on a country road, we would shoot the car and you'd see that there is no stop sign because you're not in a real place. There are no roads and the cars don't have plates. It was an interesting challenge.

You made three films about Québec, which were located in Québec, and the fourth one is set in a non-place. Are you moving away from Québec as a location?

No, it is Québec. Like in our new project, it's Québec, but it's Québec if it's compared to another place. So, people can't understand Québec if you're not in Toronto first, at the beginning of the film, or if you're not in a traditional North American city like New York and then character goes from there to Québec. Then we can understand how lost this character is in the Québec area – the language difference, the architectural standards are different, the urban sprawl is different. The naiveté of *Le Confessional* and *Polygraphe* was in thinking that people would get that just by showing Québec. Like Angelopoulos' great film *Ulysses' Gaze,* he starts in a place that you think you know, he's in Greece and we're in a port and it's everything you expect and then he brings you to a place you never would have imagined and suddenly you have the impression you know it very well because the way he brings you there and what it looks like becomes *so* important. It's the main character. But it starts in a place you know and a place where you say, 'Okay, yes, yes, he's in Athens or whatever'. But if he starts in the middle of the Balkans somewhere, we go 'Where are we? What is this?' With *Ulysses' Gaze,* locations are one of the great dramaturgical references, because he starts in a place everybody knows. Then he goes to a place that nobody knows so we are as lost as he is and at the same time, and that I think is interesting. If you're not from New York or L.A., or from Paris or London, or the colonisers' domain and you want to talk about where you live and what it is that you live, you have to start where they are and then bring them. You can't be in the middle and that was one of the problems with the first two films.

In Le Confessional, there is question of the past – 'where am I coming from?' – demonstrated in the quote where you say that 'the past carries the present on its shoulders'. You ask, 'Who am I?' in Le Polygraphe, 'Where am I going?' in Nô and 'What's my reality?' in Possible Worlds. Memory, myth and search for self – would you say that these are the main themes of your work?

With each important period or era in the world, you know what it's about by what follows. For example, the sexual liberation of the 1960s. Everybody was suddenly into sex, sex liberation and the revolution. Then, after that, you have the AIDS epidemic. So the AIDS epidemic says that, 'Okay, we've just been through ten-fifteen years of sexual exploration but there's a danger to that, there's a backlash, so now we have to bring the swing back in the other direction and find a balance'. The next wave was Alzheimer, the word Alzheimer. I have people in the family who had Alzheimer's when I was a kid, but nobody calls that 'Alzheimer's'. Why today does everybody know what it is? It's as if it's a new disease, a new epidemic, but it's always been there. Is it a consequence of the last ten years of the identity problem, of society going 'Okay, who are we, what are we? What's my past about, where do I come from?' We all put the emphasis on memory and identity, because that's what Alzheimer's is about, it's about loss of identity. But it's not just a physiological thing, there's a generalised Alzheimer epidemic socially, because we were brought up in small areas with a certain identity and we can't be that if we want to survive. We have to be something else, we have to speak another language, accommodate new languages and new universal standards. The more the world becomes a global village and then one big culture, the more you have this identity because it's not just the memory of your language and where you were brought up, it's your values, your ideas, your morals. The more we're moving towards one big identity, one generalised identity, the more we break into small ones I think. That's why the communist ideal didn't work in the twentieth century, because it's all about every man is the same and we're all equal. And you say, 'Yes, but if I accept that how about my specificity? How about my identity that is a bit different because I live on a different street corner and the wind doesn't blow as hard along that side?' There will always be something naturally unequal. Nature is an unequal, unsymmetrical thing. So how can we make societies that are symmetrical and equal? That's why I'm interested in science more and more, and DNA, because I think that politics and identity has a lot more to do with biology and about how a lot of our identity is predetermined by our DNA. We even have a suicide gene in our DNA. There are some people here at University Laval who are working on this cure for cancer by trying to find a way to give the information to the sick cell: 'No don't try to reproduce, you're supposed to kill yourself'. So the concept of suicide is in our cells, it's there, and people still address it, only as a social, psychological phenomenon, but it's more than that, it's a natural thing. It's something that's in our nature. What it says basically is 'reproduce' but if something goes wrong, stop reproducing and destroy. So I'm interested in that, I think 'Oh, there's drama there, there's tragedy, there's identity crisis, there's contradiction, there's fate, there's all these great elements to tell stories'.

Can film or theatre reflect that?

I think so. There is a huge book of conversations with Orson Welles and it starts with Orson Welles explaining what film is for him. He tells a little metaphor, and that metaphor is used in the film *The Crying Game*. It's the story of the scorpion who wants to go across the river.[2]

On the frog?

On the frog. So the moral is that when the scorpion bites the frog, the frog says, 'I don't understand, it's not logical what you're doing here, you're killing us both', and he says, 'Yes, but it's in my nature, my nature is to bite'. So Orson Welles starts by saying that the moment you understand that characters are interesting is when they have a specific natures that contradict their logic.

Is the editing process difficult for you or is it only an extension of how you shoot your mise-en-scène?

The more you accept the film, the more the film shows itself to you. My illusion at the beginning, I thought that you know what to shoot, you look at the rushes and you think you've seen everything, you think you know how things work. Then you try to put them together and they run away. The film has it's own life and it's going in a direction that you don't want to go and you're stuck and you're trying to harness it and bring it back to where you want it, but it's always running away from you because it has its own life. So, from the moment you understand and learn to accept that, you shoot differently, you write differently, you expect different things. I've learnt to change my expectations. When I'm in the editing room now, I'm more neutral so that the material surprises me, but I've only done four films. If I had been trained, it would bring me somewhere more comfortable and more exciting, so editing is less and less difficult I'd say.

When you are shooting a scene how many takes do you have?

It depends what we're shooting. Now, because you can put things on digital to work and then print, I'd say at least five, six takes, but sometimes it goes to twenty

In one of your new projects, you combine theatre and film method work and technology....

I have this project *Tourism* that I've been working on for the past year and a half. It's not difficult creatively, actually it's very, very close to the way I work in theatre, I just don't know if it's ever going to be shot because we keep postponing it. It's a film about organ trafficking, the organ market. It's a story of a guy who needs to buy a kidney and he buys a kidney of a young man. Deciding later to go and visit him, he discovers that he is dead. It's also a bit of a metaphor. It's about a man, a uni-lingual English Canadian guy in Toronto from the upper classes, who buys a kidney from a young Québecois guy from the lower class. It's interesting because he has to come to Québec where he doesn't speak English and it's all about tourism because it's about medical tourism and it's also about sexual tourism. It's about Québec City, which is a huge tourist town. At the beginning it was also called *Vampires and Cannibals*. It was also about a vampire society. We consume each other, we buy each other's services – it goes from prostitution to buying somebody's organ or blood. It has become more and more standardised so we can vampirise or cannibalise, and of course it's always the people who can afford it. Then there's a need for it and a need to sell because people need money to survive. Organ trafficking has its own system. All of this is illegal and denounced, but it goes on and it's this huge market, as huge as the drug market. China executes political prisoners every day by the thousands and they shoot them in the back of the neck so that it doesn't damage the eyes, the lungs, the heart, the liver and the kidneys. They have medical teams that come in the field and they open them up and they take organs and they sell them. So, that's what we've been developing. But also we've decided to take the time to do it, not to rush into any kind of crazy schedule – it takes time.

On your website you're signed 'Robert Lepage Film and Theatre director'. Are you planning to continue making films?

I think that I've been borrowing a lot from the cinema to stage a different style of theatre and that seems to interest people and it moves them. So, I go, 'Oh, well maybe I should push it further', and I was hoping that I could do the same thing in the other direction, but it's too big a system in cinema. Cinema is like a huge empire and it's all about money. I think there's something in the middle. The audience is bored by theatre that doesn't offer what film has to offer and bored by cinema that doesn't give you the live experience that events or concerts give you. For a while people thought that multi-media was the answer to that. I've been doing a lot of opera work in the last couple of years and up until almost the end of the nineteenth century, opera was the 'mother art'. It was the place where all forms of art would go and any new expression was invited into opera, but opera stopped doing that. I think that the twentieth century found a replacement for opera when it started to do big arena rock shows and offered something that opera couldn't offer. I think there is a form of art, there's something out there... When people say 'What is La Caserne?' I always say 'Well, it's a garage for that car to come in and park itself. It's just that we don't know where it is now and we hope that it is going to arrive.'

NOTES

CHAPTER ONE

1   Lepage often points to Québec's linguistic isolation in a mainly Anglophonic North America: 'Québecers have that need to be understood, and to have access to the market, to be invited all over the world so that people follow you and don't say "Oh, it's not in English I don't want to see it". You have to make this extra effort to get the story clear, to illustrate it, to give another layer to it.' (Quoted in McAlpine 1996: 150).

2   Lepage's theatre productions develop over years transforming and changing their narratives, and in the case of solo shows they continue to be performed by another actor. Dates provided indicate this development process, which often coincides with the production run.

CHAPTER TWO

1   After 16 years in power, Union Nationale lost an election to the Québec Liberal Party whose campaign slogan was 'it's time for a change'. This was a period of rapid transformation in Québecois society that took place between 1960 and 1966 and was known as the Quiet Revolution. During this period, Québec moved from a conservative, closed society that defended outdated traditional values to one that had a genuine desire to modernise, industrialise and, most importantly, stake out international rights to represent their own identity worldwide.

2   Film theory from the 1970s onwards, particularly organised around the British journal *Screen*, focused exclusively on the reception and social significance of film, divulging the economic factors that influenced its shape.

3   For more on the relation between Canadian film and NFB see Gary Evans (1991) 'In the National interest: A Chronicle of the National Film Board of Canada from 1949 to 1898'. Toronto: University of Toronto Press.

CHAPTER THREE

1   The dancer's name is 'Mouse', but a French speaker, who misspells her name as 'Mowse', has tattooed her. The tattoo is displayed in the scene in which she meets Pierre.
2   Susan Hayward explains that 'the desired effect, realism, is of course totally artificial given that the cinematic apparatus is not presently real-life to us – either through its images or its narrative. Use of lighting that does draw attention to itself is in some way challenging to this effect of realism and is, therefore, crucial in consideration of *mise-en-scène* precisely because it disrupts and distorts the reality effect' (2000: 211).

CHAPTER FOUR

1   In 'Lettres aux Américains' Cocteau writes about the creative process: 'Je profite de n'être sur aucun territoire pour écrire, mais dans un ciel nocturne qui simule encore quelque zones de liberté.' ['I take advantage of not being in any territory to write, but in a night sky that still simulates some zone of liberty.'] The last part of Cocteau's quotation, 'Quelques zones de liberté', was used as the title for Remy Charest's book of Lepage's interviews.

CHAPTER FIVE

1   Brassard explains that 'at one point in the movie one of the main characters is talking about renaissance, about the rebirth of nature in the city of Hiroshima, and says: 'les sept branches de...' We thought it was such a beautiful and poetic way of putting it. This is the reason why we originally called each part a box, and we had seven boxes that we wanted to explore. We were amazed to see that the river divides itself into seven streams. That's where the title comes from. (Interview with the author, 1996).

CHAPTER SIX

1   Lepage explains that 'words have to do with the way you think. The way the language is organised is the way your mind is organised. It is more than the language; it is a way of thinking.' (1999a)
2   Generally, criticism that emphasises commercial values agreed that the plot of these films was difficult to follow by the audience, particularly in the case of *Mulholland Drive* and *Vanilla Sky*, because of the fragmentary non-linear structure and absence of a clearly demarcated time frame. Rather, loss of memory is readily and safely employed as a justification device for a well-structured, action-oriented narrative as exemplified in the Hollywood blockbuster *The Bourne Identity* (2002).

CONCLUSION

1   Interview with Robert Lepage was in Québec City at his office in La Caserne on 8 January 2002.

2   There is a small island upon which a scorpion is stranded due to a terrible flood. He asks a passing frog if he can be transported to safety upon the frog's back. The frog says 'No, because you are sure to kill me.' 'If I kill you, I will drown anyway. Why would I kill you if you had saved my life? I'll be your friend forever', the scorpion tells him. Midway through their journey, the scorpion stings the frog in the back. As the frog drowns, he asks with the last of his energy, 'Why did you do this? Now you will also die.' The scorpion replies with his last breath, 'I can't help it. It's in my nature.'

FILMOGRAPHY

As Director

Le Confessionnal (1995, Can/GB/Fr, 101 min) Director: Robert Lepage; Produced: Philippe Carcassonne, Daniel Louis, David Puttnam, Denise Robert; Script: Robert Lepage; Cinematography: Alain Dostie; Original music: Sacha Puttnam; Editing: Emmanuelle Castro; Production Design and Art Direction: Francois Laplante; Casting: Lucie Robitaille; Costume Design: Barbara Kidd; Cast: Lothaire Bluteau, Patrick Goyette, Jean-Louis Millette, Kristin Scott Thomas, Ron Burrage, Richard Fréchette.

Le Polygraphe (1996, Can/Fr/Ger, 104 min) Director: Robert Lepage; Produced: Bruno Jobin; Script: Robert Lepage, Marie Brassard; Cinematography: Guy Dufaux; Editing: Emmanuelle Castro, Jean-François Bergeron; Art Direction: Monique Dion; Original Music: Robert Caux; Cast: Patrick Goyette, Marie Brassard, Peter Stormare, Maria De Madeiros, Josée Deschénes.

Nô (1998, Can, 85 min, b/w & col) Director: Robert Lepage; Produced: Bruno Jobin; Script: Robert Lepage, André Morency; Cinematography: Pierre Mignot; Editing: Aube Foglia; Art Direction: Fanfan Baudreau; Original Music: Michelle F. Côté, Bernard Falaise; Cast: Marie Brassard, Anne-Marie Cadeaux, Richard Fréchette , Alexis Martin, Marie Gignac, Eric Bernier.

Possible Worlds (2000, Can, 93 min) Director: Robert Lepage; Produced: Sandra Cunningham, Bruno Jobin; Script: Robert Lepage, John Mighton; Cinematography:

Jonathan Freeman II; Editing: Susan Shipton; Art Direction: Collin Niemi; Costume Design: Michèle Hamel; Cast: Tilda Swinton, Tom McCamus, Sean McCann, Gabriel Gascon, Rick Miller I.

As Actor

Jésus de Montréal (1989, Can/Fr, 120 min.) Director: Denys Arcand; Produced: Roger Frappier, Pierre Gendron II, Monique Létourneau; Script: Denys Arcand; Cinematography: Guy Dufaux; Original music: Jean Marie Benoît I, François Dompierre, Yves Laferrière; Editing: Isabelle Dedieu; Production Design: François Séguin; Costume Design: Louise Jobin; Cast: Lothaire Bluteau, Catherine Wilkening, Johanne-Marie Tremblay, Rémy Girard, Robert Lepage, Gilles Pelletier, Yves Jacques.

Stardom (2000, Can/Fr, 100 min, b/w & col) Director: Deny Arcand; Produced: Philippe Carcassonne, Robert Lantos, Denise Robert; Script: Denys Arcand, Jacob Potashnik; Cinematography: Guy Dufaux; Editing: Isabelle Dedieu; Art Direction: Jean Morin II; Production Design: Zoé Sakellaropoulo; Original Music: François Dompierre; Costume Design: Michelle Robidas; Cast: Jessica Paré, Dan Aykroyd, Carles Berling, Robert Lepage, Camilla Rutherford, Thomas Gibson I.

BIBLIOGRAPHY

Althusser, Louis (ed.) (1971) *Lenin and Philosophy*. New York: Monthly Review Press.

Altman, Rick (1999) *Film/Genre*. London: BFI.

Andrew, Geoff (1999) '*Nô*', in John Pym (ed.) *Time Out Film Guide, 8th Edn*. London: Penguin Books.

____ (2001) '*Possible Worlds*', *Time Out*, 18–25 July, 91.

Anon. (1993) 'Lepage Inc.'s worldly view comes to Harbourfront', *The Toronto Star*, 31 March, D5.

Anon. (1996) '*Le Polygraphe*', *24 Images*, 85, 47.

Arnheim, Rudolph (1958) *Film as Art*. London: Faber and Faber.

Armes, Robert (1968) *The Cinema of Alain Resnais*. London: A. Zwemmer and New York: A.S. Barnes.

Artaud, Antonin (1958) *The Theatre and its Double*. Trans. M. C. R. Evergreen. New York: Grove Press.

Bal Mieke & Bryan Gonzales (eds) (1999) *Practice of Cultural Analysis: Exposing Interdisciplinary Interpretation (Cultural Memory in the Present)*. Stanford University Press.

Baldick, Chris (1990) *Oxford Concise Dictionary of Literary Terms*. Oxford: Oxford University Press.

Barthes, Roland (1972) *Mythologies*. Trans. A. Lavers. London: Jonathan Cape.

____ (1977) *Image-Music-Text*. Trans. S. Heath. New York: Hill and Wang.

Baudrillard, Jean (1976) *Simulations*. Trans. P. Foss. New York: Semiotext(e).

Bazin, André (1971) *What is Cinema?* Vol. 1. Berkeley: University of California Press.

____ (1971) *What is Cinema?* Vol.2. Berkeley: University of California Press.

____ (1972) 'Hitchcock versus Hitchcock', in Albert J. La Valley (ed.) *Focus on Hitchcock*. Englewood Cliffs: Prentice Hall, 60–9.

____ (1978) 'Théâtre et Cinéma', in *Qu'est-ce-que le cinema? Édition definitive*. Paris:

Editions du Cerf: 129–78.

Bhabha, Homi (ed.) (1990) *Nation and Narration*. London: Routledge.

Bilodeau, Michel (2000) 'L'impossible Rêve', *Le Devoir*. 13 September, 19.

Birringer, Johannes (1993) *Theatre, Theory, Postmodernism*. Bloomington: Indiana University Press.

Björkman, Stig (1995) *Woody Allen on Woody Allen: In Conversation with Stig Björkman*. London: Faber and Faber.

Bondanella, Peter (2002) *The Films of Federico Fellini*. Cambridge: Cambridge University Press.

Bordwell, David (1985) *Narration in the Fiction Film*. Madison: University of Wisconsin Press.

____ (1989) *Making Meaning: Inference and Rhetoric in the Interpretation of Cinema*. Cambridge: Harvard University Press.

____ (1996) 'La Nouvelle Mission de Feuillade; or, What was mise-en-scène?', *Velvet Light Trap*, 37, 10–29.

____ (2000) *Planet Hong Kong: Popular Cinema and the Art of Entertainment*. Cambridge: Harvard University Press.

Bovet, Jeanne (1991) 'Une Impression de Décalage: Le Plurilinguisme dans la Production du Théâtre Repère', Unpublished Master's thesis. Québec: Université Laval.

____ (2000) 'Identity and Universality: Multilingualism in Robert Lepage's Theatre', in Joseph Donohoe Jr. & Jane M. Koustas (eds) *Theater Sans Frontières: Essays on the Dramatic Universe of Robert Lepage*. East Lansing: Michigan State University Press.

Branigan, Edward (1992) *Narrative, Comprehension and Film*. London: Routledge.

Brassard, Marie (1996) Interview with Robert Lepage (2 October, London).

____ (1997) *Polygraph*. London: Methuen.

Brassard, Marie & Robert Lepage (1993) *Polygraph*. Trans. Gyllian Raby, in Alan Filewood (ed.) *CTR Anthology*. Toronto: University of Toronto Press.

Breton, André (1962) *Manifestoes of Surrealism*. Trans. R. Seaver & H. R. Lane. Ann Arbor: University of Michigan Press.

Brewster, Ben & Lea Jacobs (1997) *Theatre to Cinema*. Oxford: Oxford University Press.

Brunette, Peter & David Wills (1989) *Screen Play/Derrida and Film Theory*. New Jersey: Princeton University Press.

Buckland, William (1998) *Film Studies*. London: Hodder and Stoughton.

Burgoyne, Robert (ed.) (1992) *New Vocabularies in Film Semiotics*. London: Routledge.

Burnett, Ron (1990) 'Denys Arcand – Jesus of Montréal: A Discussion', *Melbourne Sunday Herald*, 29 June.

Buss, Robin (1994) 'Introduction', in Jean Cocteau, *The Art of Cinema*. London: Marion Boyars.

Carlson, Tom (1996) 'Gorgeous Distortions and Brilliant Perceptions.' Available at: m/euphony/articles/needlesandopiumreview-tc.html (15 October).

Carney, Ray & Leonard Quart (2000) *The Films of Mike Leigh: Embracing the World*. Cambridge: Cambridge University Press.

Carroll, Noel (1988) *Mystifying Movies*. New York: Columbia University Press.

____ (1998) *Interpreting the Moving Image*. Cambridge: Cambridge University Press.

Carson, Christi (2000) 'The Intercultural Experiments of Robert Lepage', in Joseph

Donohoe Jr. & Jane M. Koustas (eds) *Theater sans Frontières: Essays on the Dramatic Universe of Robert Lepage*. East Lansing: Michigan State University Press, 74.

Caughie, John (ed.) (1981) *Theories of Authorship, A Reader*. London: Routledge.

Chabot, Claude (1989) *Le Cinéma Québécois d'annés 80*. Montréal: Cinematèque Québécois.

Chabrol, Claude (1979) *Hitchcock: The First Forty-four Films*. New York: Ungar.

Charest, Rémy (1995) *Robert Lepage: Quelques Zones de Liberté*. Québec City: L'Instant Même/Ex Machina.

_____ (1997) *Robert Lepage: Connecting Flights in Conversation with Rémy Charest*. Trans. Wanda Romer-Taylor. London: Methuen.

Cocteau, Jean (1994) *The Art of Cinema*. Trans. Robin Buss & Claude Gauteur. London: Marion Boyars.

Connerton, Paul (1989) *How Societies Remember*. Cambridge University Press.

Collingham, John (2000) 'Descartes: Descartes' Philosophy of Mind', in Ray Monk & Frederic Raphael (eds) *The Great Philosophers*. London: Phoenix.

Coulombe, Michel (1995) 'Entretien avec Robert Lepage', *Cinebulles*, 14, 4, 18–25.

_____ (1998) 'Entretien avec Robert Lepage', *Cinebulles,* 17, 2.

De Bois, Marco (1995–96) 'L'iconoclast de Québec', *24 Images: La Revue Québécoise du Cinéma*, 80.

Deleuze, Gilles (1986) *Cinema 1: The Movement-Image*. Trans. H. Tomlinson & B. Habberjam. London: Athlone Press.

_____ (1989) *Cinema 2: The Time-Image*. Trans. H. Tomlinson & R. Galeta. London: Athlone Press.

Denzin, Norman K. (1991) *Images of a Post-modern Society: Social Theory and Contemporary Cinema*. New York: SAGE Publications.

Derrida, Jacques (1978) *Of Grammatology*. Baltimore and London: John Hopkins University Press.

Dickinson, John & Young Brian (eds) (2003) *A Short History of Québec*. Montréal: McGill-Queen's University Press.

Dionne, Rene (1986) *Litterature Québecoise Et Cinema (Histoire Litteraire Du Québec Et Du Canada Francais No. 11)*. Ottawa: University of Ottawa Press.

Donohoe, Joseph Jr. (ed.) (1991) *Essays on Québec Cinema*. East Lansing: Michigan State University Press.

Donohoe, Joseph Jr. & Jane M. Koustas (eds) (2000) *Theater Sans Frontieres: Essays on the Dramatic Universe of Robert Lepage*. East Lansing: Michigan State University Press.

Dormachi, Jean & Jaccques Doniol-Valcroze (1985) 'Hiroshima Notre Amour', in John Hillier (ed.) *Cahiers du Cinema: The 1950s Neo-realism, Hollywood, New Wave*. Cambridge: Harvard University Press: 59–70.

Dossier 'Robert Lepage' (1995a) 'La Première Confession de Robert Lepage', *Séquences*, 180, September/October, 24–28.

Dossier 'Robert Lepage' (1995b) 'Lepage/Hitchcock: Leçons D'Histoire(s)', *Séquences*, 180, September/October, 29–34.

Durgnat, Raymond (1974) *The Strange Case of Alfred Hitchcock*. Cambridge: MIT Press.

During, Simon (ed.) (1993) *The Cultural Studies Reader*. London: Routledge.

Duynslaegher, Patrick (1997) 'The Accidental Tourist', *Sight and Sound*, 12, 14–18.

Dvorak, Marta (1997) 'Représentations Récentes des Sept Branches de la Rivière Ota et d'Elseneur de Robert Lepage', in Bednardski & Oorc (eds) (1997) *Nouveaux Regards sur le Théâtre Québécois*. Montréal: XYZ.

Dyer, Richard (1979) *Stars*. London: BFI.

_____ (1990) *How you see it*. London: Routledge.

Eisenstein, Sergei (1968) *Film Essays*. Trans. Jay Leyda. London: Dennis Dobson.

_____ (1975) *The Film Sense*. Trans. Jay Leyda. San Diego, New York and London: Harvest Books.

Feldman, Susan (1991) 'When Cultures Collide', Theatrum, 24, 9–13.

Féral, Josette (1992) 'Pour Une Autre Pédagogie du Théâtre: Entretien avec Alain Knapp', *Jeu*, 63, 55–64.

_____ (2001) 'Robert Lepage', in *Mise-en-scène et Jeu de l'acteur. Tome 2: Le Corps en Scène*. Montréal: Editions Jeu/Editions Lansman, 160–85.

Filewood, Alan (1998) 'Beyond Collective Creation', *Canada Theatre Review*, 55, Summer, 38–52.

Forbes, Jill & Michael Kelly (eds) (1995) *French Cultural Studies: An Introduction*. Oxford: Oxford University Press.

Foucault, Michel (1970) *The Order of Things: An Archaeology of the Human Sciences*. Phanteon Books.

_____ (1995) *Madness and Civilization: A History of Insanity in the Age of Reason*. London: Routledge.

Freeman, Edward (1992) Introduction to *Orphée* by Jean Cocteau. Bristol: Bristol Classical Press, vii–xii.

Fusco, Coco (1995) *English is Broken Here: Notes on Cultural Fusion in the Americas*. New York: The New Press.

Gabriel, Peter (1994) *Secret World Live* (video). Los Angeles: Geffen HomeVideos.

Gajan, Philippe (2001) 'Le Réel en Parte de Vitesse', *24 Images*, 105, 25.

Garrity, Henry R. (2000) 'Robert Lepage's Cinema of Time and Space', in Joseph Donohoe Jr. & Jane M. Koustas (eds) *Theater Sans Frontièrs: Essays on the Dramatic Universe of Robert Lepage*. Ann Arbor: Michigan State University Press, 95–107.

Gibbs, John (2001) *Mise-en-scène: Film Style and Interpretation*. London: Wallflower Press.

Gibson, Pamela Church & John Hill (2000) *Film Studies Critical Approaches*. Oxford University Press.

Gocic, Goran (2001) *The Cinema of Emir Kusturica: Notes from the Underground*. London: Wallflower Press.

Gombrich, Ernst (1961) *Art and Illusion: A Study in the Psychology of Pictorial Representation*. New York: Bollingen Foundation/Pantheon Books.

Gomery, Douglas & Robert Clyde Allan (1985) *Film History Theory and Practice*. New York and Toronto: McGraw-Hill.

Gottlieb, Susan (1995) *Hitchcock on Hitchcock*. London: Faber and Faber.

Gramsci, Antonio (1971): *Selections from the Prison Notebooks*. London: Lawrence & Wishart.

Gurevitch, Michael, Tony Bennett, James Curran & Janet Woollacott (eds) (1982) *Culture, Society and the Media*. London: Methuen.

Hall, Stuart (1987) 'Minimal Selves', in *The Real Me: Post-Modernism and the Question of*

Identity. London: Institute of Contemporary Arts.

Halprin, Lawrence (1969) *The RSVP Cycles: Creative Processes in the Human Environment.* New York: George Braziller.

Hannerz, Ulf (1996) *Transnational Connections: Culture, People, Places.* London and New York: Routledge.

Hauer, Denise (dir.) (1992) 'Who is this Nobody from Québec?' BBC Videocassette, Founder's Library. Royal Holloway, University of London.

Hauser, Arnold (1985) *The Sociology of Art.* Chicago: University of Chicago Press.

Hayward, Susan (2000) *Key Concepts: Cinema Studies,* 2nd edn. London: Routledge.

Hébert, Chantal (1995) 'The Theatre: Sounding Board for the Appeals and Dreams of the *Québécois* Collectivity', in *Essays on Modern Québec Theatre.* East Lansing: Michigan State University Press, 27–46.

Hiroshi, Takahagi (1995) 'Shakespeare at the Globe in Tokyo', *Canadian Theatre Review,* Winter, 84.

Hodgdon, Barbara (1993) 'Splish Splash and The Other: Lepage's Intercultural Dream Machine', *Essays in Theatre/Etudes Théâtrale,* 12, 1.

Hunt, Nigel (1989) 'The Global Voyage of Robert Lepage', *The Drama Review,* 33, 2, 104–18.

Hutcheon, Linda (1988) *The Canadian Postmodern: A Study of Contemporary English Canadian Fiction.* Toronto: Oxford University Press.

Hutcheon, Linda & Michael Hutcheon (1996) *Opera: Desire, Disease, Death.* Lincoln and London: University of Nebraska Press.

Hutton, Patrick (1993) *History as an Art of Memory.* Vermont: University of Vermont.

Huxley, Michael & Noel Witts (eds) (1996) 'Robert Lepage in Discussion with Richard Eyre,' in *The Twentieth-Century Performance Reader.* London: Routledge, 237–47.

____ (2001) '19 Answers by Heiner Müller', in *The Twentieth-Century Performance Reader.* London: Routledge 16–22.

Jackson, Russell (2000) 'From Play-script to Screenplay', in Russell Jackson (ed.) *Shakespeare on Film.* Cambridge: Cambridge University Press.

James, Nick (2002) 'Introduction: Back to the Brats', in Yoram Allon, Del Cullen & Hannah Pattersons (eds) *Contemporary North American Film Directors: A Wallflower Critical Guide,* 2nd edn. London: Wallflower Press, xvi–xix.

Jean, Marcel (1991) *Le Cinéma Québécois.* Montréal: Boréal.

Jencks, Charles (1989) *What is Post-Modernism?* 3rd edn. London: St. Martin's Press.

Johnson, Brian J. (1998) 'A Festival Zeros in on Québec: Robert Lepage Re-examines the October Crisis in His New Feature', *Maclean's,* 7 September, 52–3.

Jung, Carl Gustav (1960) 'Instinct and the Unconscious', *The Structure and Dynamics of the Psyche,* Vol. 8, London: Routledge.

____ (1971) *Psychological Types.* Trans. H. G. Baynes. *The Collected Works of C. G. Jung,* Vol. 6. London: Routledge and Kegan Paul.

Kasbekar, Asha (1996) 'An Introduction to Indian Cinema,' in Jill Nelmes (ed.) *An Introduction to Film Studies.* London: Routledge, 366–7.

Kellner, Douglas (1995) *Media Culture.* London: Routledge.

King, Geoff (2002) *New Hollywood Cinema,* New York: Columbia University Press.

Kirkland, Bruce (1995) 'Le Confessionnal', *Toronto Star,* November 24, C5.

Klawans, Stuart (1999) 'Global Indigestion', *The National,* 17 May, 26.

Klein, Naomi (2001) *No Logo*. London: Flamingo.

Landesman, Cosmo (2002) 'Insomnia', *The Sunday Times* Culture supplement, 1 September, 8.

Lapsley, Robert & Michael Westlake (1988) *Film Theory: An Introduction*. Manchester: Manchester University Press.

Larouche, Michel (ed.) (1996) *L'Aventure du cinéma québécois en Français*. Montréal: XYZ.

La Rochelle, Réal (2001) 'La Trilogi Orphique de Cocteau en DVD', *24 Images*, 106, 6–8.

La Rochelle, Réal & Gilbert Maggi (1971) 'Situation politique du cinema québécoise', *Champ Libre*, 1 July, 53, 66.

Leach, Jim (1999) *Claude Jutra Filmmaker*. Montréal: McGill-Queen's University Press.

Lebovici, E. (1995) 'Dans le Secret du Confessionnal', *Libération*, 19 May.

Lefebre, Martin (1998) 'Sense of Time and Place: The Chrontope in *I Confess* and *Le Confessional*', *Québec Studies*, 26, 92.

Le Goff, Jacques *et al.* (1996) *History and Memory*. New York: Columbia University Press.

Lepage, Robert (1992) 'Robert Lepage in Conversation with Richard Eyre', *Platform Papers 3*, London: Royal National Theatre.

_____ (1996a) Interview, in Maria Delgado & Paul Heritage (eds) *In Contact with the Gods: Directors Talk Directing*. Manchester and New York: Manchester University Press, 140–1.

_____ (1996b) Press Release for *Le Confessionnal*. Available at: http://www.canada/films/forthnight/confessional/confessional.html. (24 July 1996).

_____ (1999a) Talk at the National Theatre, London, 3 April.

_____ (1999b) Interview with the Author. Québec City, 9 December.

_____ (2002) Interview with the Author. Québec City, 8 January.

Lepage, Robert & Ex Machina (1996) *The Seven Streams of the River Ota*. London: Methuen Drama.

Lévesque, Solange (1988) 'Polygraphe', *June*, 48, 153.

Levi-Strauss, Claude (1967) 'The Structural Study of Myth', in Levi-Strauss (ed.) *Structural Anthropology*. Garden City, New York: Anchor Books, 202–28.

Loiselle, André (1999) 'Subtly Subversive or Simply Stupid: Notes on Popular Québec Cinema', *Post Script*, 18, 2, 75–83.

MacKenzie, Sam (2000) 'A Screen of One's Own: Early Cinema in Québec and the Public Sphere 1906–28', *Screen*, 41, 2, 183–202.

Magder, Ted (1993) *Canada's Hollywood: The Canadian State and Future Fims*. Toronto: University of Toronto Press.

Mansfield, Nick (2000) *Subjectivity: Theories of the Self from Freud to Haraway*. New York: New York University Press.

Manvell, Robert (1979) *Theatre and Film: A Comparative Study?* Rutherford: Associated University Press.

Marshall, Bill (2001) *Québec National Cinema*. Montréal: McGill-Queens University Press.

Mast, Gerald (1976) 'Film History and Film Historians', *Quarterly Review of Film Studies*, August.

Mast, Gerald & Marshall Cohen (eds) (1995) *Film Theory and Criticism*. Oxford: Oxford University Press.

Mathews, Shirley (1997) 'High-Tech Elsinore is More like Cinema than Theater', *Connecticut Post*, 19 September, F4.

Mettler, Peter (dir.) (1992) *Les Plaques Tectoniques/Tectonic Plates*. Adaptation of the play by Robert Lepage & Théâtre Repère. Videocassette. Toronto: Rhombus Media.

Michaels, Anne (2002) Interview, in 'Frozen Acrobatics of Memory: Branko Gorjup Speaks with Anne Michaels', *The Reader*. University of Liverpool, 10, 8–17.

Mighton, John (1992) *Possible Worlds & A Short History of Night*, Toronto: Playwrights Canada Press.

____ (2002) Interview with the author. Toronto, 12 January.

Mirzoeff, Nicholas (1999) *An Introduction to Visual Culture*. London: Routledge.

Monaco, James (1997) *How to Read a Film: Movies, Media, Multimedia*, 3rd edn. New York: Oxford University Press.

____ (1976) *Cinema and Society*. New York: Elsevier.

Nadeau, Chantal (1990) 'Américanité ou américanisation: l'exemple de la coproduction au Québec', *Cinémas* 1, 1–2, 61–71.

Nelmes, Jill (ed). (1996) *An Introduction to Film Studies*. London: Routledge.

Nowell-Smith, Geoffrey (ed.) (1996) *Oxford History of World Cinema*. Oxford: Oxford University Press.

Pavis, Patrice (ed.) (1996) *The Intercultural Performance Reader*. London and New York: Routledge.

Pallister, Janis L. (1995) *The Cinema of Québec: Masters in their own house*. Fairleigh Dickinson University Press.

Perreault, Luc (2000) 'Une Bizarre Impression d'étrangeté', *La Press*, 13 September, 12.

Petterson, Richard (1994) 'Culture Studies Through the Production Perspective: Progress and Prospects', in Diane Crane (ed.) *The Sociology of Culture: Emerging Theoretical Perspectives*. Oxford: Blackwell, 163–89.

Phelps, Guy & Ralph Stephensen (1989) *The Cinema as Art*. London: Penguin Books.

Posner, Michael (1993) *Canadian Dreams: The Making and Marketing of Independent Films*. Vancouver: Douglas and McIntyre.

Possible Worlds (2000) press release, La Caserne archives.

Privet, Georges (2001) 'L'universalisme', *24 Images*, 105, 15.

Provencher, Normand (2000) 'L'anglais … Pour le Réalisme', in *Le Soleil Extra*. 24 October, B12.

____ (2000) 'Un étrange Canvas', in *Le Soleil Extra*, 24 October, 12.

Remy, Jacques (2000) 'Une Histoire d'amour Cubiste.' *Le Soleil*. 13 September: 23

Richard, B. (1997) 'Totally Clueless', in Lynda Boose & Burt Richard (eds) *Shakespeare the Movie: Popularising the Plays on Film, TV, and Video*. London: Routledge, 11.

Ricoeur, Paul (1988) *Time and Narration*. Volume 3. Trans. Kathleen Blarney & David Pellauer. Chicago: University of Chicago Press.

Rist, Peter (2001) *Guide to the Cinema[s] of Canada*. Westport, CT: Greenwood.

Roseberry, William (1989) *Anthropologies and Histories: Essays in Culture, History, and Political Economy*. New Brunswick and New Jersey: Rutgers University Press.

Rousseau, Yves (2001) 'Bavardages', *24 Images*, 105, 17.

Rushdie, Salman (1991) *Imaginary Homeland: Essays and Criticism 1981–1991*. London:

Granta and Penguin Books.

Saäl Michka (2001) 'Dossier Cinéma et Exil', *24 Images*, 106, 28–9.

Said, Edward. (1991) *Orientalism: Western Concepts of the Orient.* London: Penguin Books.

Salter, Denis (1993) 'An Interview with Robert Lepage and Le Théâtre Repère', *Theater*, 24, 3.

Schechner, Richard (1996) 'Interculturalism in Contemporary Theatre', in Pavis (ed.) *The Intercultural Performance Reader.* London: Routledge, 39–54.

Schudson, Mike (1994) 'The Integration of National Societies', in Diane Crane (ed.) *The Sociology of Culture: Emerging Theoretical Perspectives.* Oxford: Blackwell, 21–43.

The Seven Streams of the River Ota (theatre programme) (1996) The Royal National Theatre, London, October.

Smith, Ian Haydn (2002) 'Robert Lepage', in Yoram Allon, Del Cullen & Hannah Pattersons (eds) *Contemporary North American Film Directors: A Wallflower Critical Guide*, 2nd edn. London: Wallflower Press, 324–5.

Stacey, Jackie & Annette Khun (eds) (1998) *Screen Histories: A Screen Reader* Oxford: Clarendon Press.

Staiger, Janet, David Bordwell & Kristin Thompson (1985) *The Classic Hollywood Cinema.* New York: Columbia University press.

Steegmuller, Francis (1970) *Cocteau: A Biography.* London: Macmillan Press.

Still, Judith & Michael Worton (eds) (1990) *Intertextuality: Theory and Practices.* Manchester: Manchester University Press.

Take One (2000) 'Faded Possibilities: A Conversation with Robert Lepage', Winter, 9 (30), 14–18.

Thompson, Kristin (1981) *Ivan the Terrible: A Neo-Formalist Analysis.* Princeton: Princeton University Press.

Thornham, Sue (1997) 'Some introductions', in Paul Marris & Sue Thornham (eds.) *Media Studies: A Reader.* Edinburgh: Edinburgh University Press.

Todorov, Tzvetan (1992) *The Conquest of America: The Question of the Other.* Trans. R. Howard. New York: Harper Perennial.

Trudeau, Pierre Elliott (1980) *Federalism and the French Canadians* Toronto: Macmillan.

Wallace, Robert (1990) *Producing Marginality.* Saskatoon: Fifth House Publisher.

Weimann, Heinz (1990) *Ciné,a de l'imaginaire québécois: de La Petite* Aurore à Jésus de Montréal. Montréal: l'Hexagone.

Williams, Raymond (1980) *Problems in Materialism and Culture.* London: Verso.

Wirth, Andrzej (1989) 'Interculturalism and Iconophilia in the New Theatre', *Performance Art Journal,* 33/34, 176–85.

Wolf, Matt (1992) 'Lepage's Version of *A Midsummer Night's Dream* Looks to be Touchstone of 90s.', in *The Gazette*, Montréal, 13 August: C5.

_____ (1992) 'Robert Lepage: Multicultural and Multifaceted', in *The New York Times*, 6 December.

Wollen, Peter (1982) *Readings and Writings.* London: Verso Editions.

INDEX

The Cinema of Emir Kusturica
Notes from the Underground

Goran Gocic

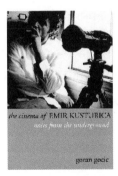

Notes from the Underground: The Cinema of Emir Kusturica is the first book on the Sarajevan film-maker to be published in English. With seven highly acclaimed films to his credit, Kusturica is already established as one of the most important of contemporary film-makers, with each of his films winning prizes at the major festivals around the world. His films include *Underground*, *Arizona Dream* with Johnny Depp, and *Black Cat, White Cat*. *Notes from the Underground* delves into diverse facets of Kusturica's work, all of which is passionately dedicated to the marginal and the outcast, and includes an exclusive interview with the director.

£14.99 pbk
1-903364-14-0
£42.50 hbk
1-903364-16-7
192 pages

Goran Gocic is a contributor to *Sight and Sound*, *Variety's International Film Guide*, *The Independent* and BBC World. He has most recently written on Andy Warhol and media representation of the Kosovo crisis.

The Cinema of
Wim Wenders
The Celluloid Highway

Alexander Graf

The Cinema of Wim Wenders is a new study of the films of this most prominent of German directors, and penetrates the seductive sounds and images for which he is best known. The book analyses the individual films in the context of a preoccupation central to all of Wenders' work and writings: why did modern cinema, a recording art, solely composed of sounds and images naturally developed into a primarily narrative medium, a domain traditionally associated with words and sentences? With its emphasis on analysing the films themselves, this book identifies and critically elucidates Wenders' chief artistic motivation: that the act of seeing can constitute a creative act in its own right.

£14.99 pbk
1–903364–29–9
£42.50 hbk
1–903364–30–2
192 pages

Alexander Graf lives in Berlin and works in film production. He has published widely on European directors and contemporary cinema.

The Cinema of
Ken Loach
Art in the Service of the People

Jacob Leigh

The Cinema of Ken Loach: Art in the Service of the People examines the linking of art and politics that distinguishes the director's work. Loach's films manifest recurrent themes over a long period of working with various collaborators, yet his handling of those themes have changed throughout his career. This book examines those changes as a way of reaching an understanding of Loach's style and meaning. It evaluates how he incorporates his political beliefs and those of his writers into his work, and augments this thematic interpretation with contextual information gleaned from archive research and new interviews.

£14.99 pbk
1–903364–31–0
£42.50 hbk
1–903364–32–9
192 pages

Jacob Leigh is Lecturer in Film Studies at the Media Arts Department at Royal Holloway, University of London.

The Cinema of
Kathryn Bigelow
Hollywood Transgressor

Edited by Deborah Jermyn
& Sean Redmond

Kathryn Bigelow has undoubtedly been one of Hollywood's most significant female film-makers, well known in popular terms for films such as *Point Break* and *Blue Steel*, yet she remains relatively unexplored in academia. This collection explores how Bigelow can be seen to provide a point of intersection across a whole range of issues at the forefront of contemporary film studies and the transformation of Hollywood into a post-classical cinema machine, with a particular emphasis on her most ambitious and controversial picture to date, *Strange Days*.

£14.99 pbk
1-903364-42-6
£42.50 hbk
1-903364-43-4
192 pages

Both editors are Lecturers in Film Studies at the Southampton Institute, UK, and have published widely on contemporary American cinema.

The Cinema of
George A. Romero
Knight of the Living Dead

Tony Williams

The Cinema of George A. Romero is the first in-depth study in English of the career of this foremost auteur working at the margins of the Hollywood mainstream. In placing Romero's oeuvre in the context of literary naturalism, the book explores the relevance of the director's films within American cultural traditions and thus explains the potency of such work beyond 'splatter movie' models. The author explores the roots of naturalism in the work of Emile Zola and traces this through to the EC Comics of the 1950s and on to the work of Stephen King. In so doing, the book illuminates the importance of seminal Romero texts such as *Night of the Living Dead* (1968), *Creepshow* (1982), *Monkey Shines* (1988) and *The Dark Half* (1992).

£14.99 pbk
1-903364-73-6
£42.50 hbk
1-903364-62-0
192 pages

Tony Williams is Professor and Area Head of Film Studies at Southern Illinois University at Carbondale. He has published widely in the areas of horror and American independent cinema.

The Cinema of
David Lynch
American Dreams, Nightmare Visions

Edited by Erica Sheen
& Annette Davison

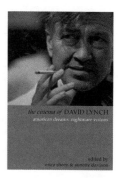

David Lynch is an anomaly. A pioneer of the American 'indie' aesthetic, he also works in Hollywood and for network television. Throughout his career he has created some of the most disturbing images in contemporary cinema, and produced startlingly innovative work in sound. The contributors of this collection offer an up-to-date range of theoretically divergent readings that demonstrate not only the difficulty of locating stable interpretative positions for Lynch's work, but also the pleasure of finding new ways of thinking about it. Films discussed include *Blue Velvet*, *Wild at Heart*, *The Straight Story* and *Mulholland Drive*.

£14.99 pbk
1–903364–85–X
£42.50 hbk
1–903364–86–8
208 pages

Erica Sheen lectures in literary theory and film at the University of Sheffield, and has published on Shakespeare, film theory and cinema history. Annette Davison is a lecturer in film music at the University of Leeds, and has published on film composition and soundtrack.

The Cinema of
Nanni Moretti
Dreams and Diaries

Ewa Mazierska &
Laura Rascaroli

The Cinema of Nanni Moretti provides an analysis of the work of the most important Italian film-maker of the past thirty years and an outstanding figure in contemporary European cinema. Interdisciplinary and wide-ranging, the authors use Moretti's films as a lens to view and discuss contemporary phenomena such as the crisis of masculinity and authority, the decline of the political Left, and the transformation of the citizen's relationship to the State. Films discussed include *Aprile*, *Dear Diary* and *The Son's Room*, winner of the Palme d'Or at Cannes 2001.

£14.99 pbk
1–903364–77–9
£42.50 hbk
1–903364–78–7
208 pages

Ewa Mazierska is Senior Lecturer in Film and Media Studies at the University of Central Lancashire. Laura Rascaroli is Toyota Lecturer in Film and Media Studies at the National University of Ireland, Cork.